MAD

SPY VS SPY

MISSIONS OF MADNESS

antonio prohias

WATSON-GUPTILL PUBLICATIONS
NEW YORK

W9-CQG-109

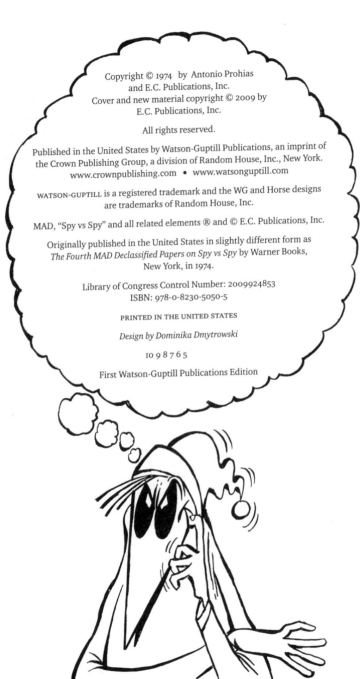

Published in the United States by Watson-Guptill Publications, an imprint of
the Crown Publishing Group, a division of Random House, Inc., New York.
www.crownpublishing.com • www.watsonguptill.com

WATSON-GUPTILL is a registered trademark and the WG and Horse designs
are trademarks of Random House, Inc.

MAD, "Spy vs Spy" and all related elements ® and © E.C. Publications, Inc.

Originally published in the United States in slightly different form as
The Fourth MAD Declassified Papers on Spy vs Spy by Warner Books,
New York, in 1974.

Library of Congress Control Number: 2009924853
ISBN: 978-0-8230-5050-5

PRINTED IN THE UNITED STATES

Design by Dominika Dmytrowski

10 9 8 7 6 5

First Watson-Guptill Publications Edition

It was July 12, 1960 when a political cartoonist from Cuba named Antonio Prohias arrived at the offices of *MAD* magazine. He had come to America two months earlier after death threats were directed at him and his family by the new Cuban dictator, Fidel Castro. Accompanying Prohias on that fateful day was his daughter, Marta, who acted as an interpreter. (Though her English at the time was only marginally better than her father's—which was nonexistent!) Also with Prohias were his drawings of two pointy-nosed characters he had created especially for *MAD*—one black, one white, both silent. Forever locked in a see-saw battle of destruction and mayhem, the conflict between the two was a metaphor for the futility of the Cold War.

Prohias first showed his creations to then Associate Editors Nick Meglin and Jerry DeFuccio. They liked what they saw and quickly ushered Prohias into the *MAD* art department, where he met Art Director John Putnam and his assistant Lenny (Gordito) Brenner. They, too, were intrigued. In no time, Prohias had met the remaining members of the *MAD* staff, Editor Al Feldstein and Publisher Bill Gaines. Prohias left the offices with a check for $800 for three of his strip adventures, which *MAD* called "Spy vs. Spy."

Overnight, a *MAD* classic was born. Prohias went on to create Spy misadventures for the next 26 years in virtually every issue of *MAD* until his retirement. Today, the strip continues in *MAD* written and illustrated by Peter Kuper.

Whether you're a longtime fan of "Spy vs. Spy" or a newcomer to the strip, this book, one of three being republished after a long absence from the shelves, will provide hours of entertainment. Just watch out for the exploding bombs and flying teeth!

John Ficarra
Editor, *MAD* magazine

SPY vs SPY

THE MODEL DETECTIVE

SHERLOCK HOLMES

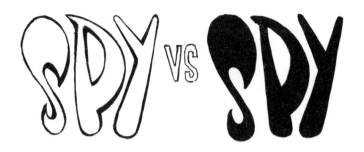

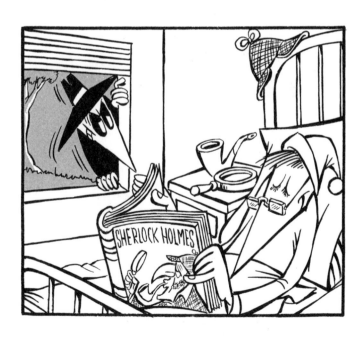

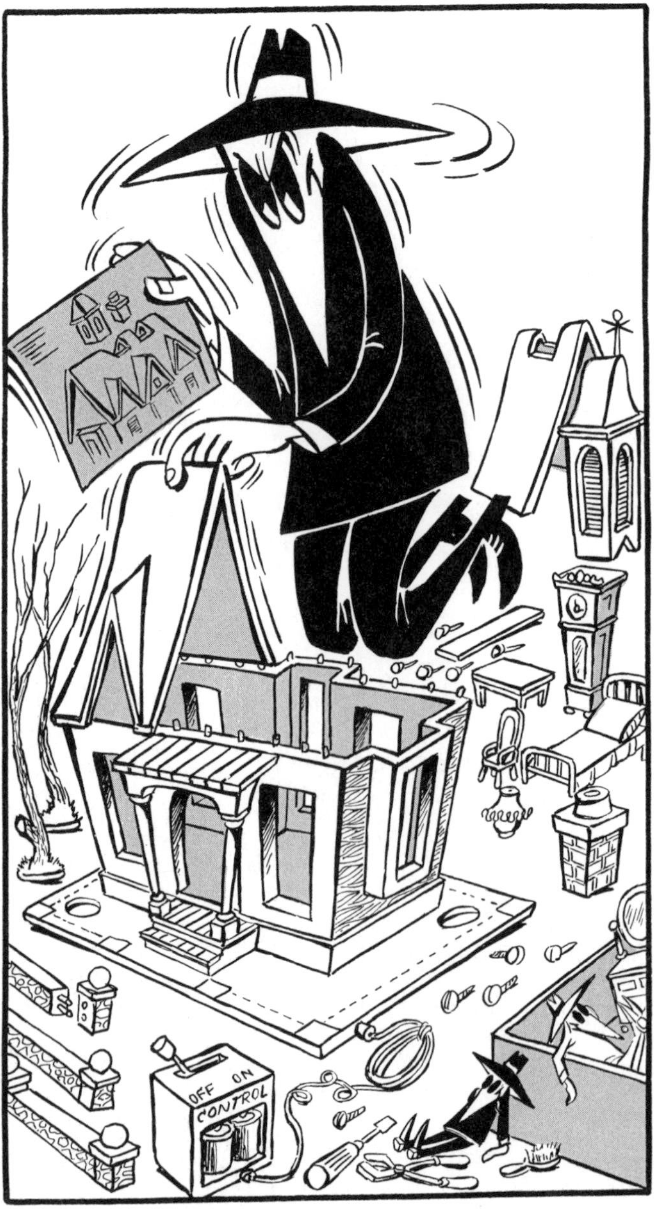
OFF ON
CONTROL

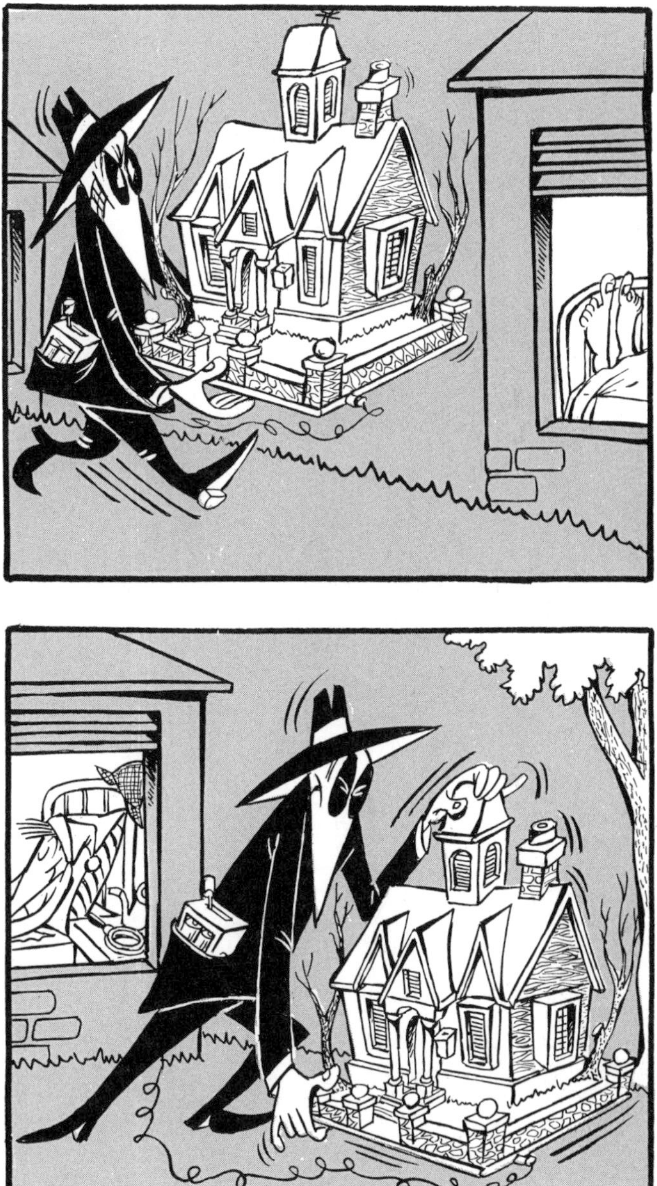

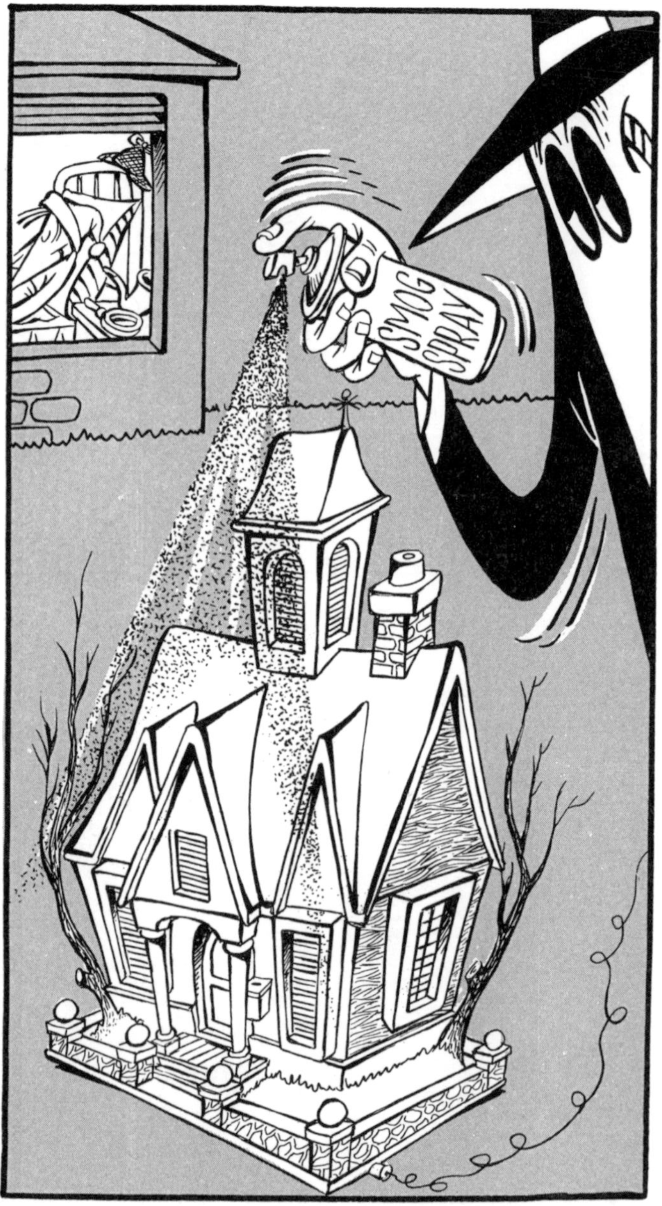
SMOG SPRAY

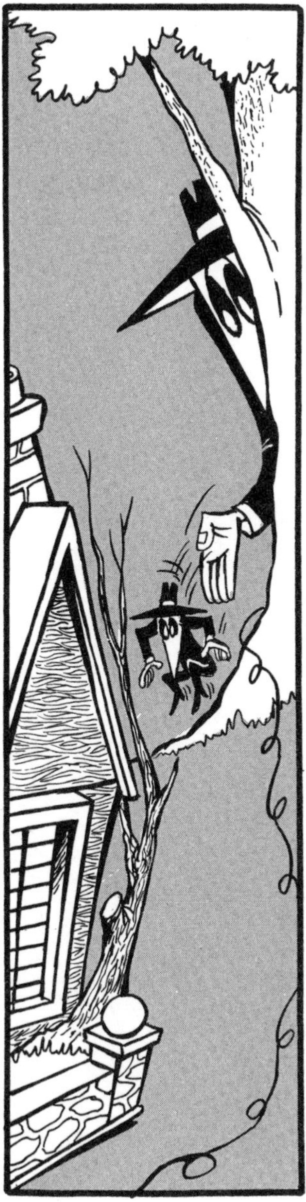

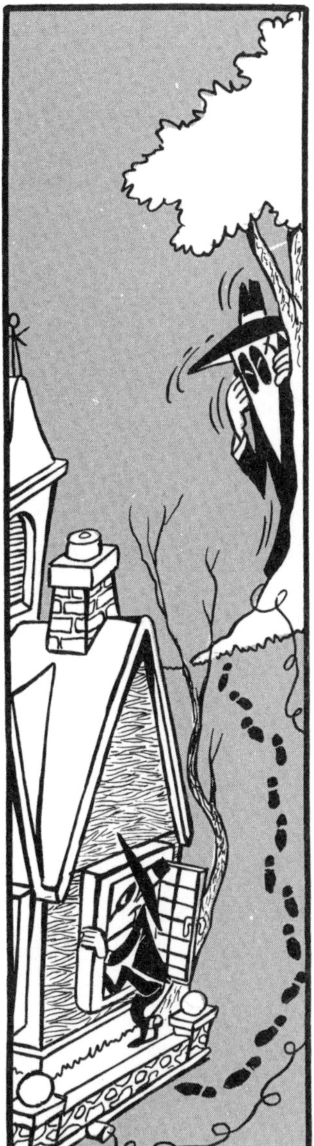

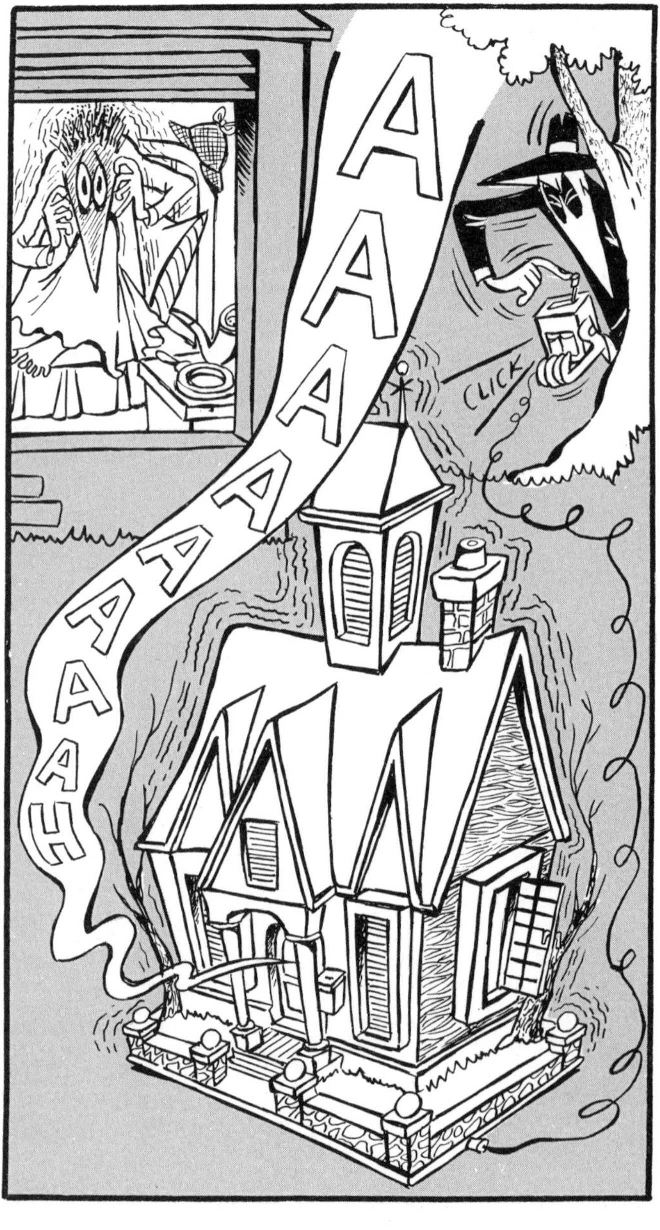
AAAAAAAAH
CLICK

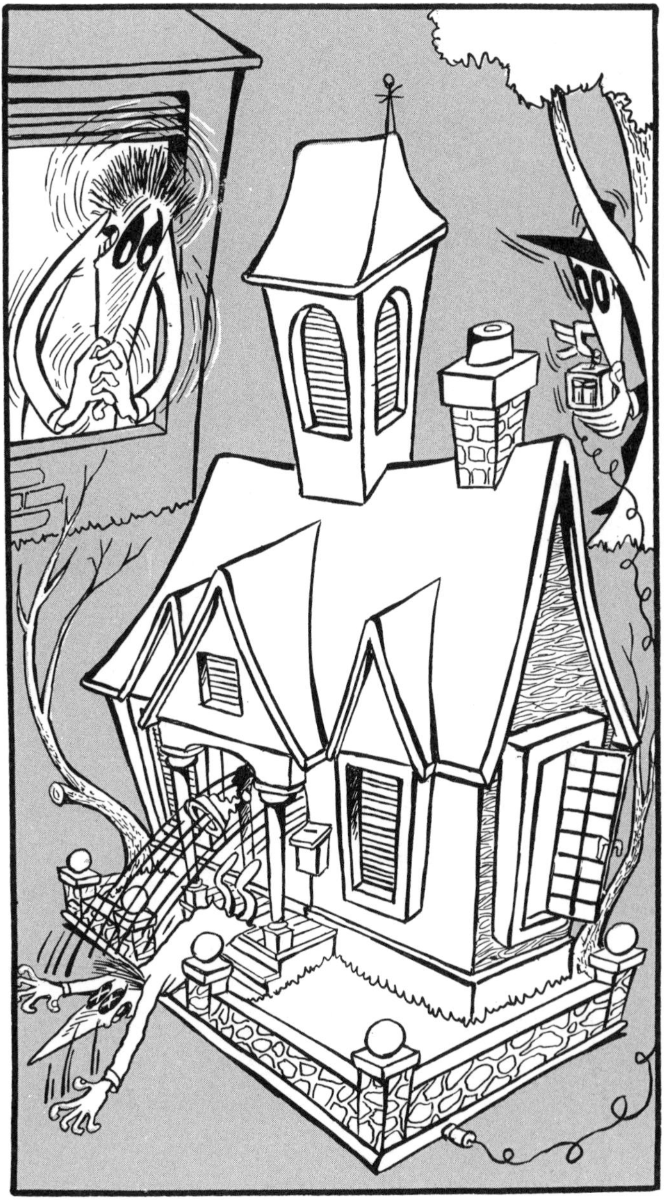

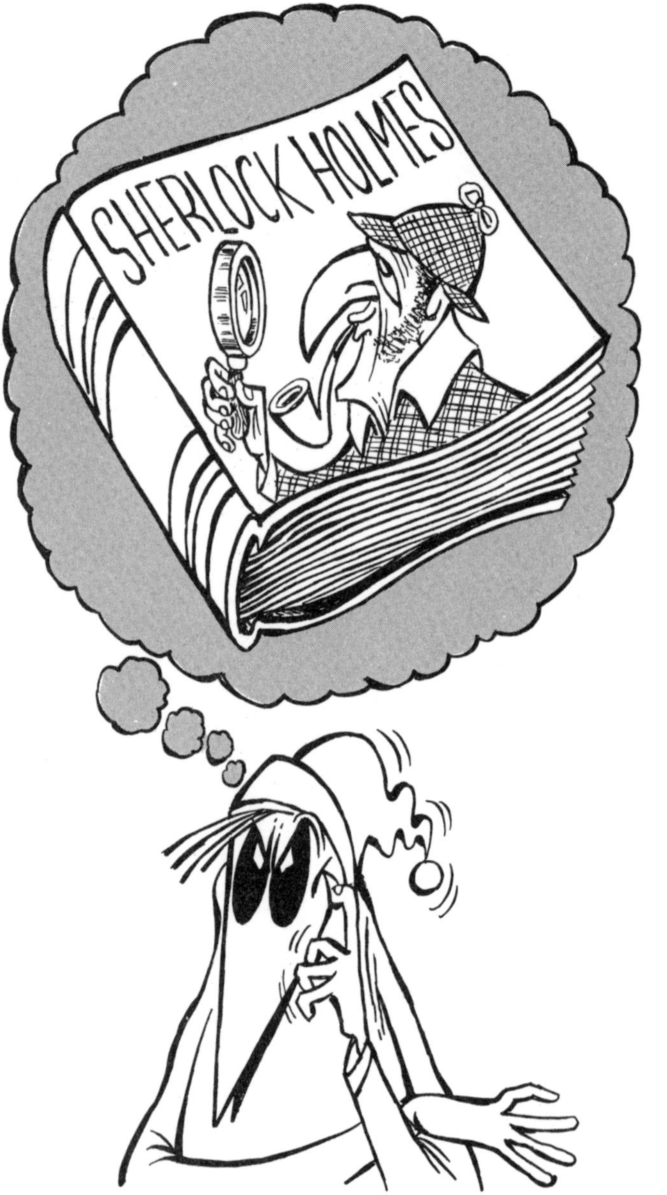
SHERLOCK HOLMES

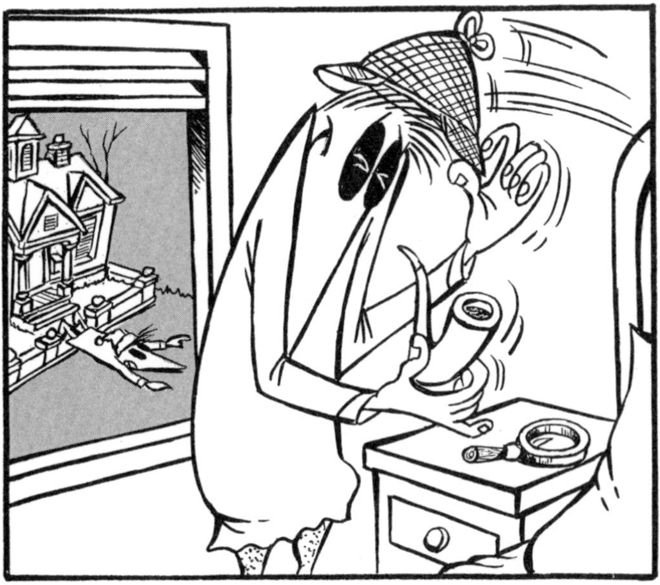

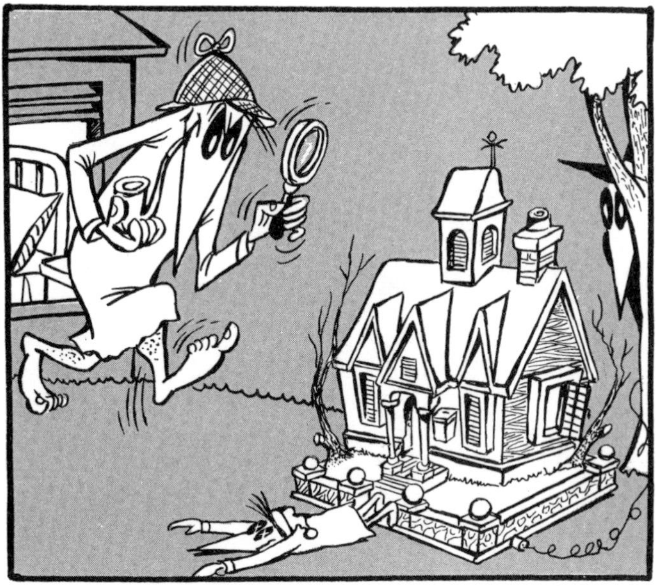

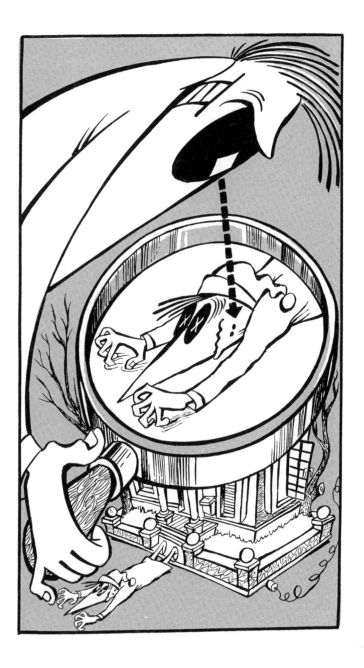

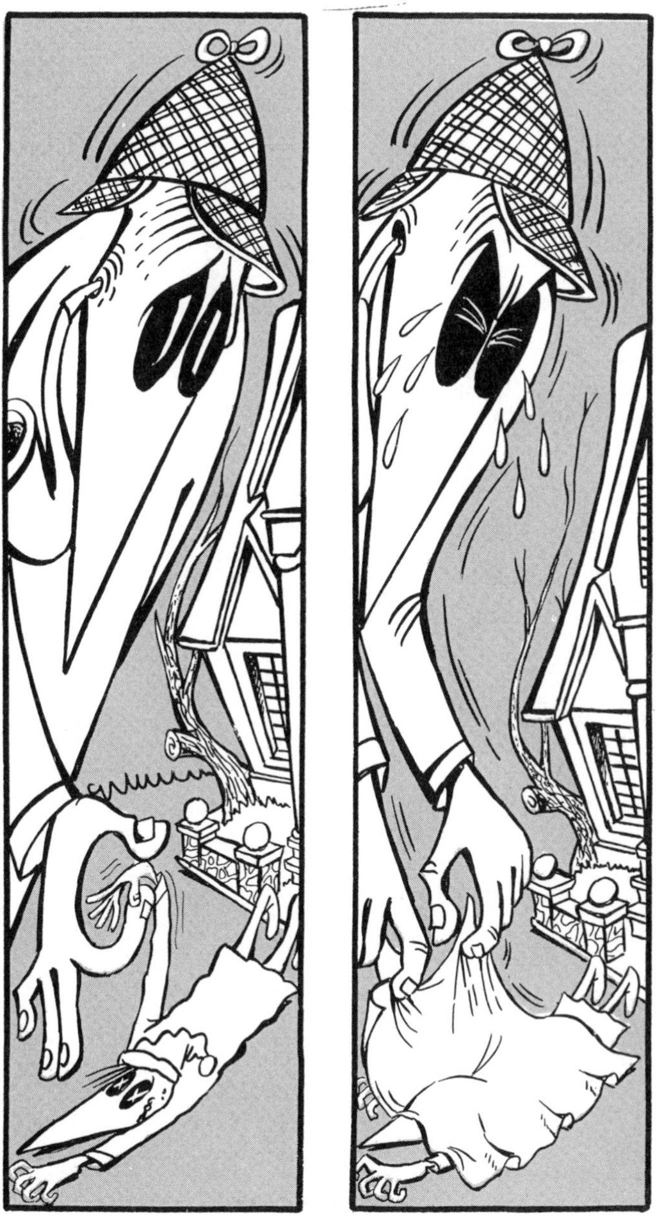

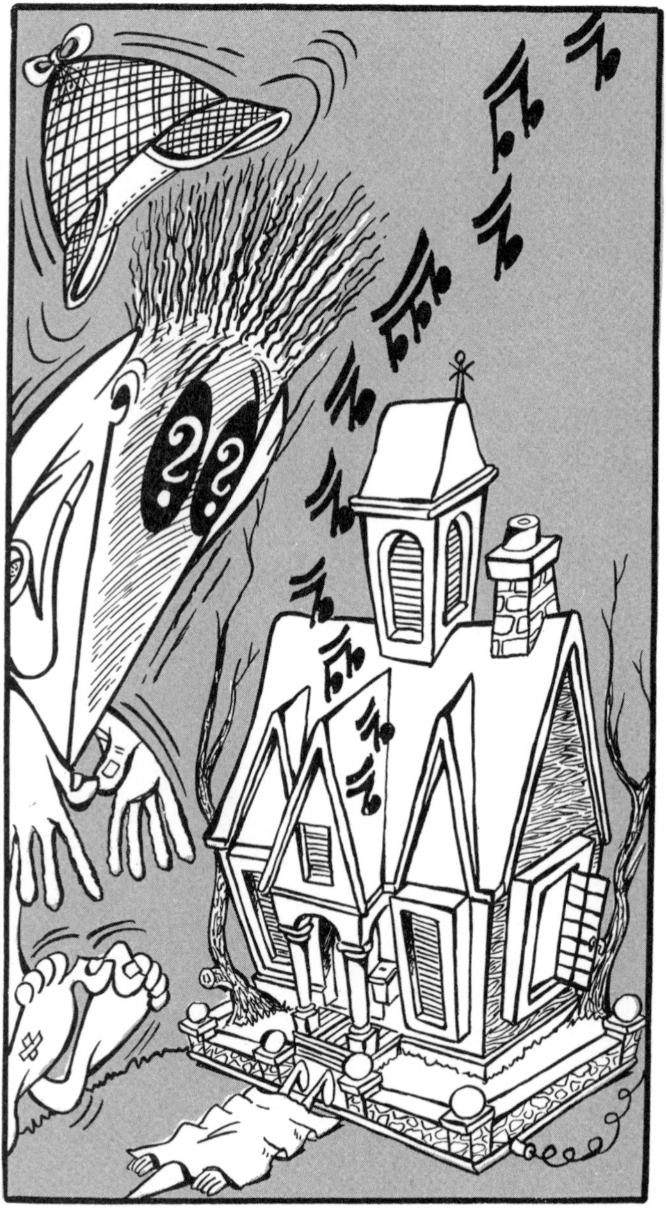

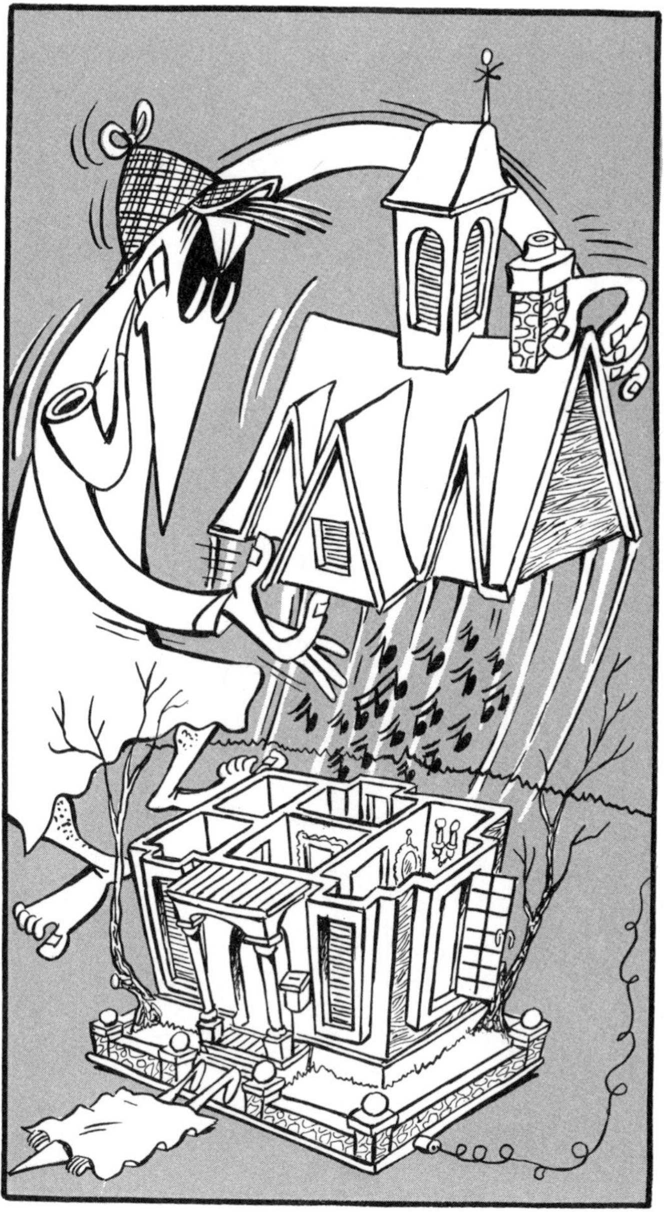

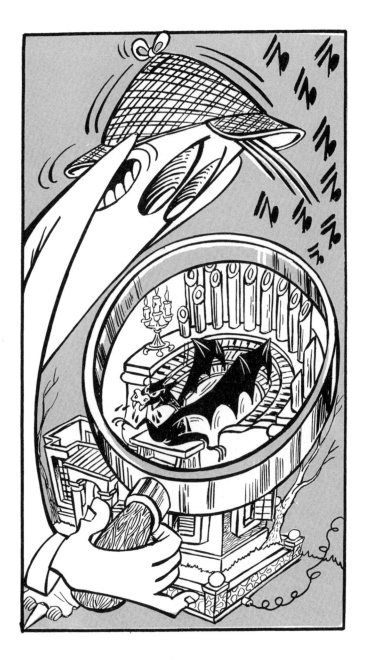

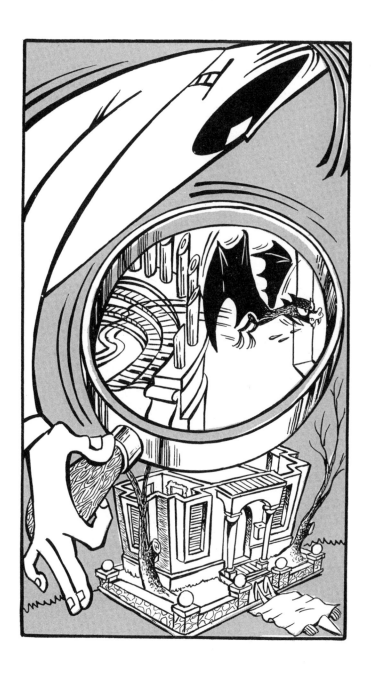

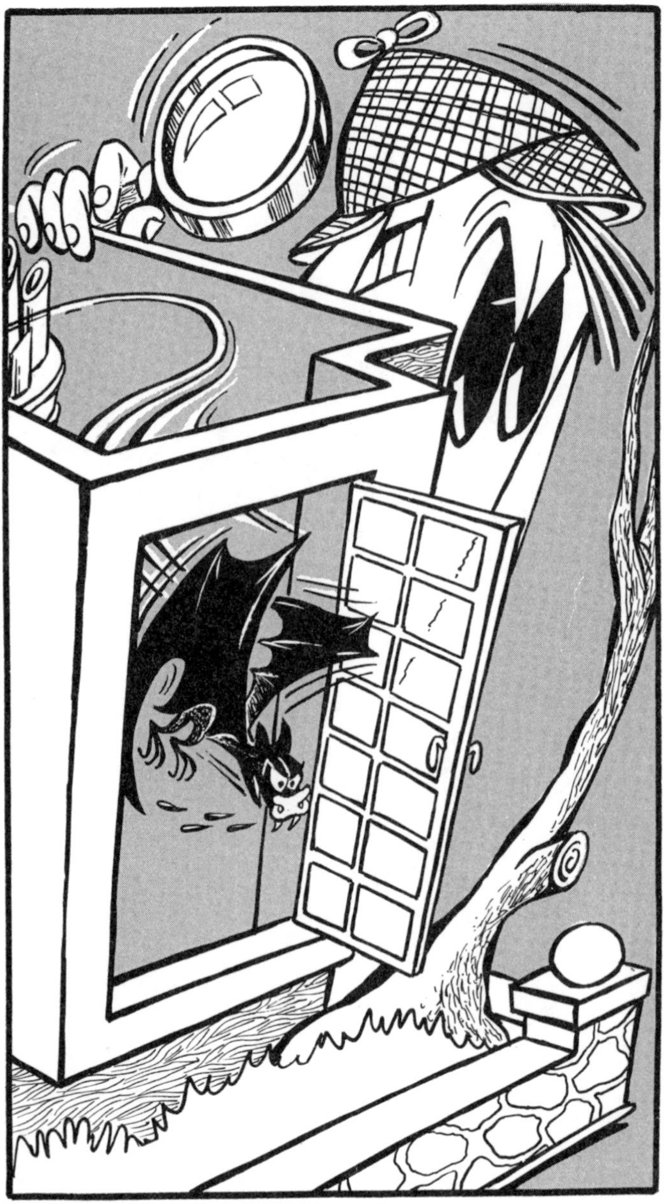

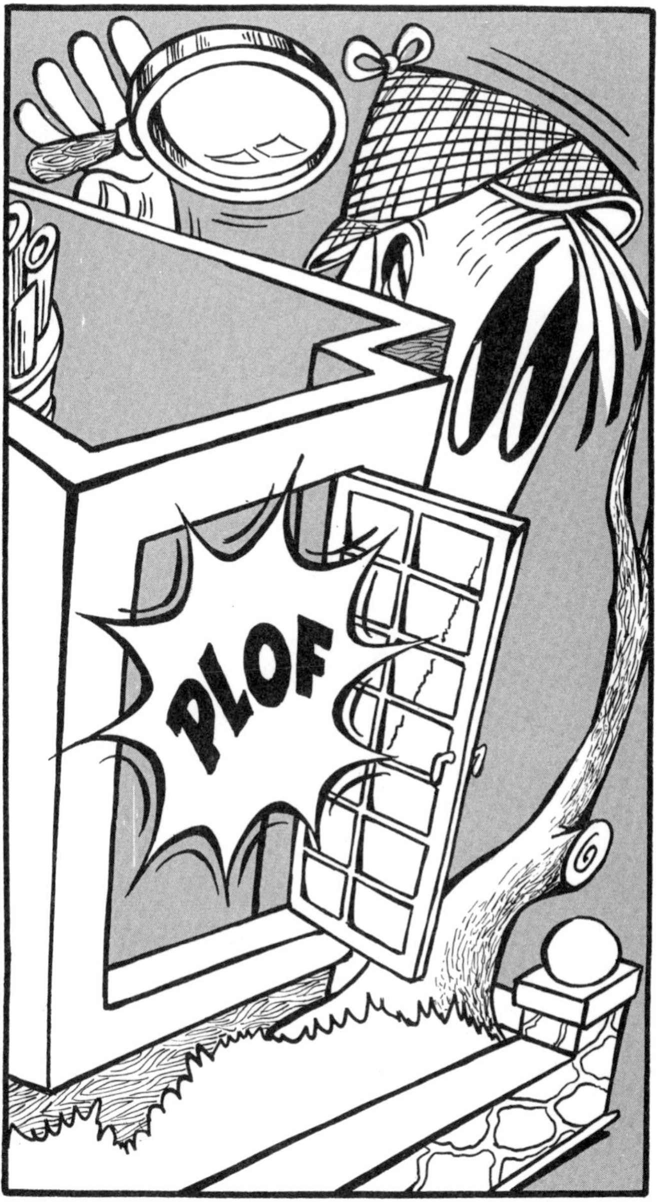
PLOF

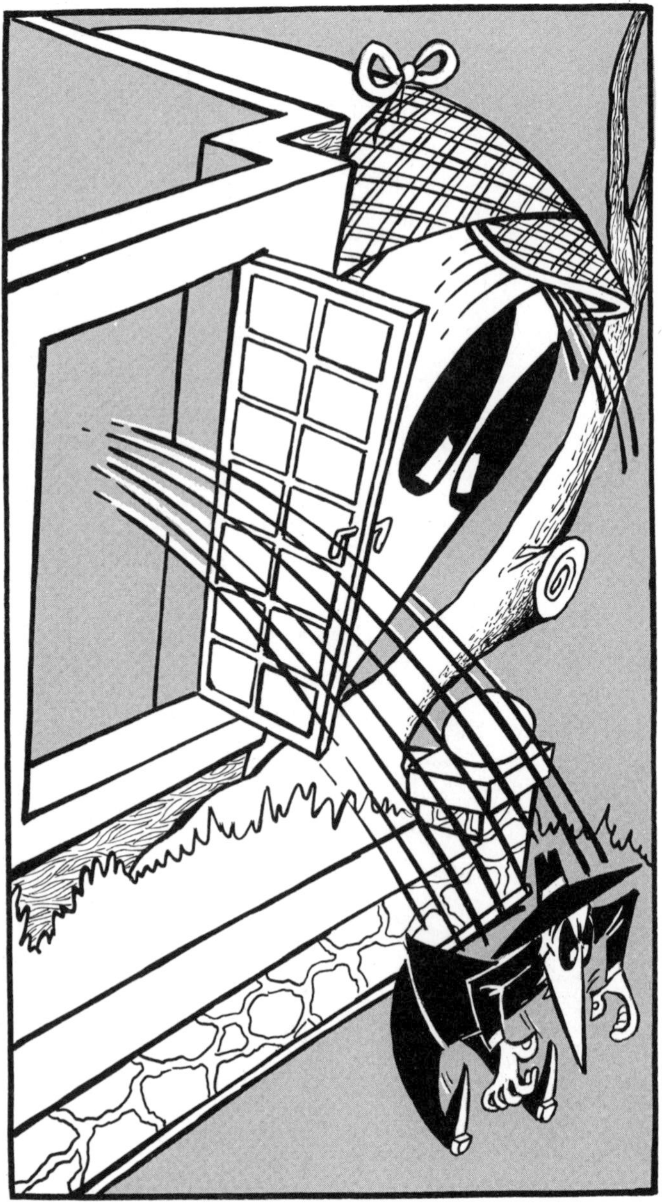

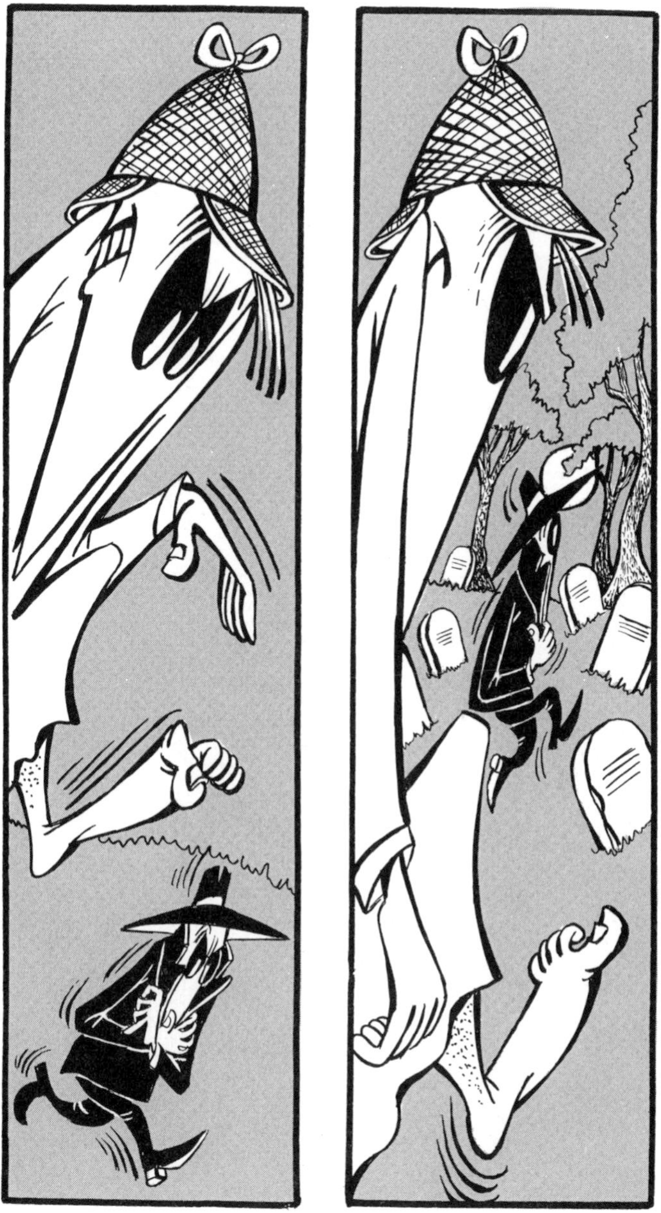

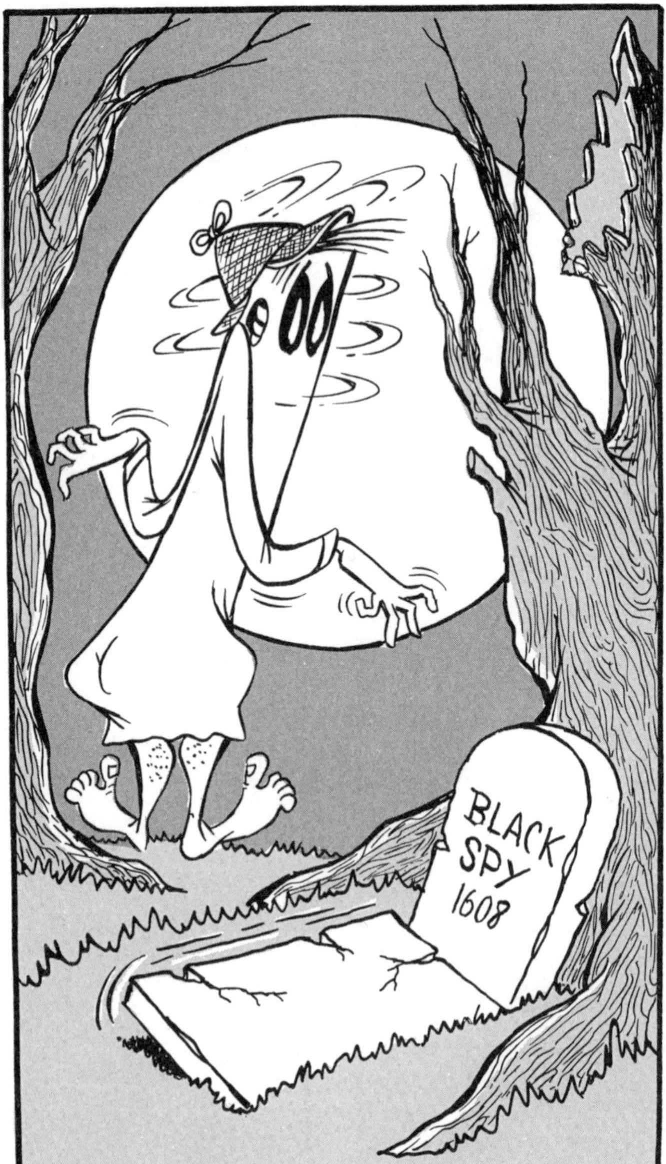
BLACK
SPY
1608

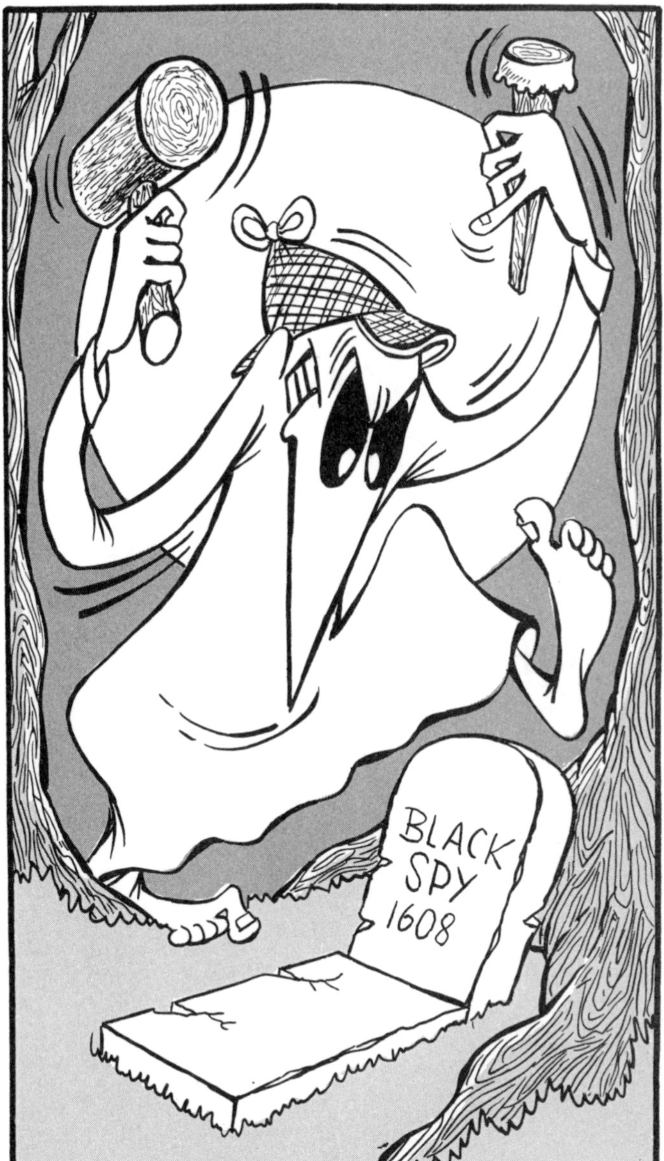
BLACK
SPY
1608

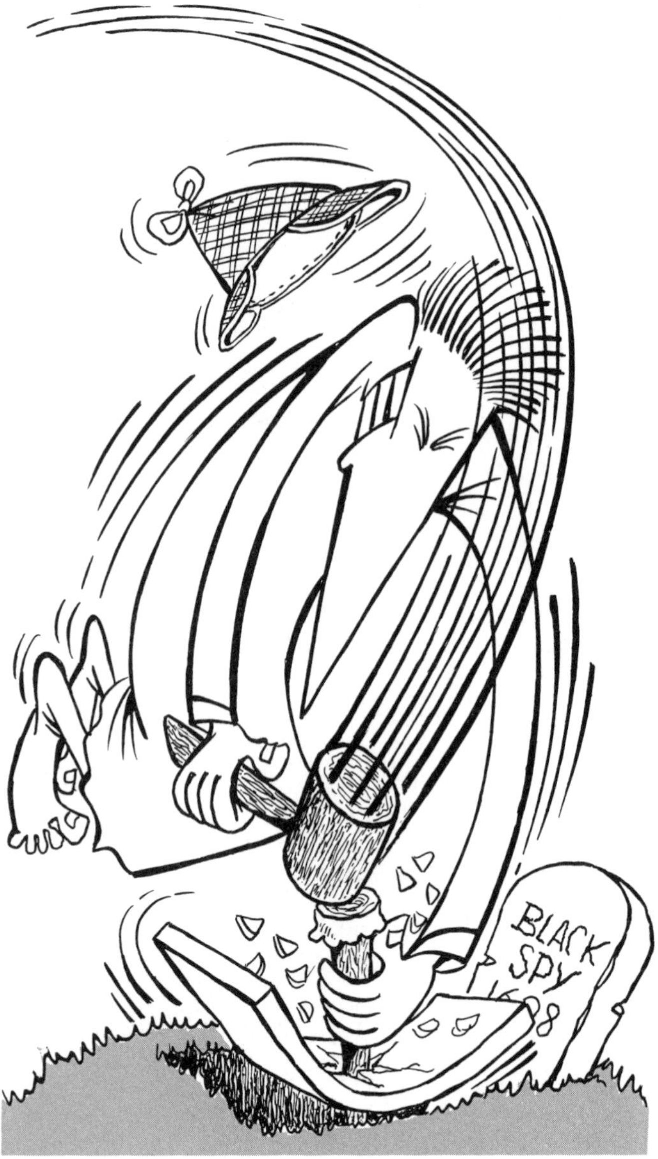
BLACK
SPY

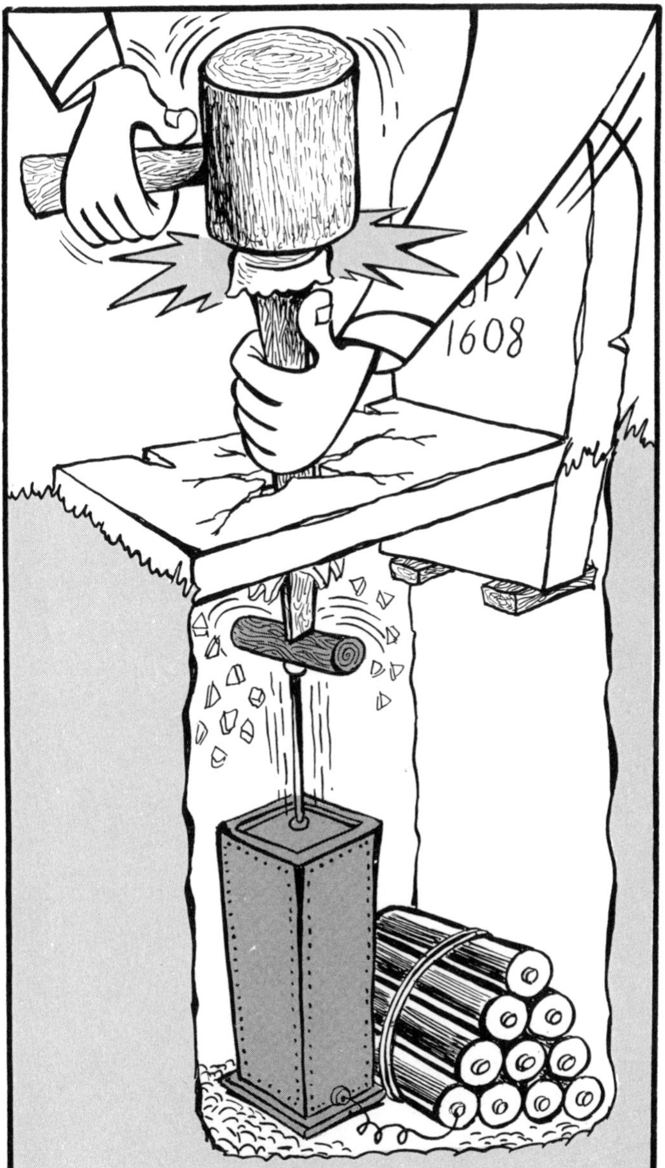
1608

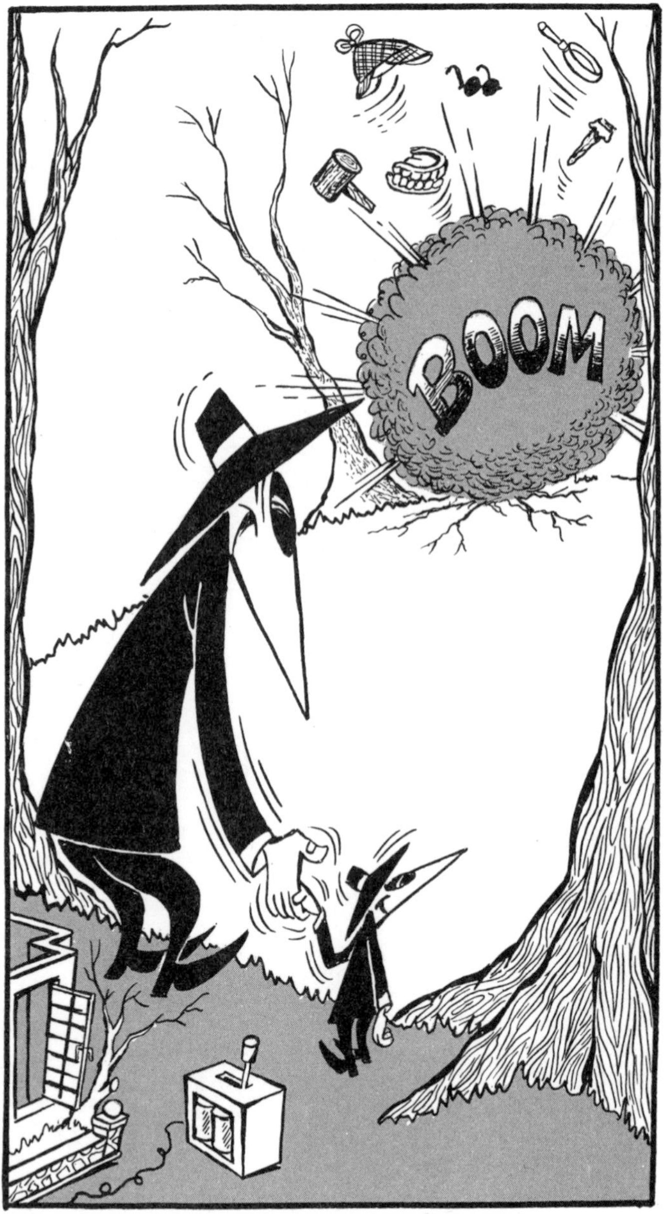
BOOM

SPY vs SPY

DEPTH'S CHARGE

TOP SECRET

BOOM
TOP SECRET

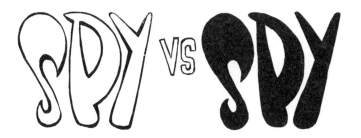

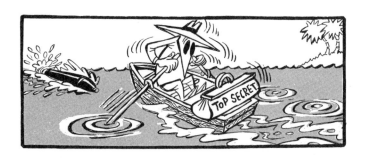

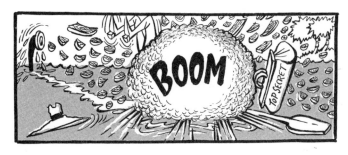

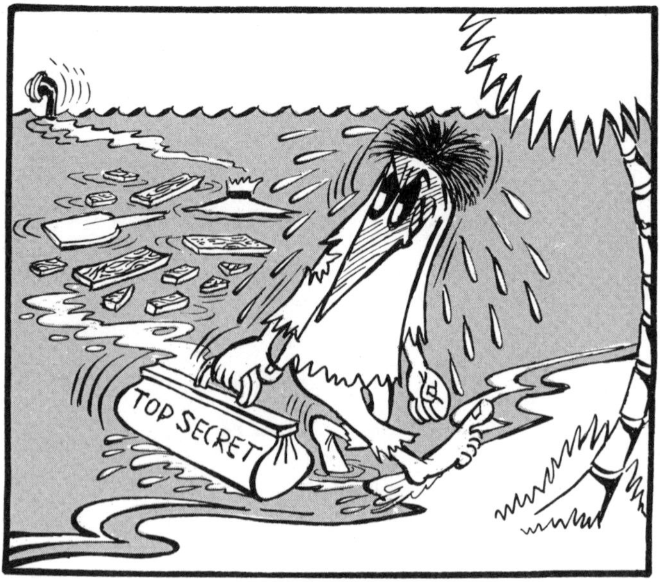
TOP SECRET

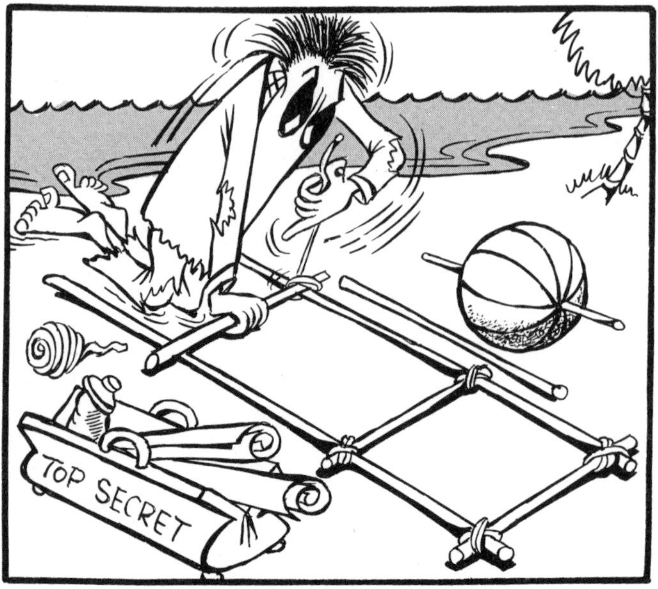
TOP SECRET

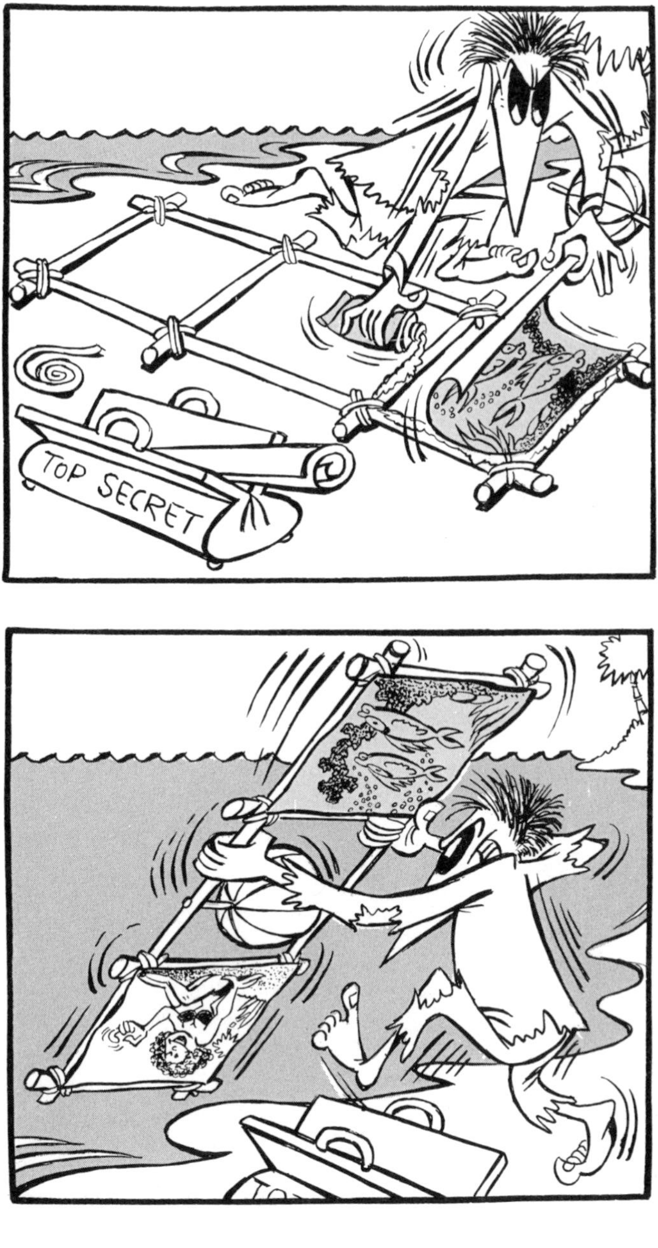
TOP SECRET

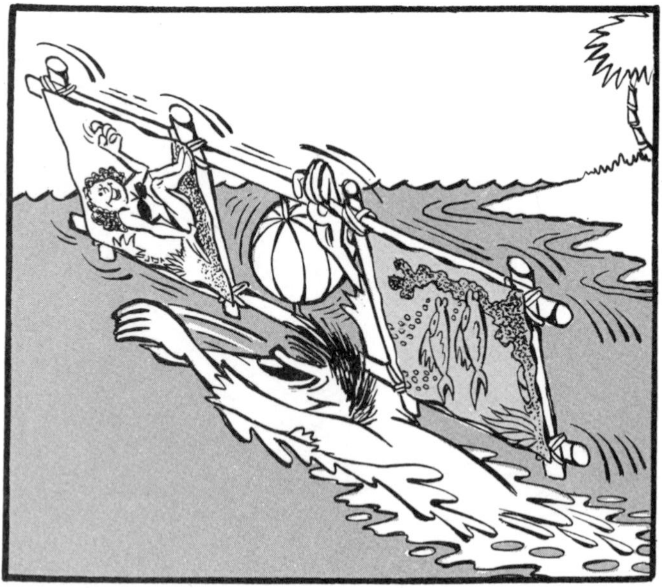

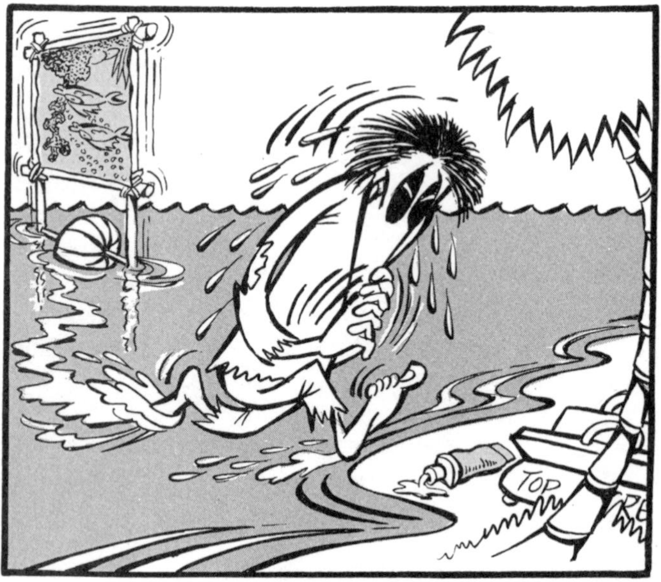
TOP

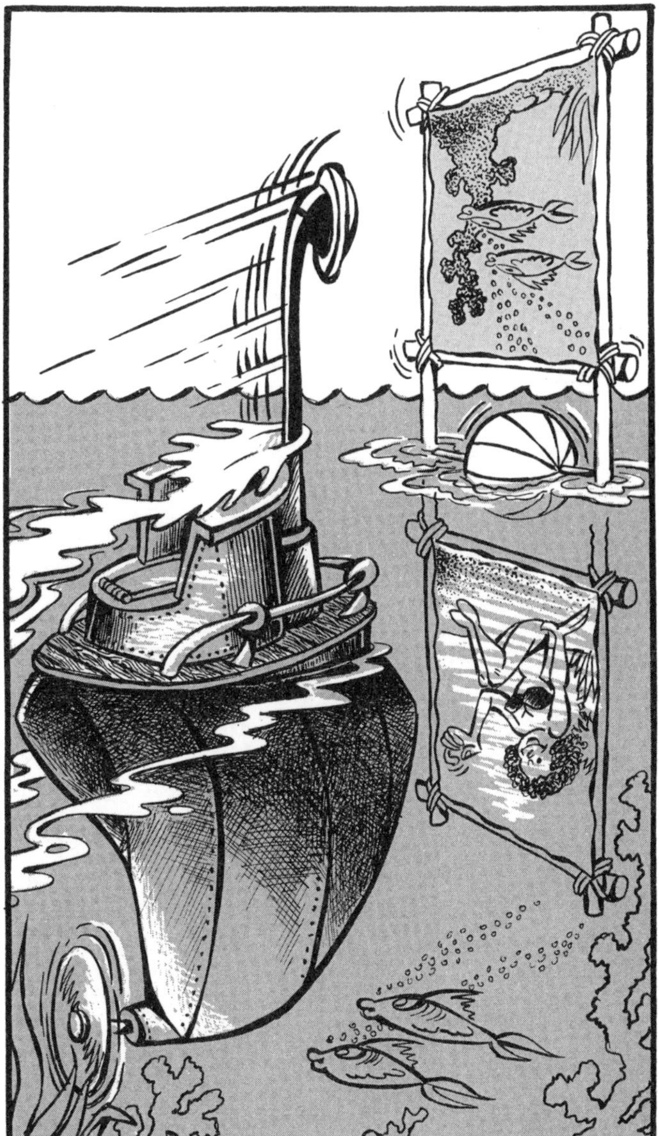

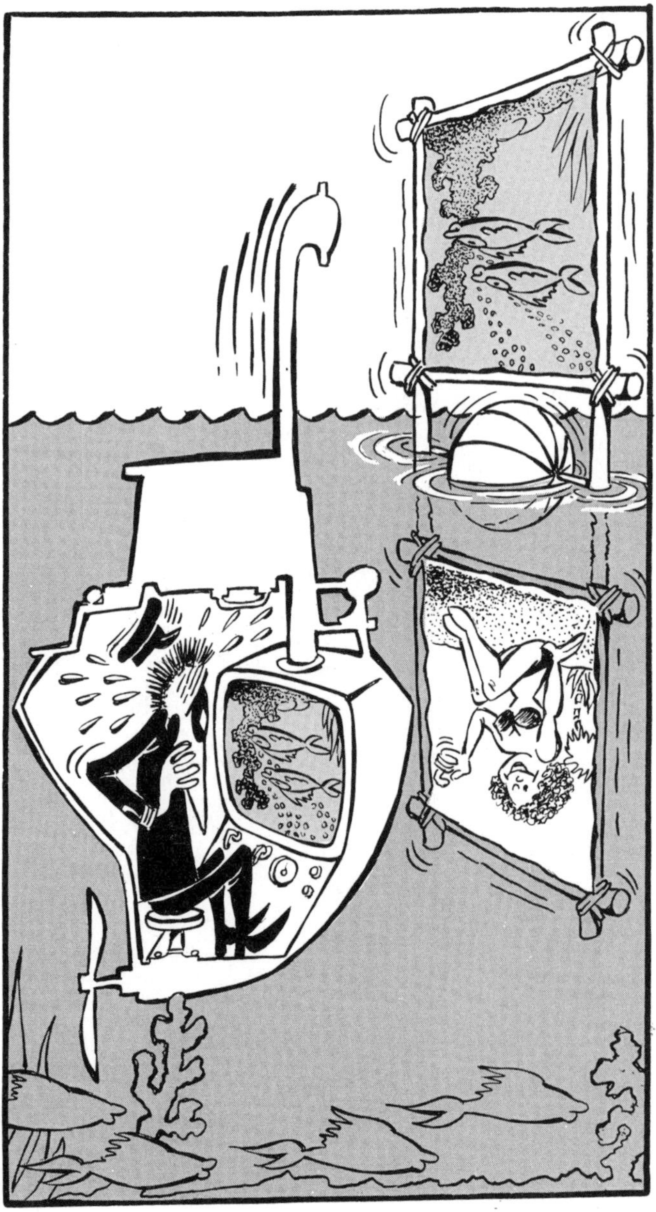

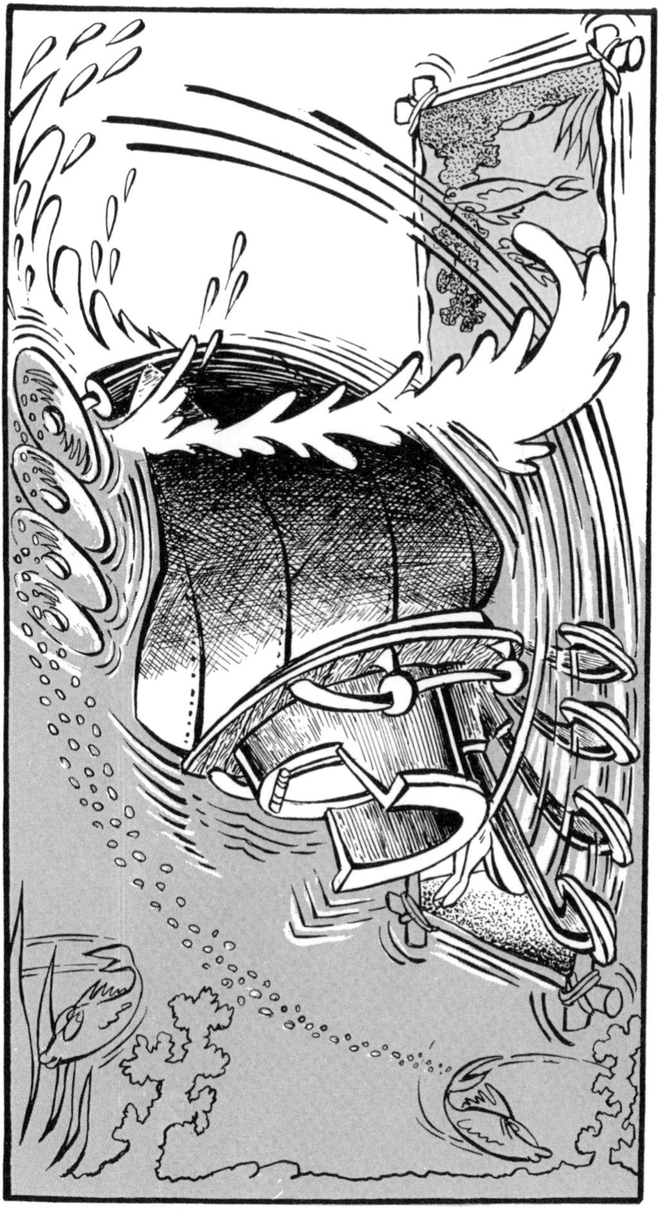

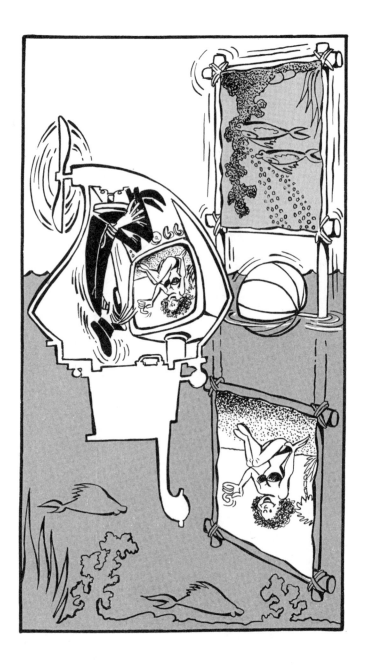

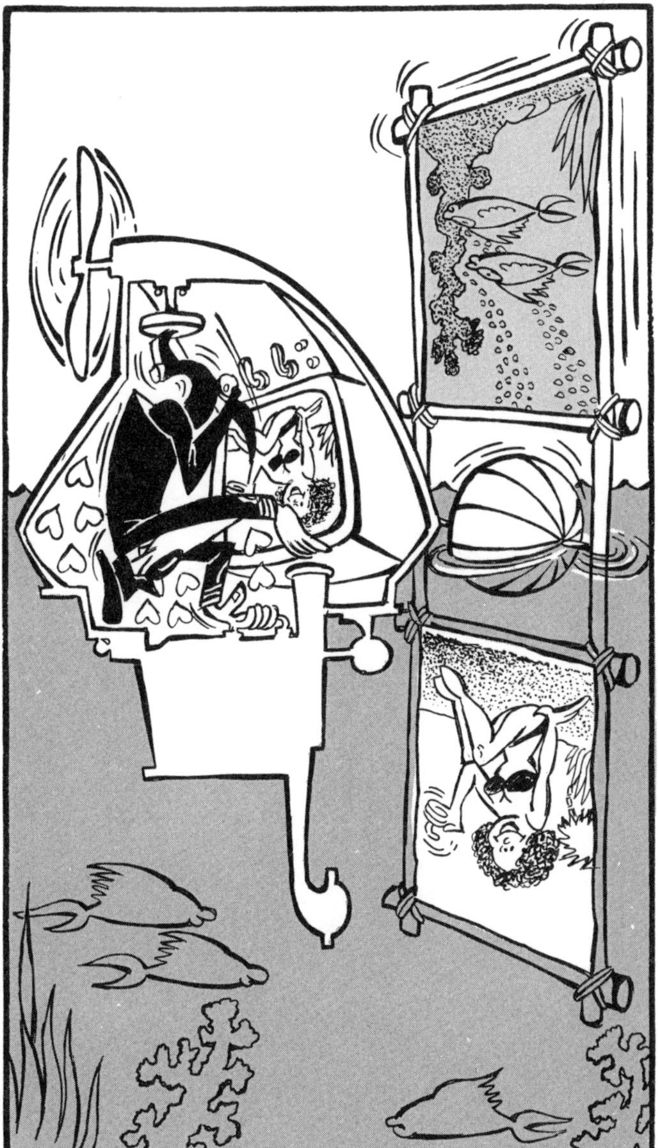

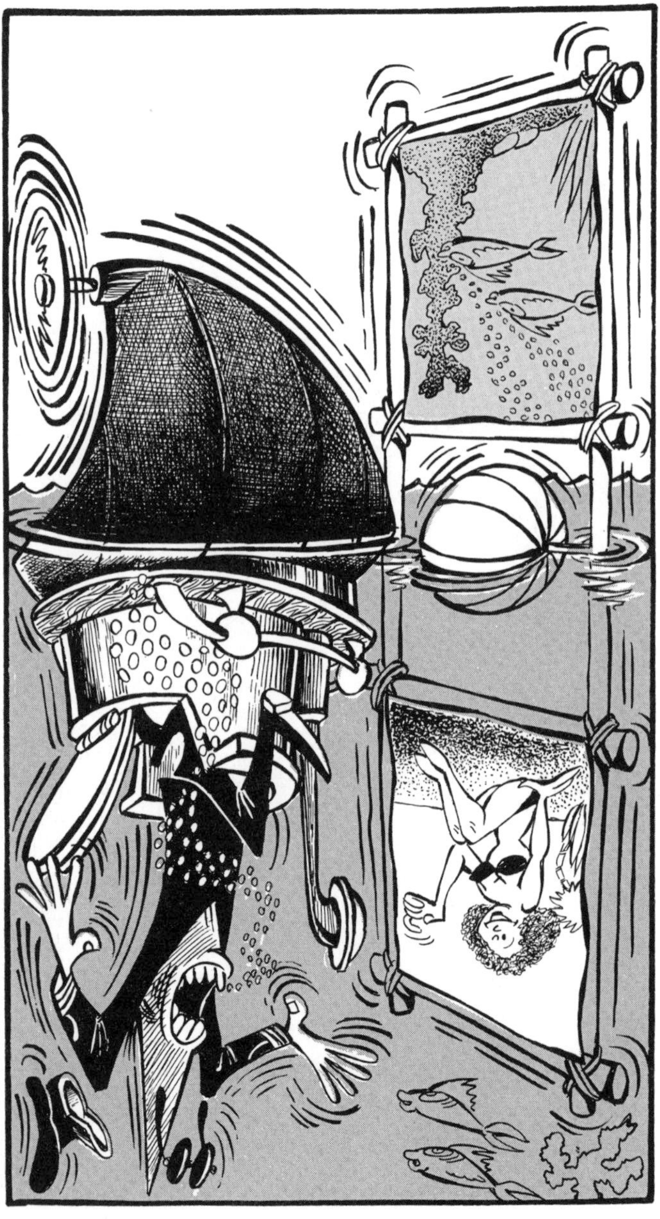

SPY vs SPY

FOR WHOM THE BELLE'S TOAD

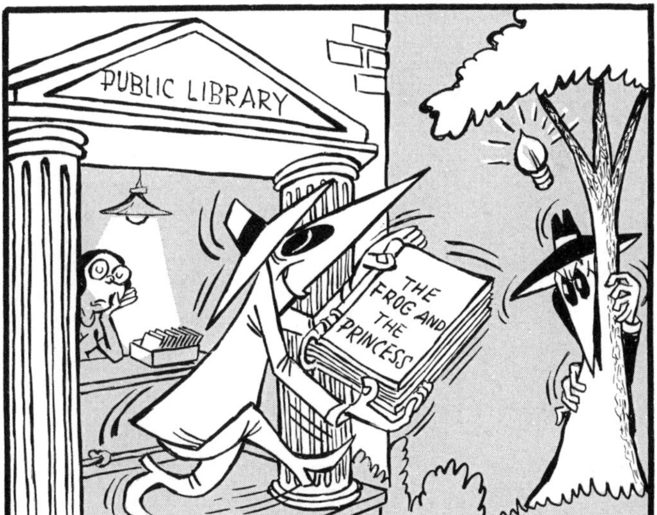
PUBLIC LIBRARY
THE FROG AND THE PRINCESS

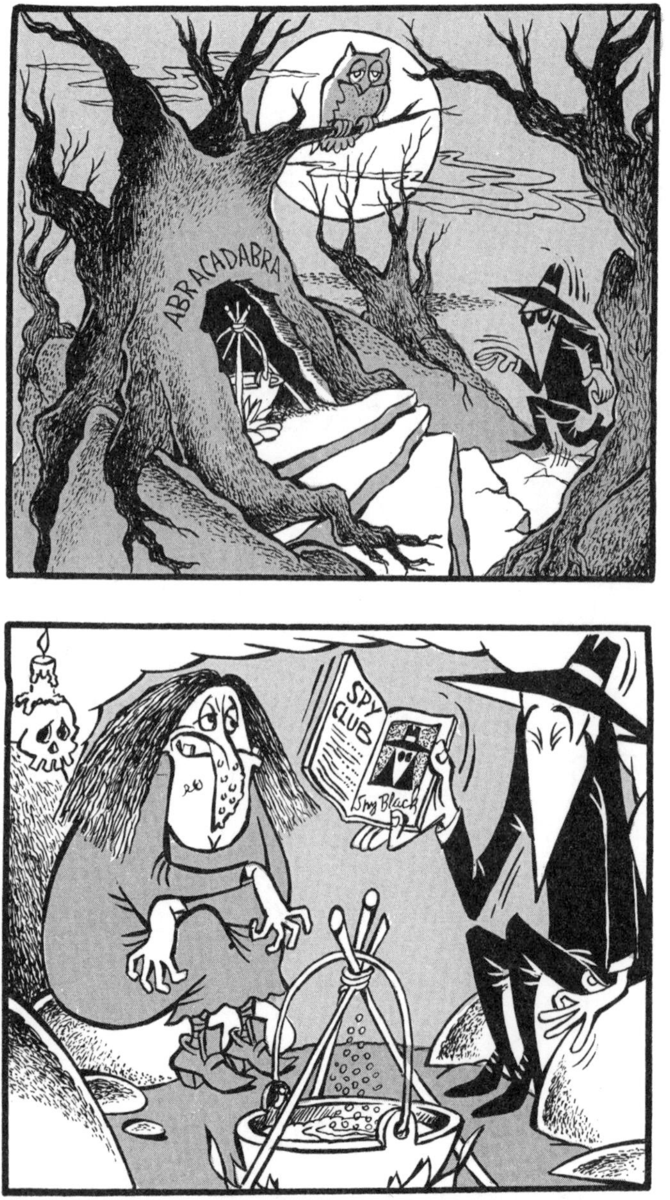
ABRACADABRA
SPY CLUB
Spy Black

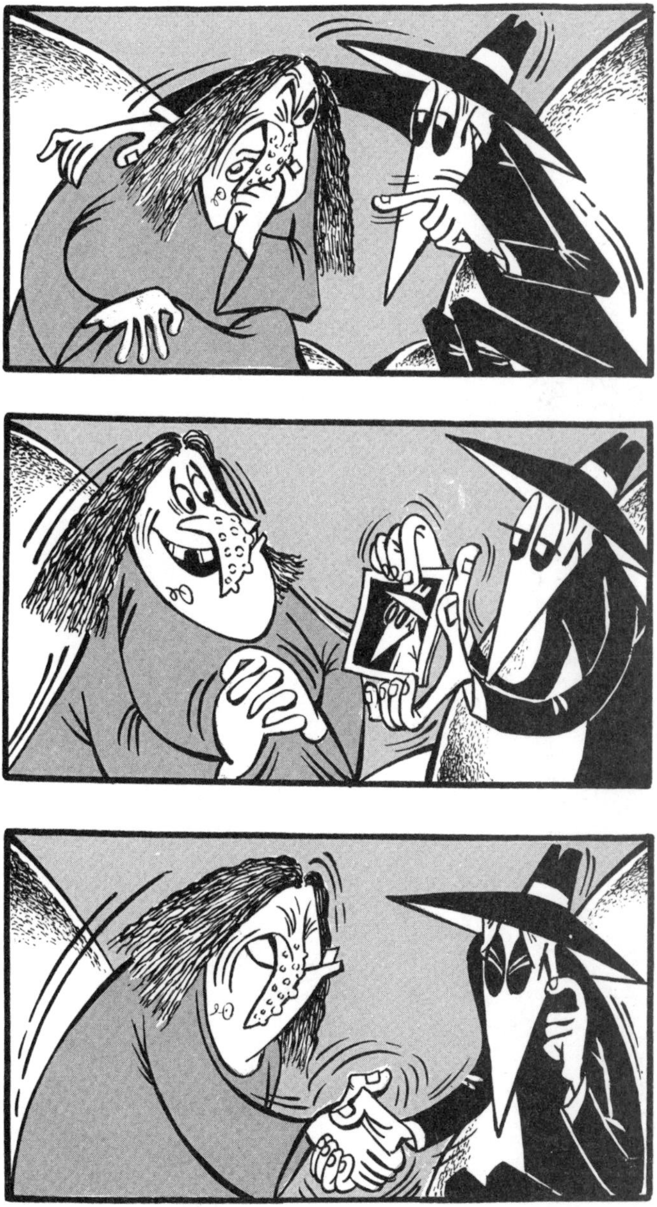

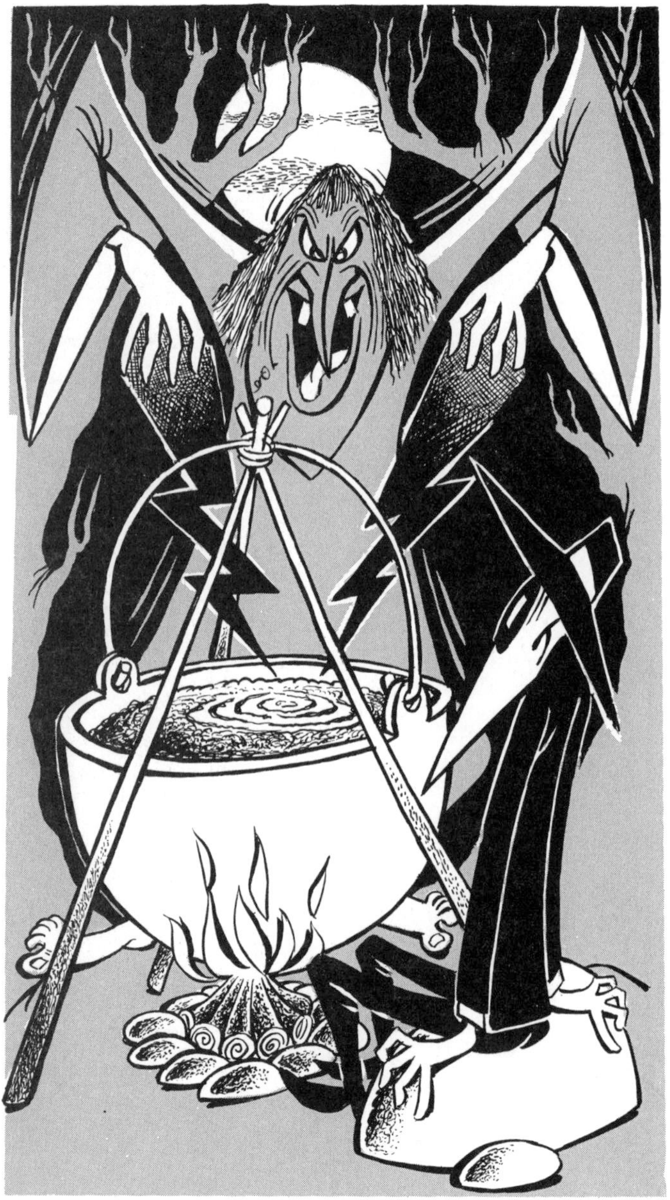

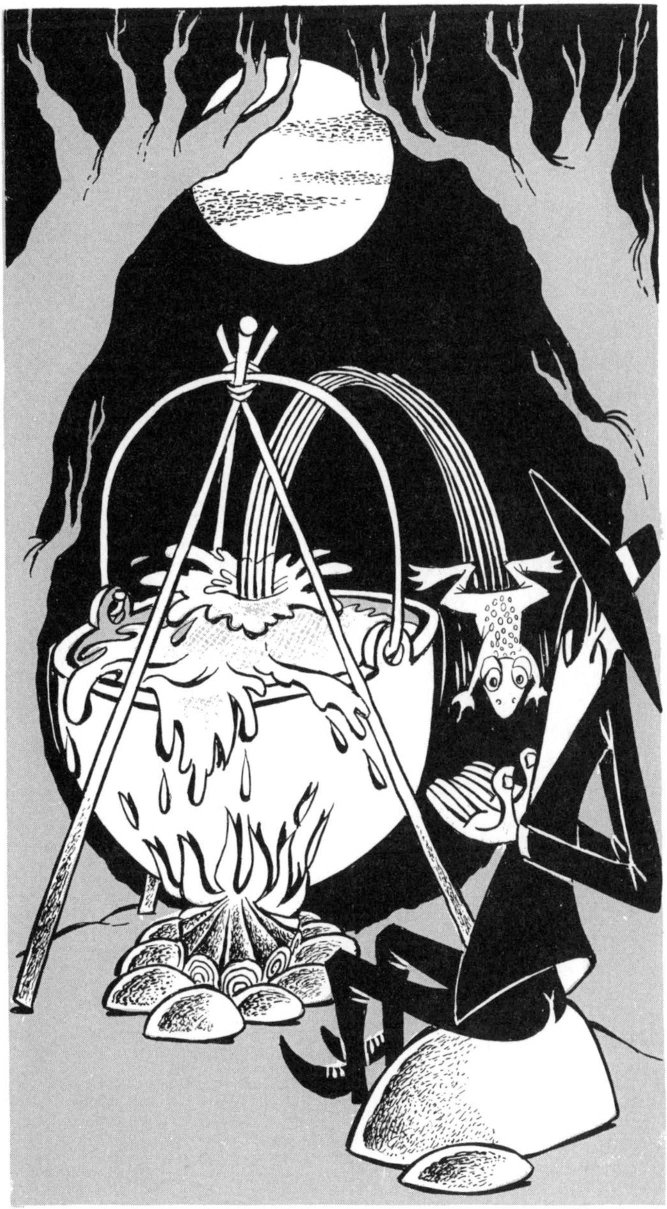

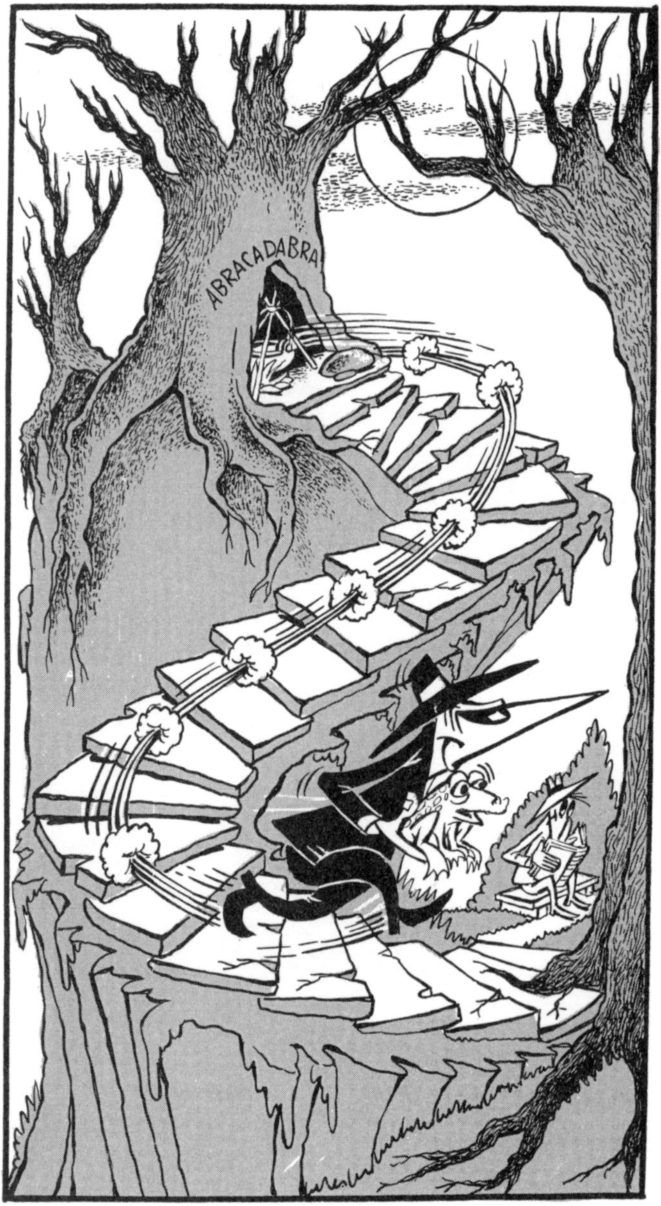
ABRACADABRA

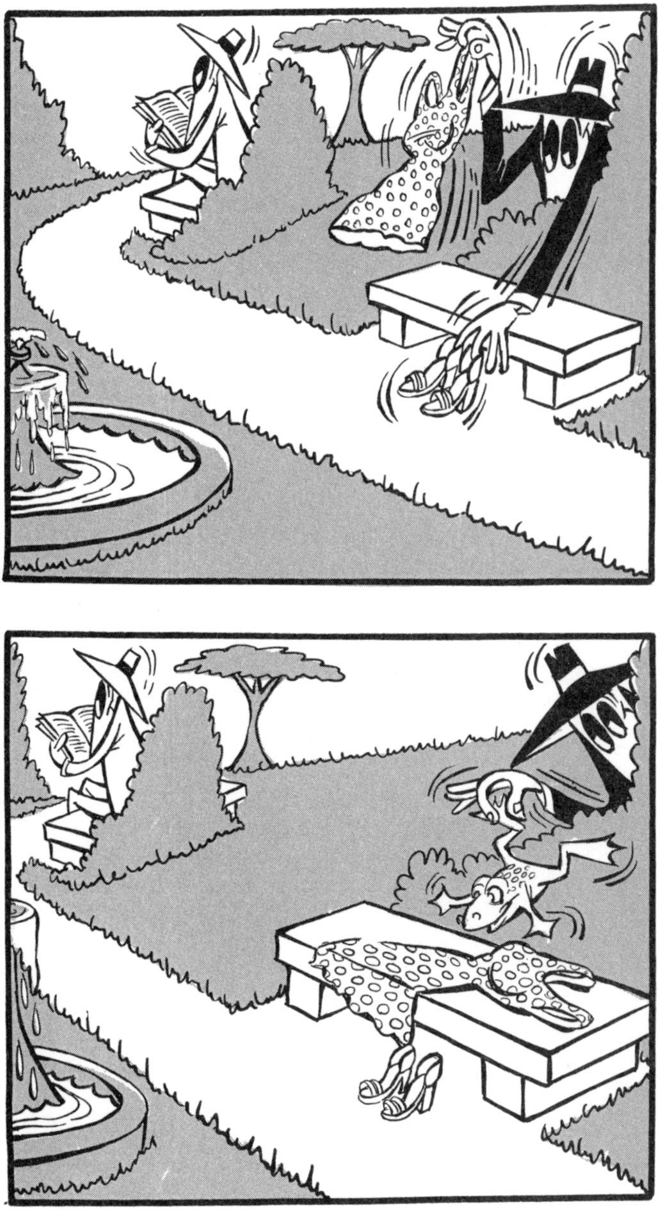

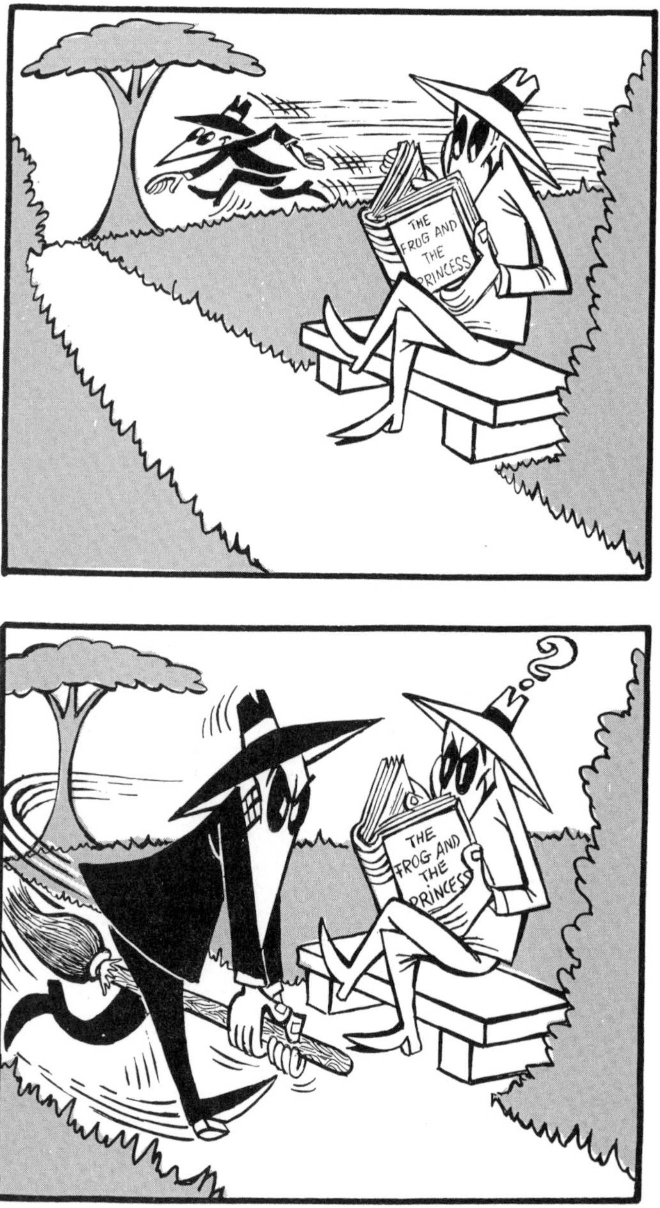
THE FROG AND THE PRINCESS
THE FROG AND THE PRINCESS

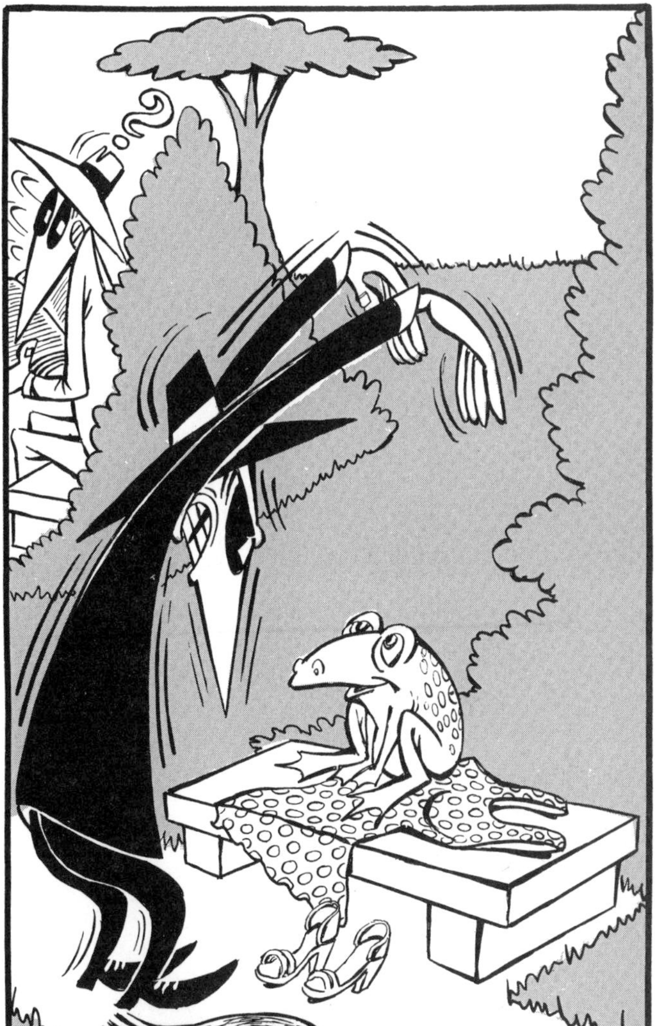

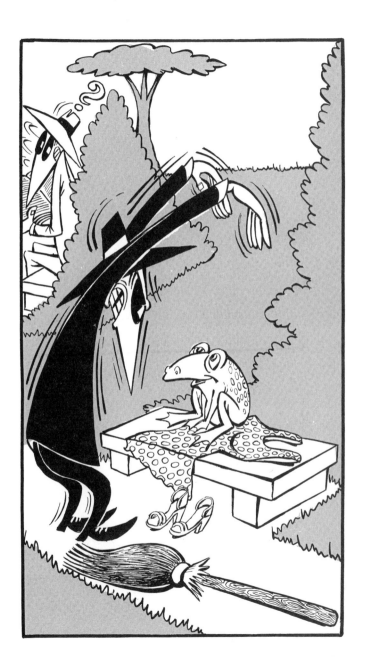

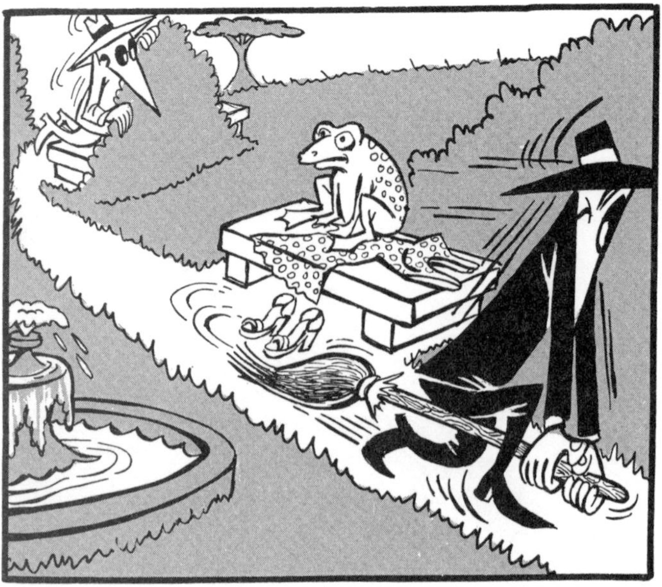

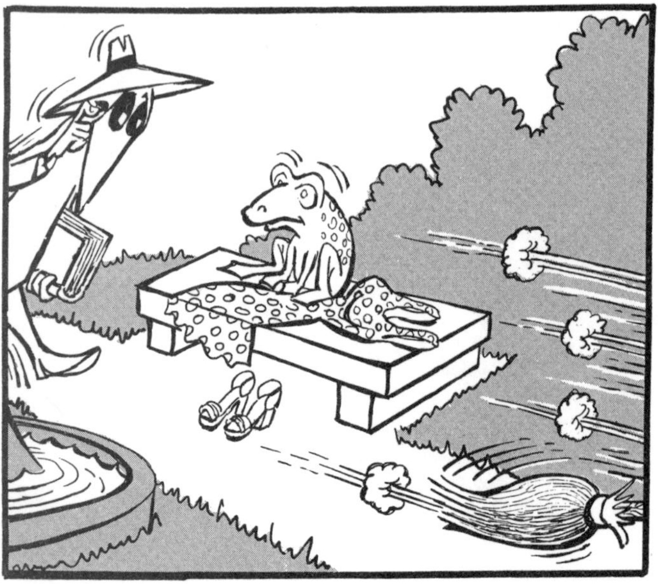

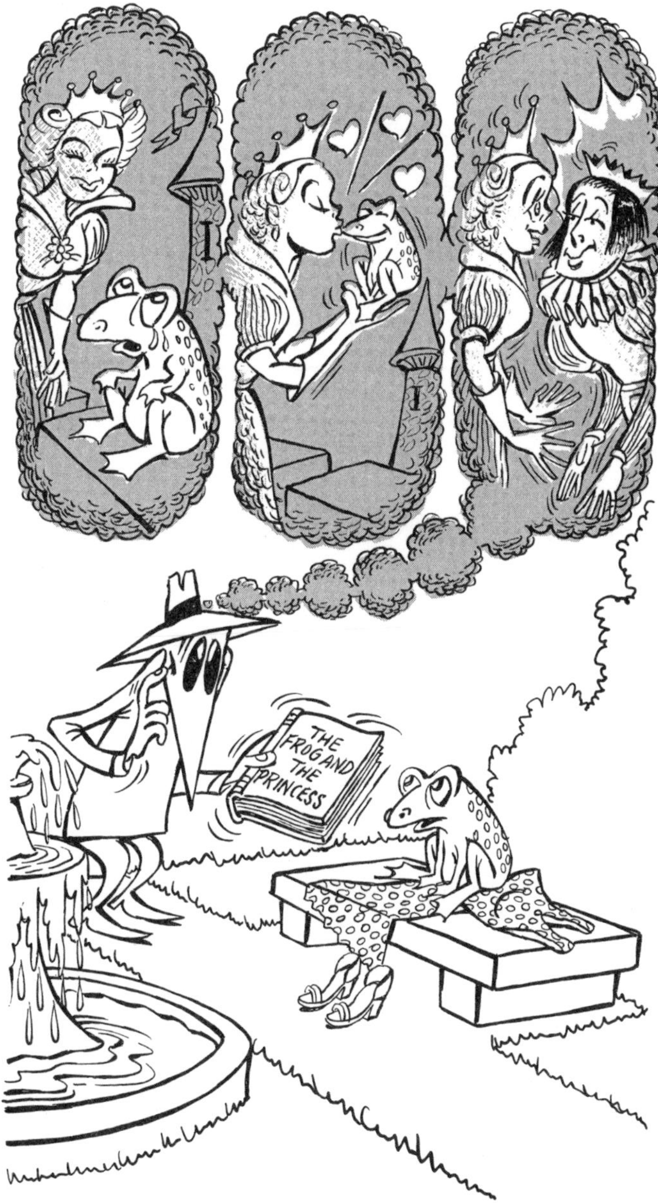
THE FROG AND THE PRINCESS

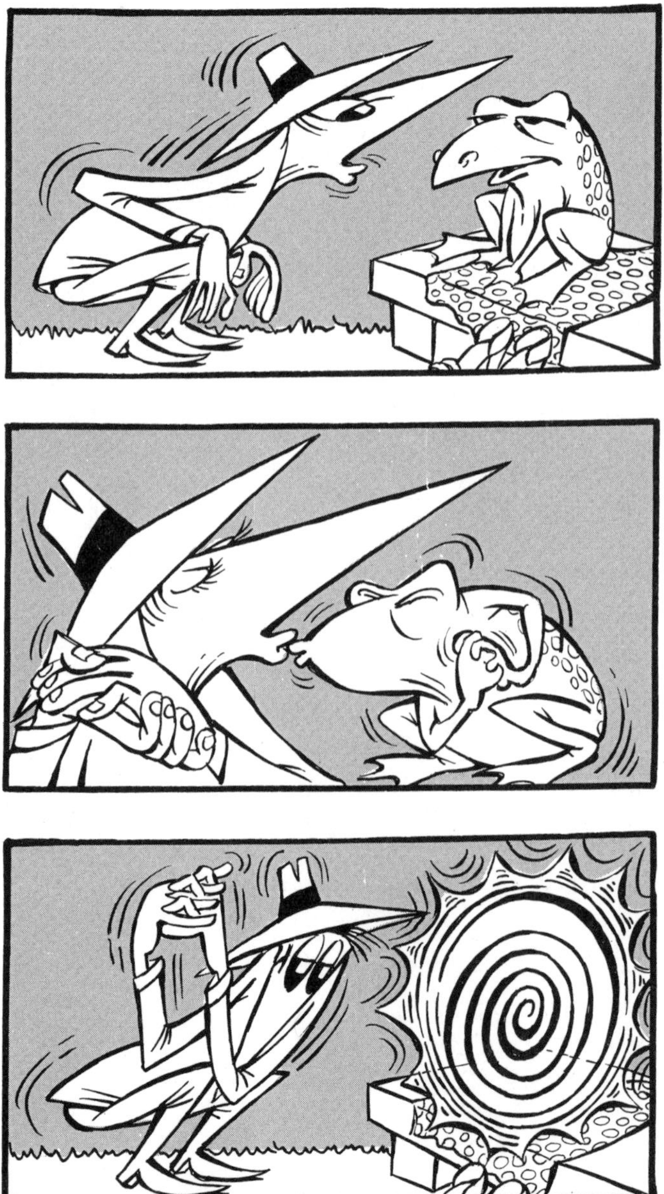

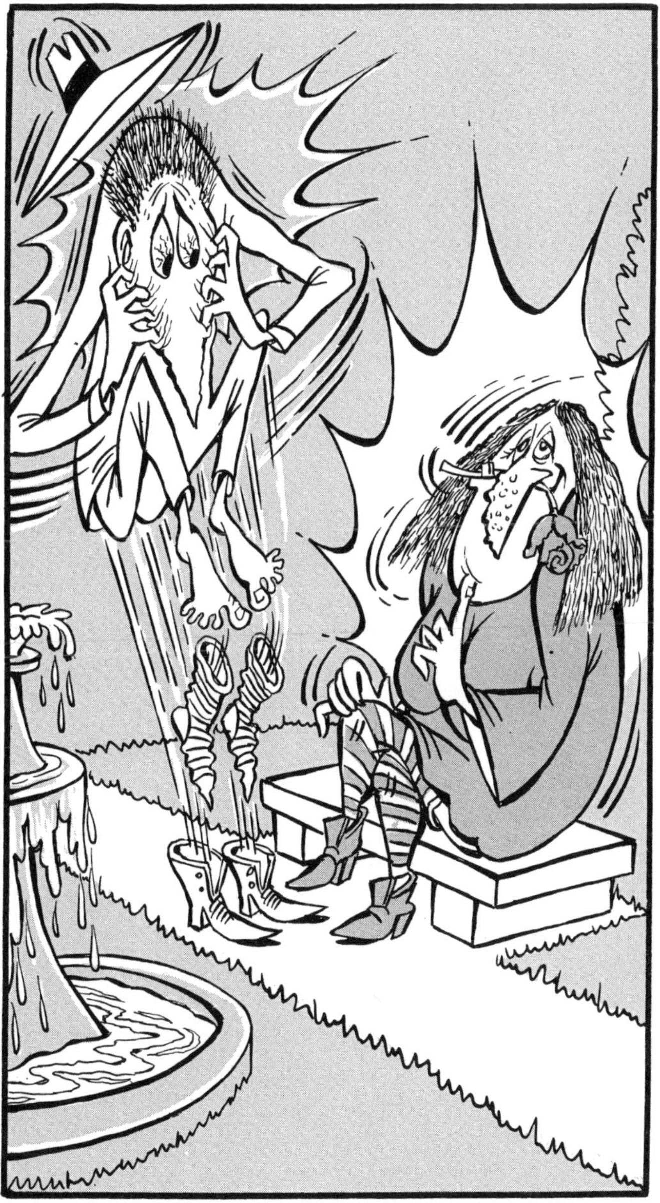

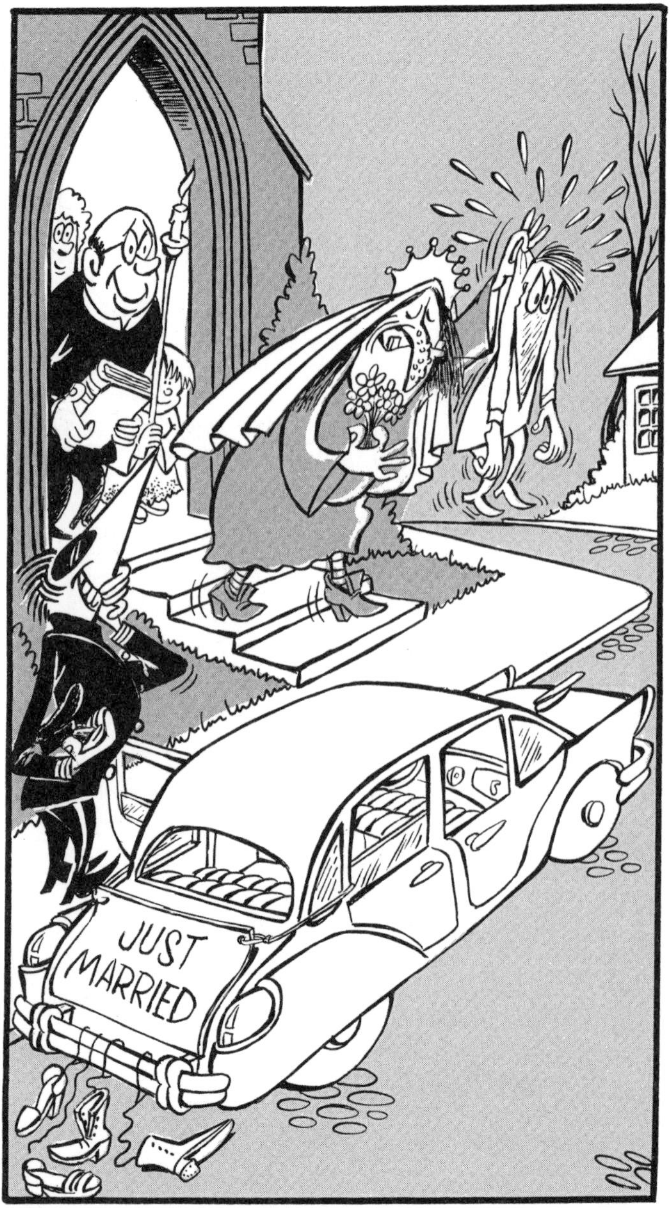
JUST MARRIED

SPY VS SPY

WHEN OPPOSITE ATTRACTS

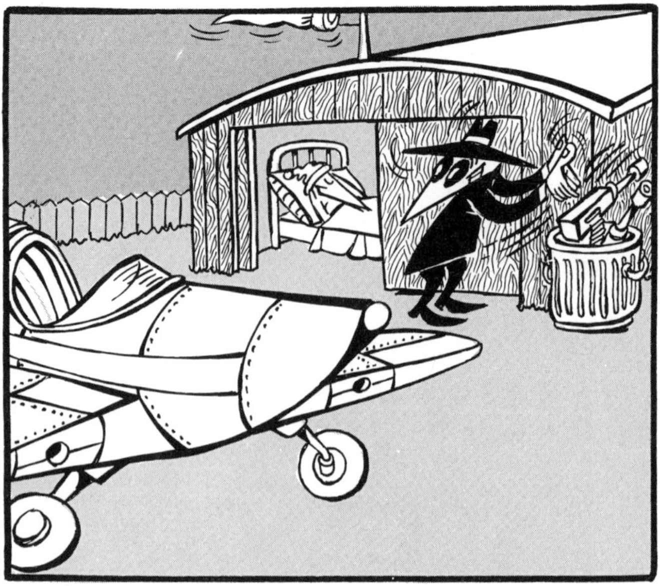

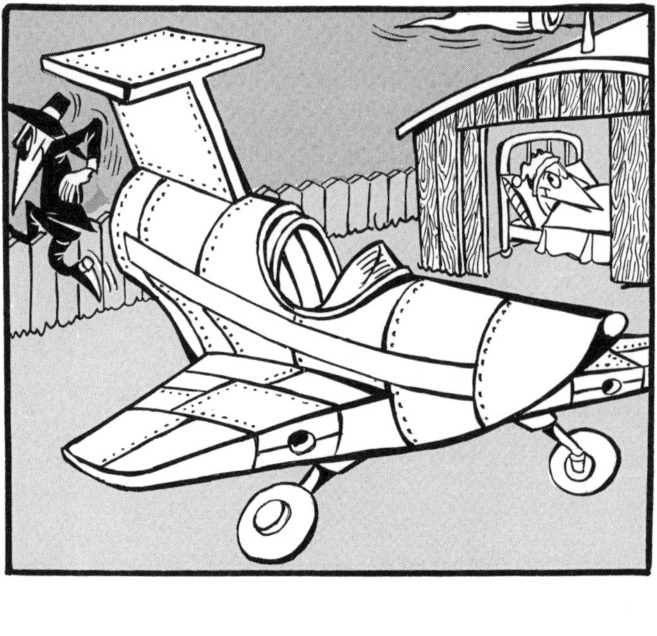

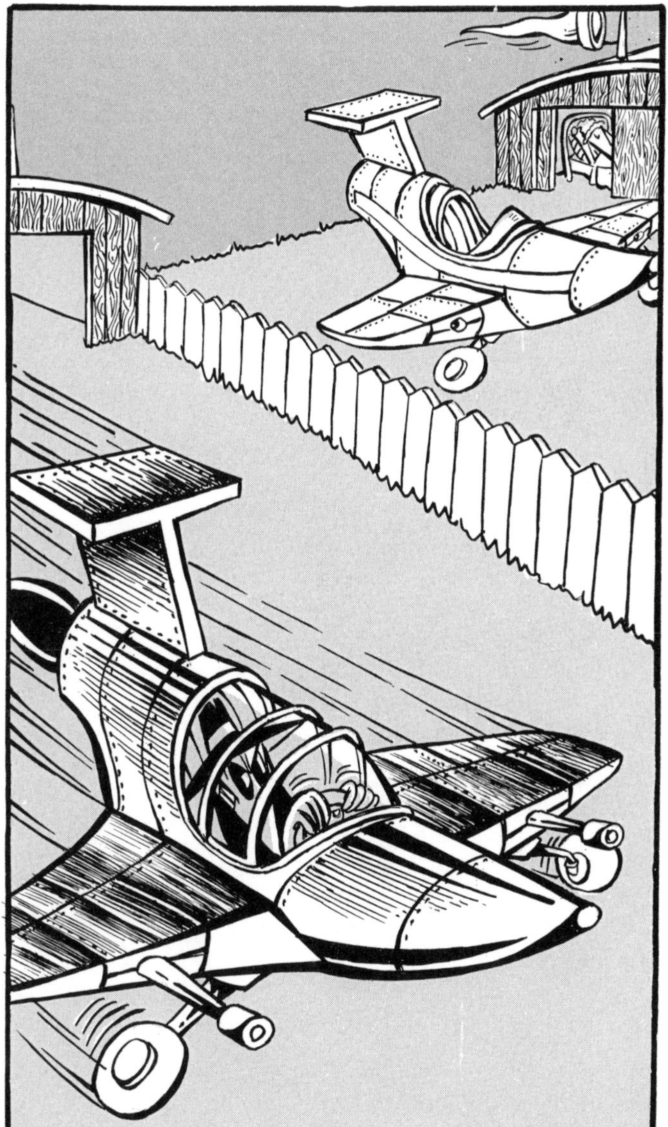

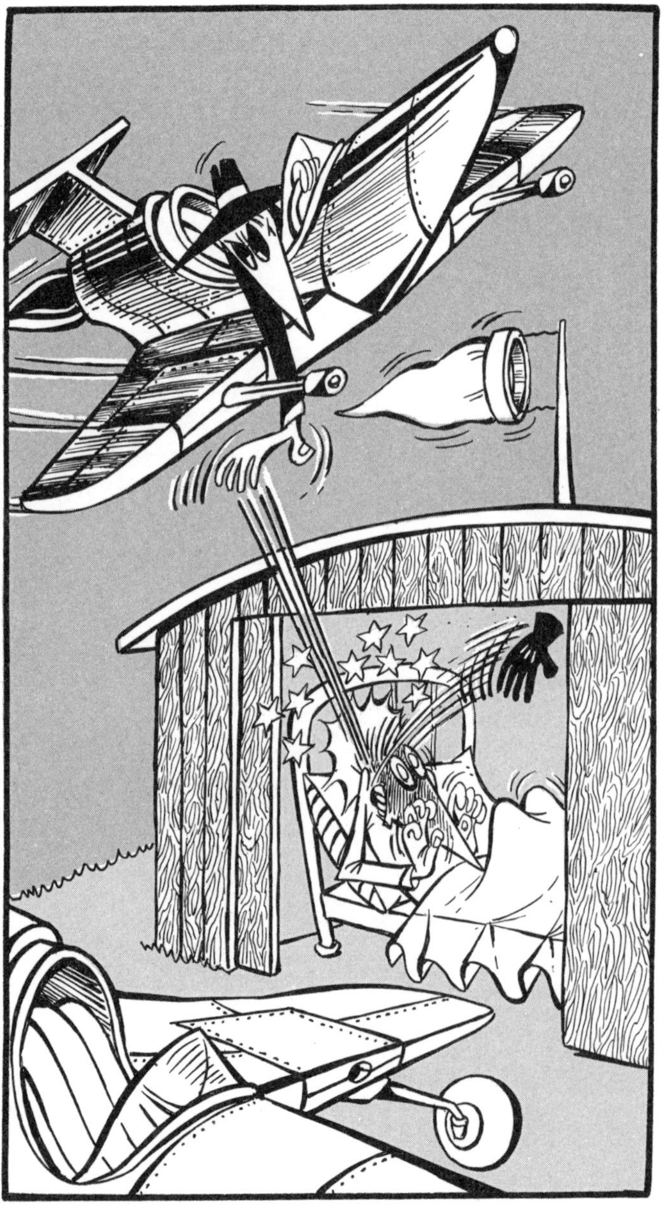

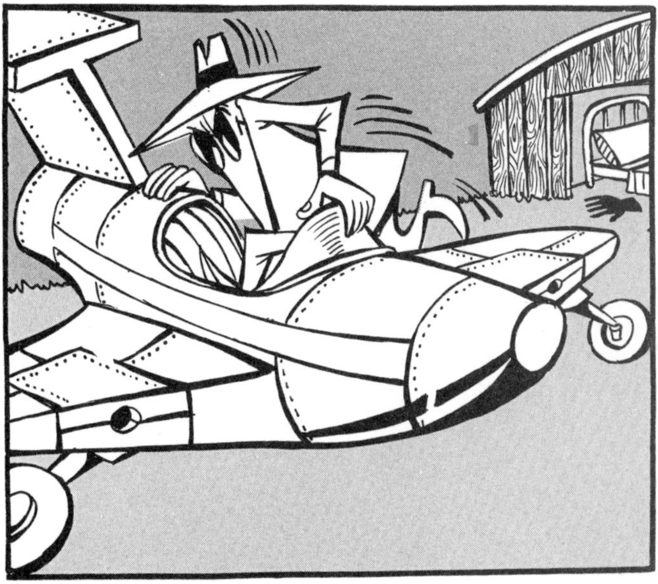

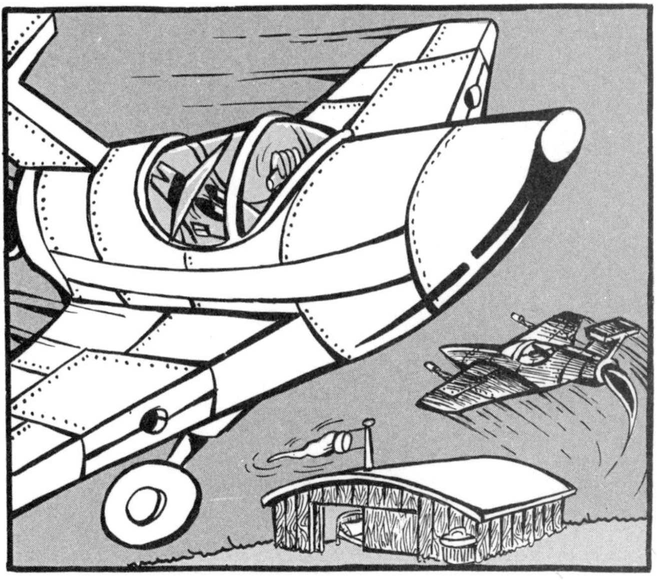

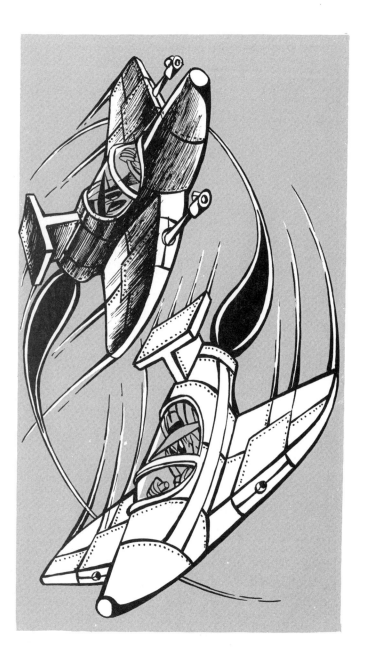

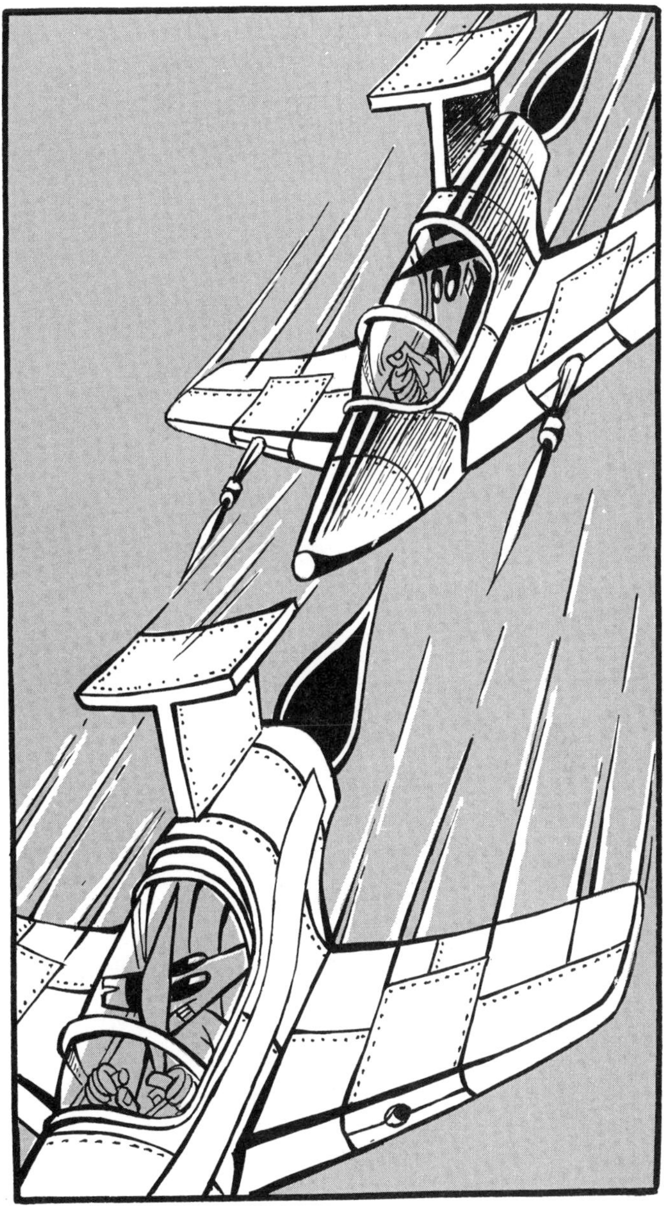

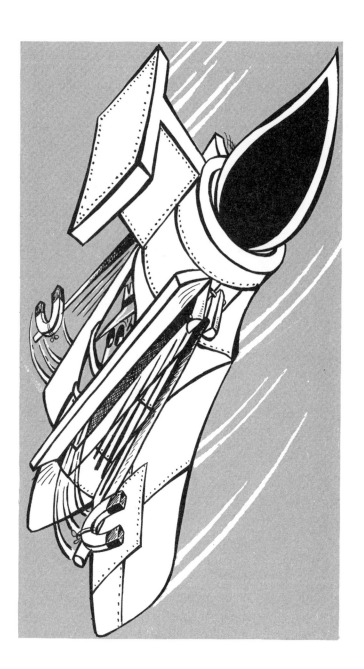

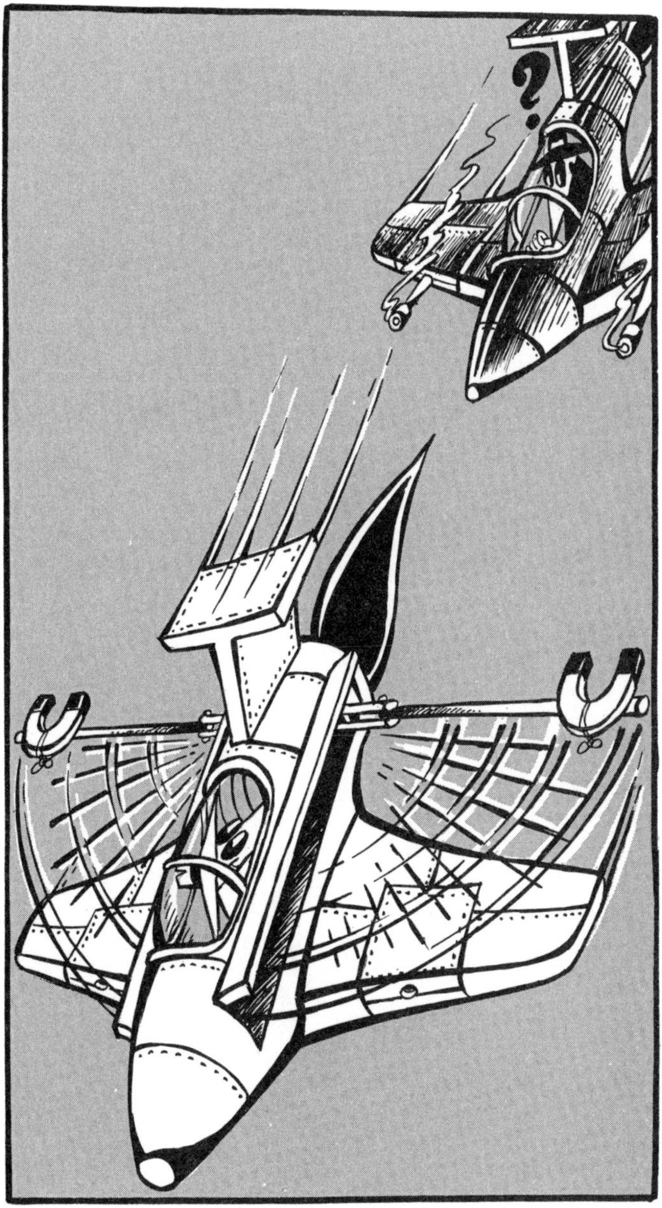

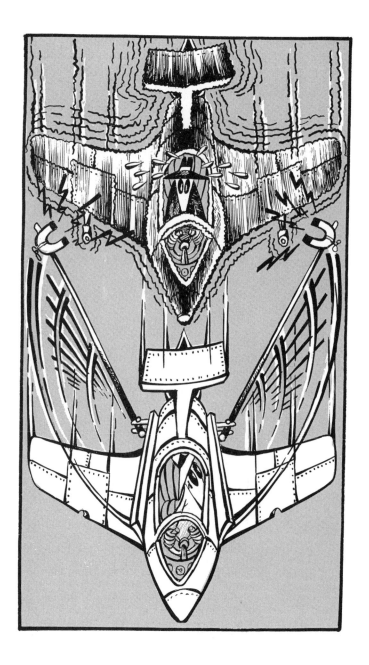

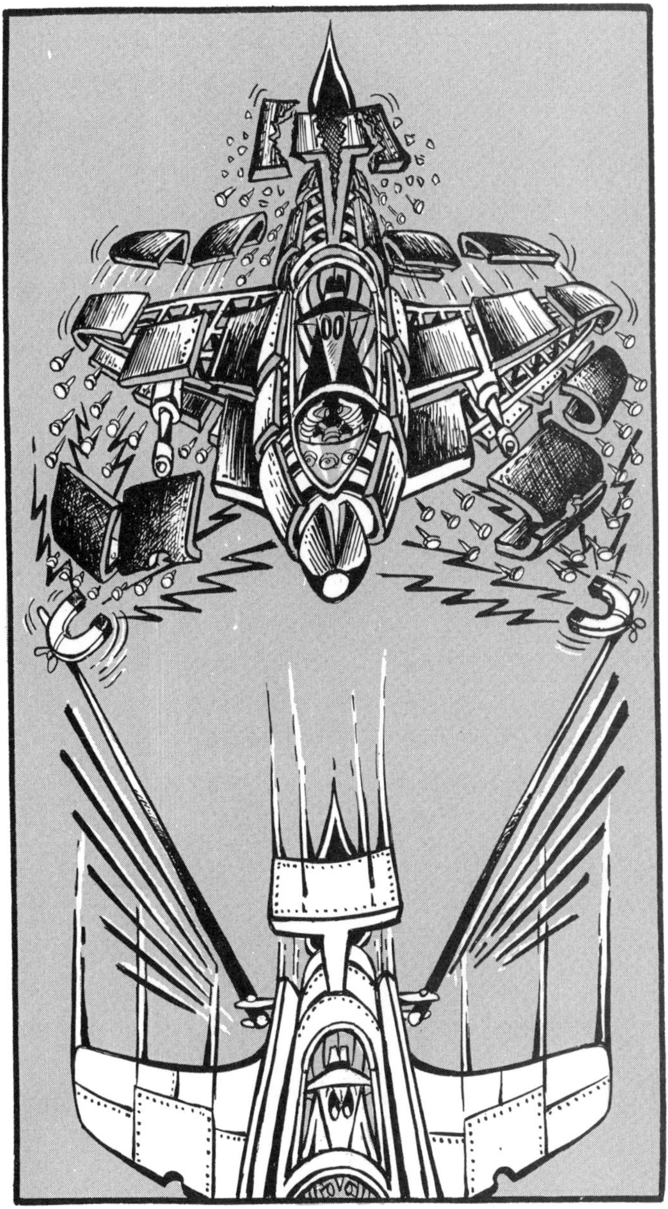

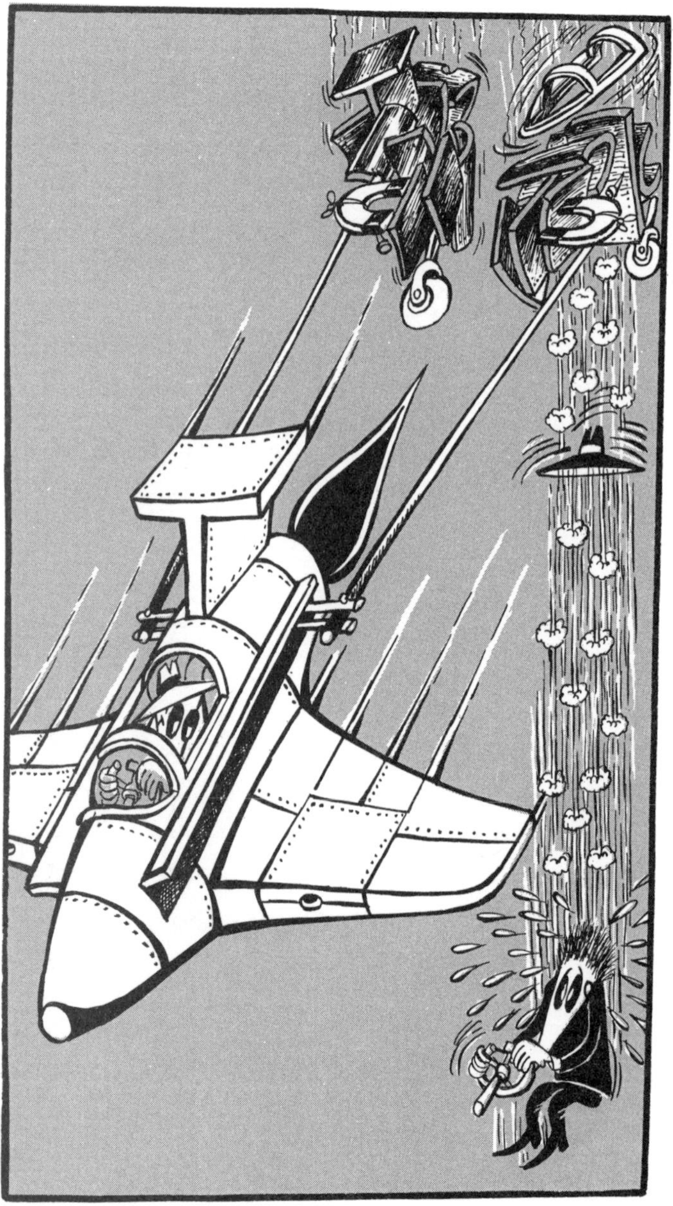

SPY vs SPY

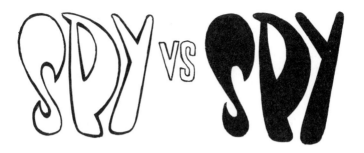

EAVES DROPPING

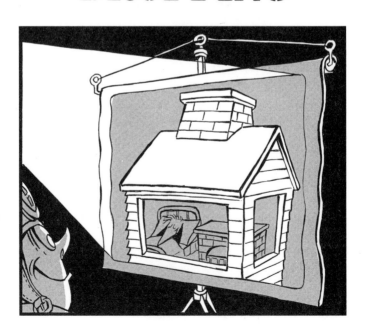

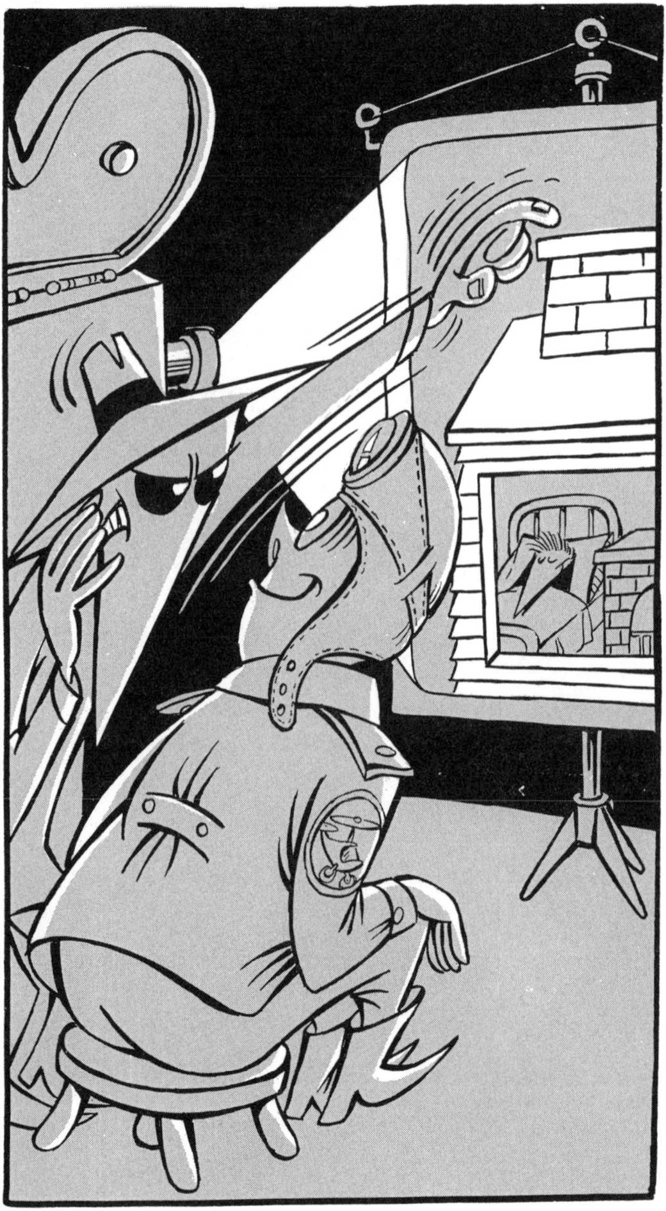

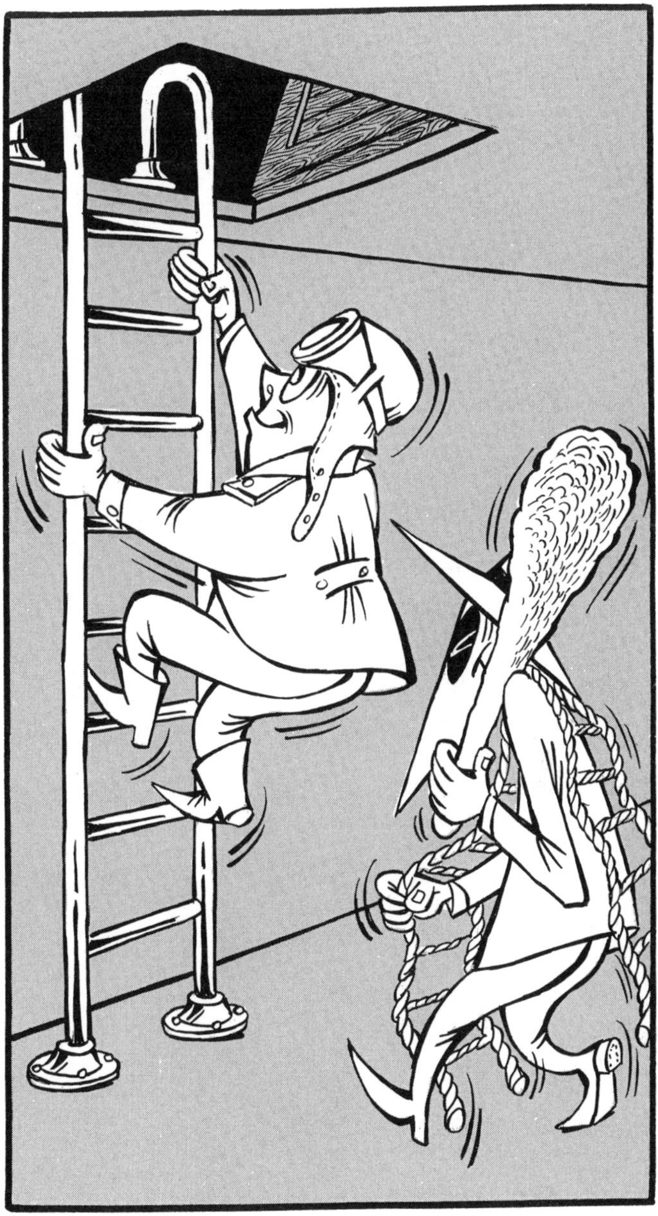

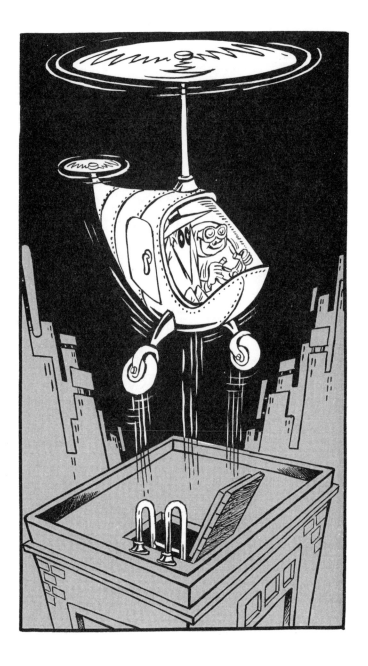

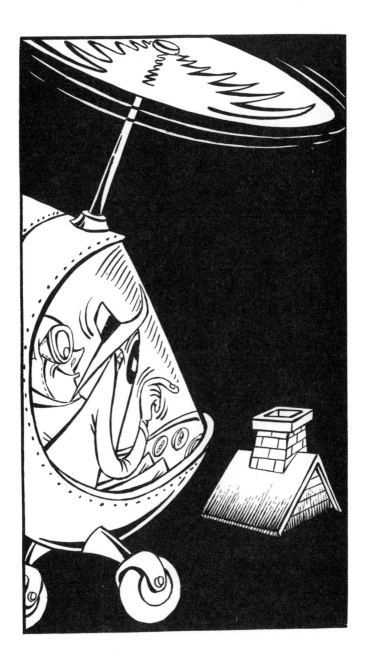

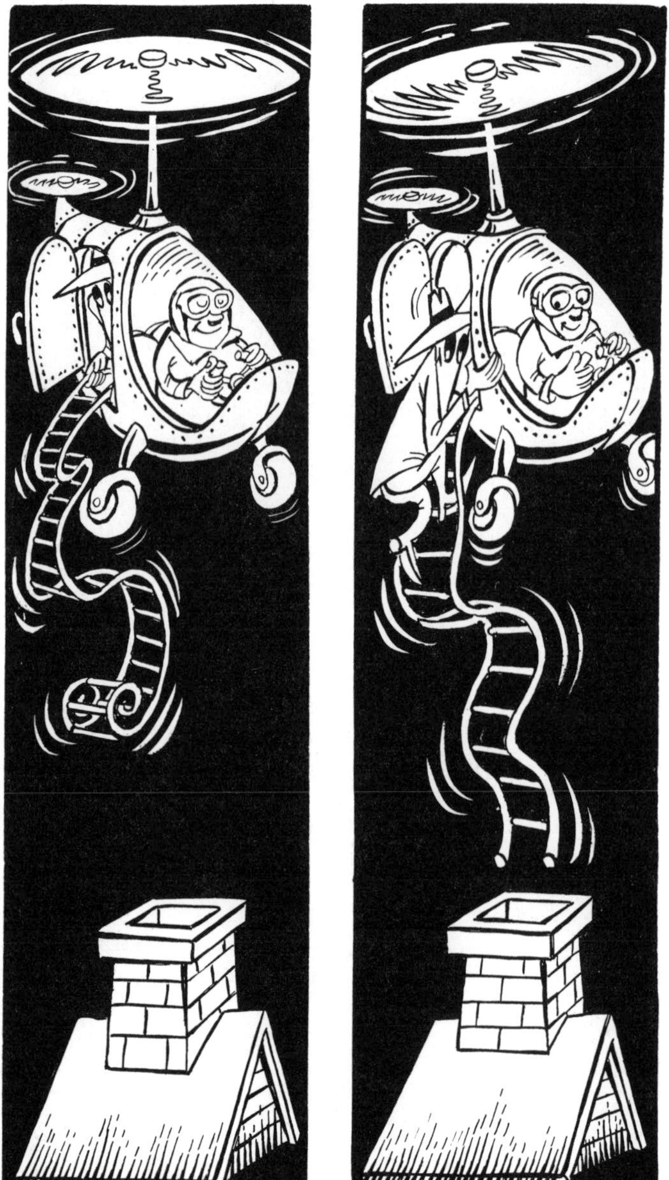

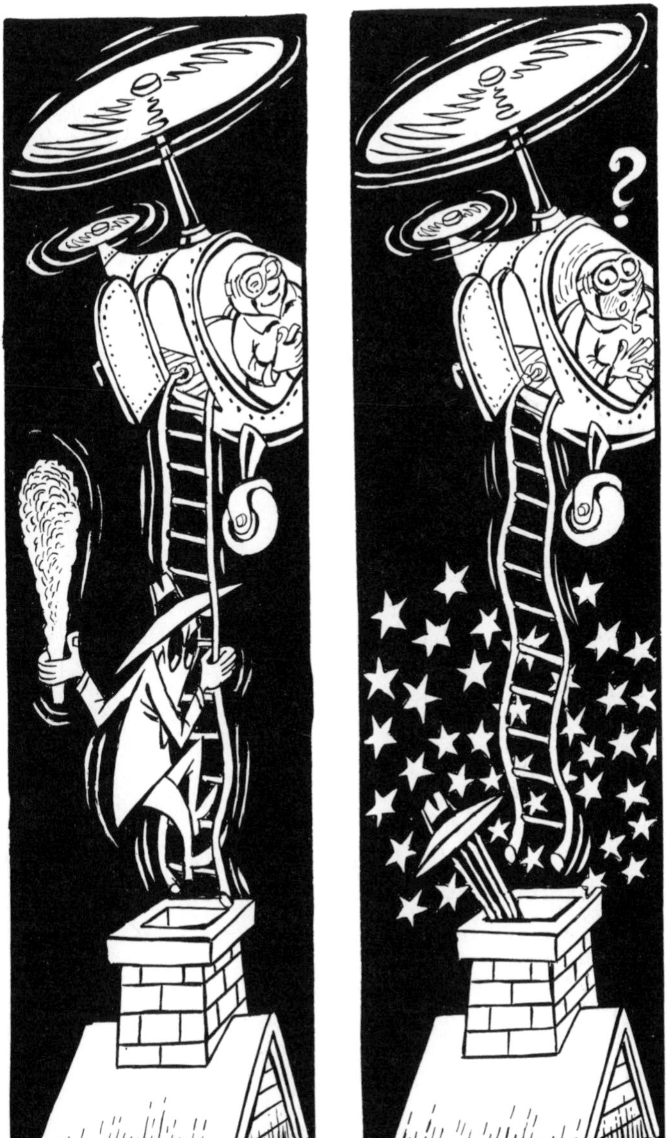
?

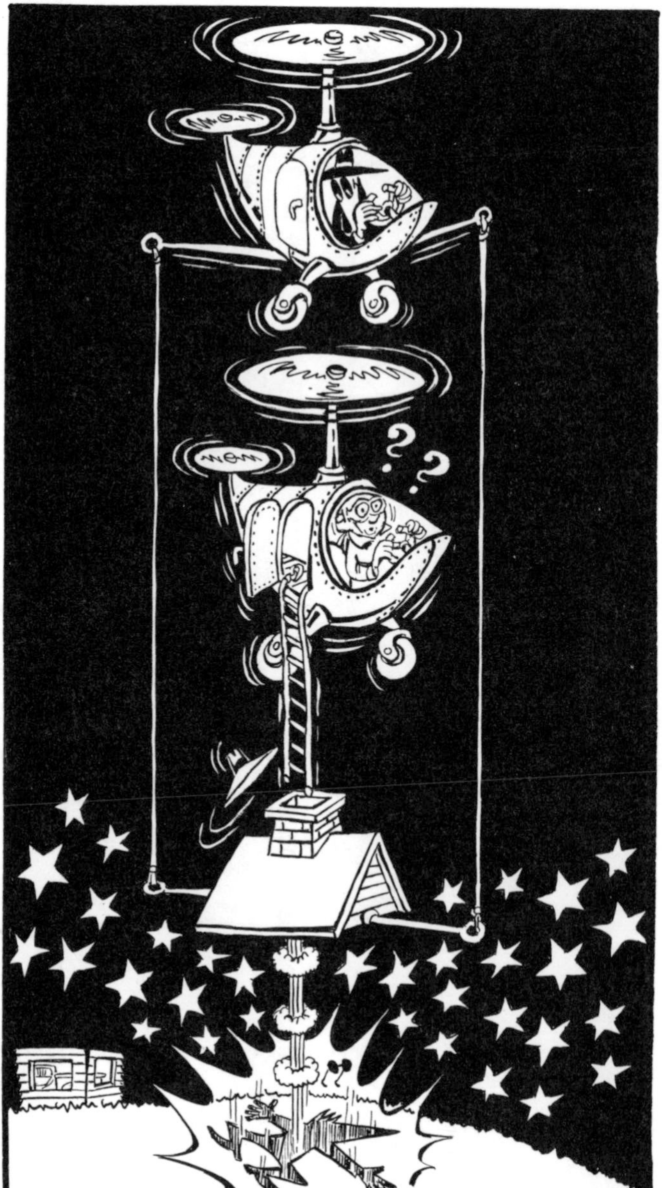

SPY vs SPY

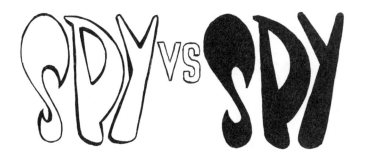

ARMOR DILLY

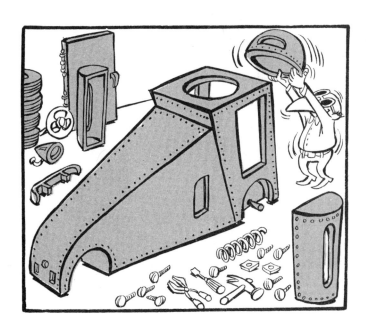

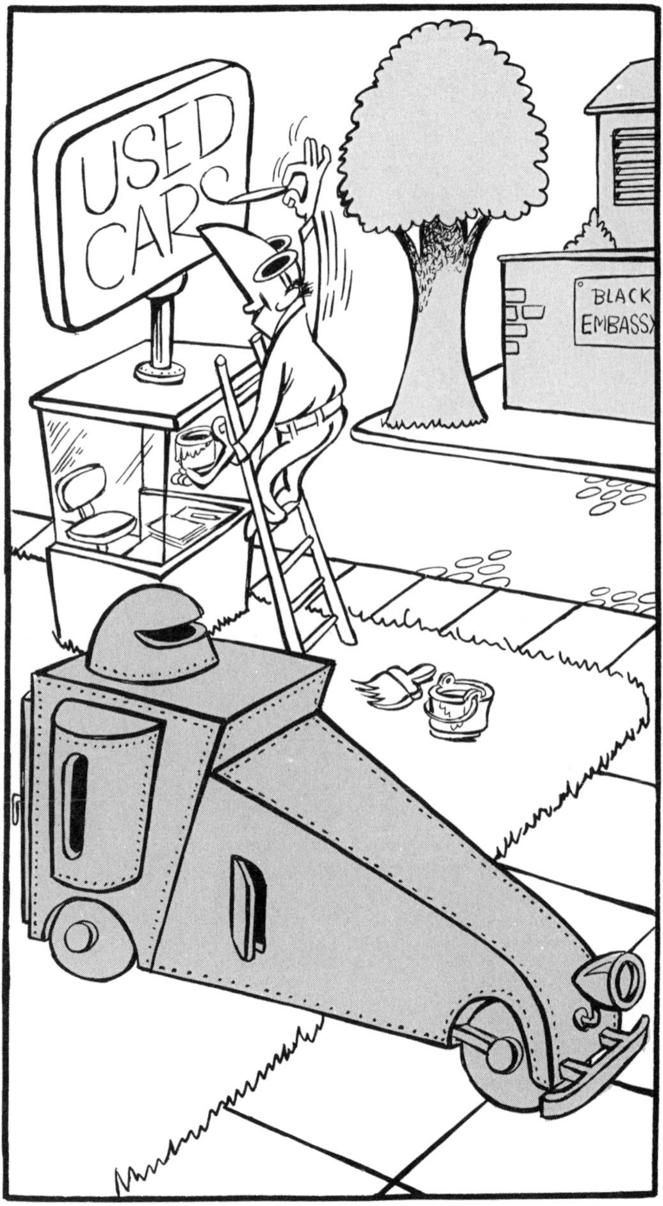
USED CARS
BLACK EMBASSY

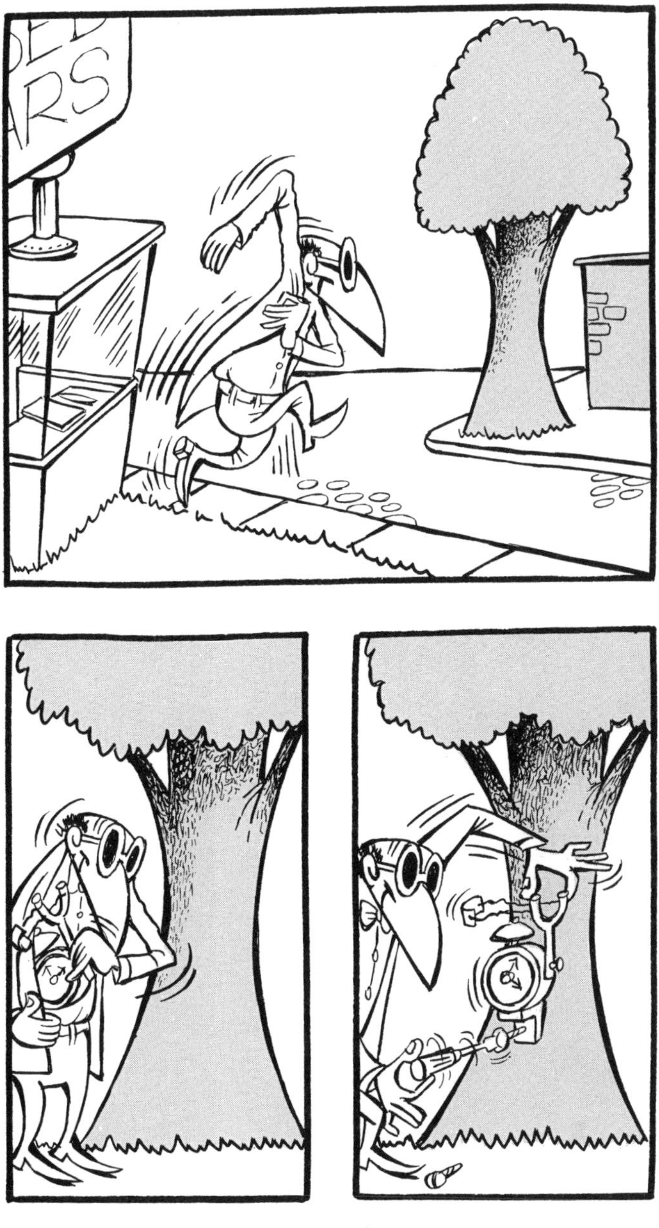

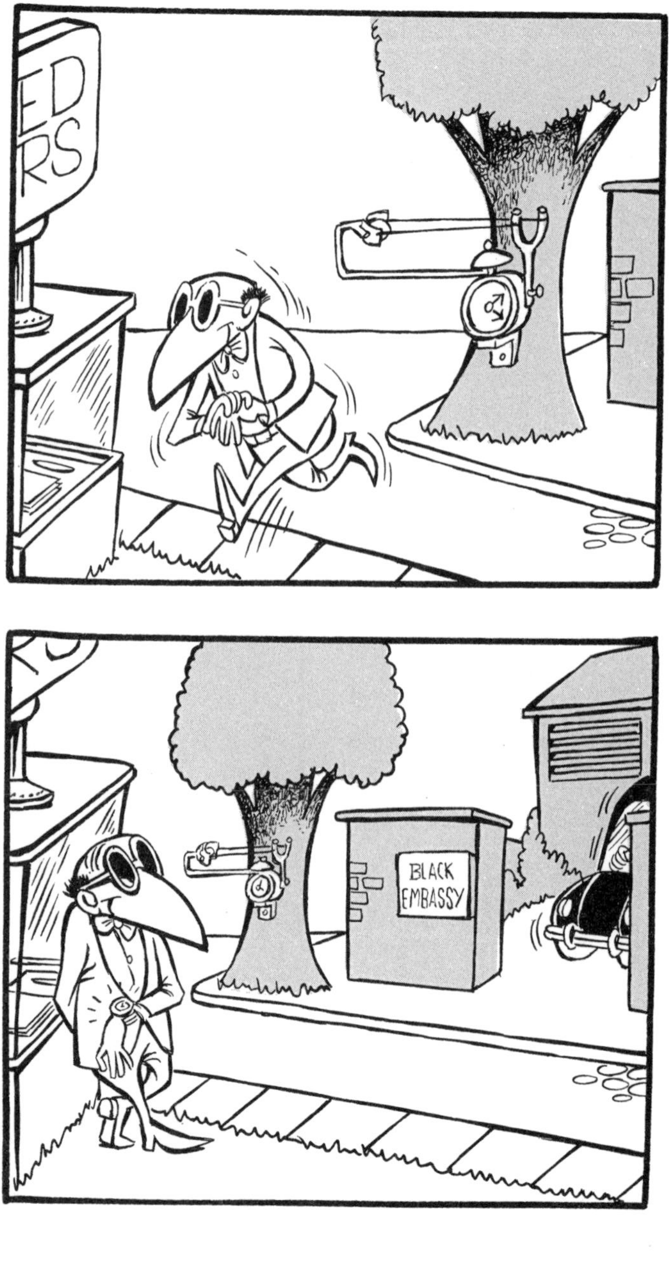
ED
RS
BLACK
EMBASSY

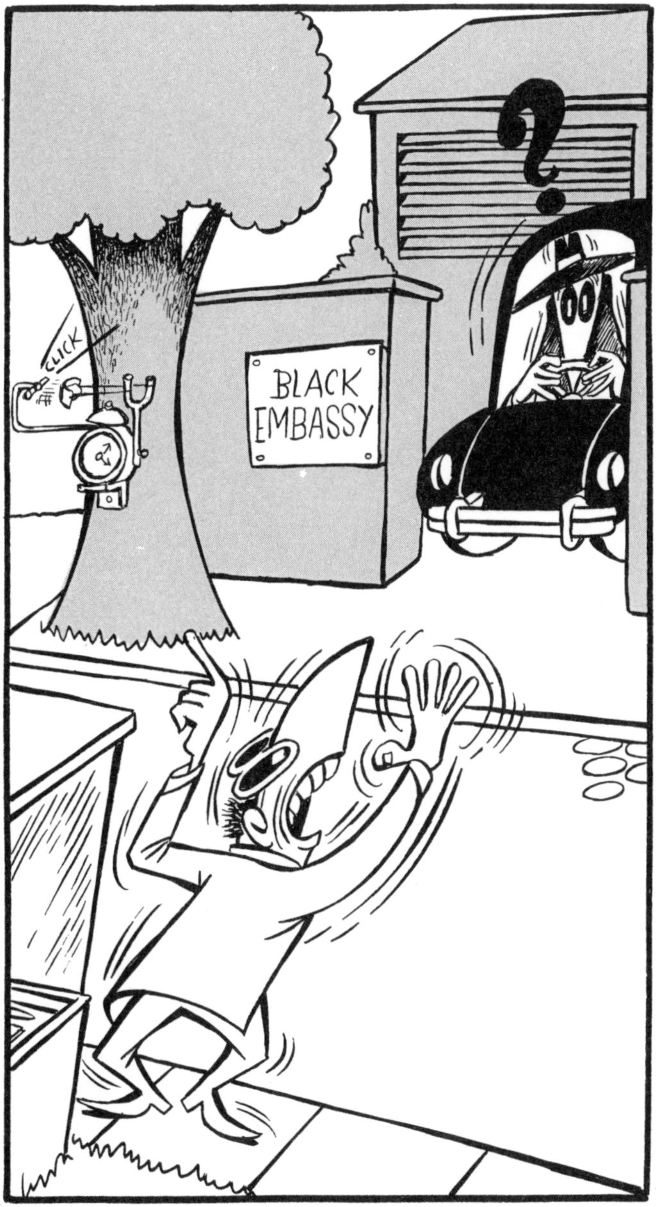
CLICK
BLACK EMBASSY

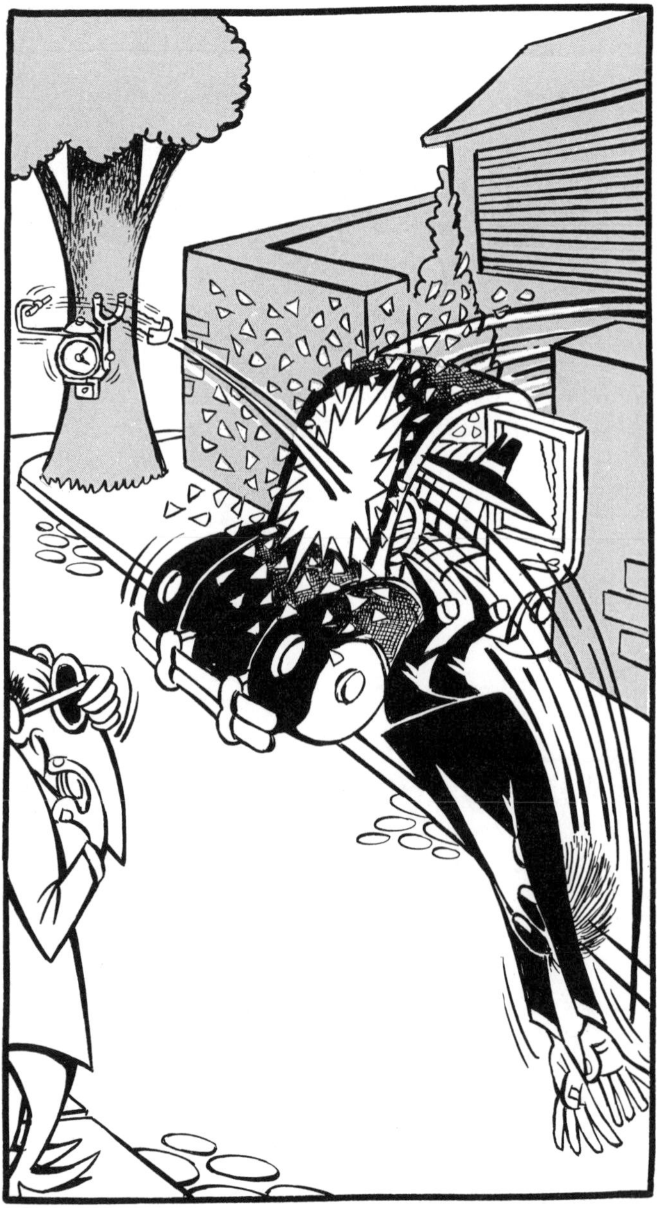

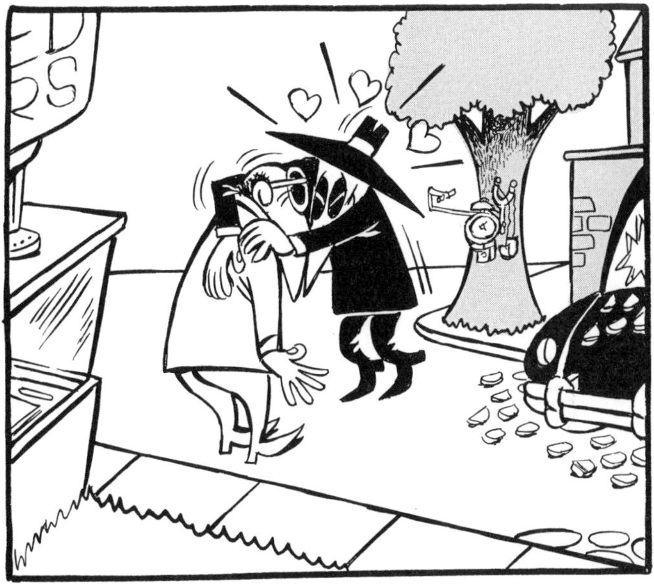

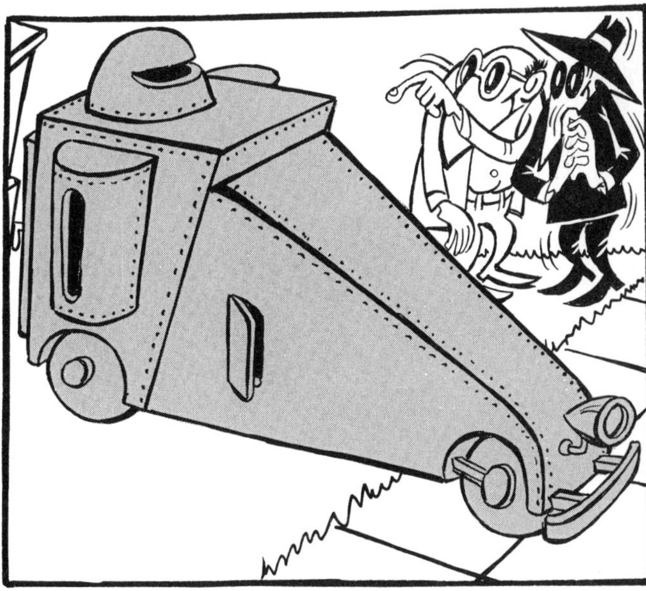

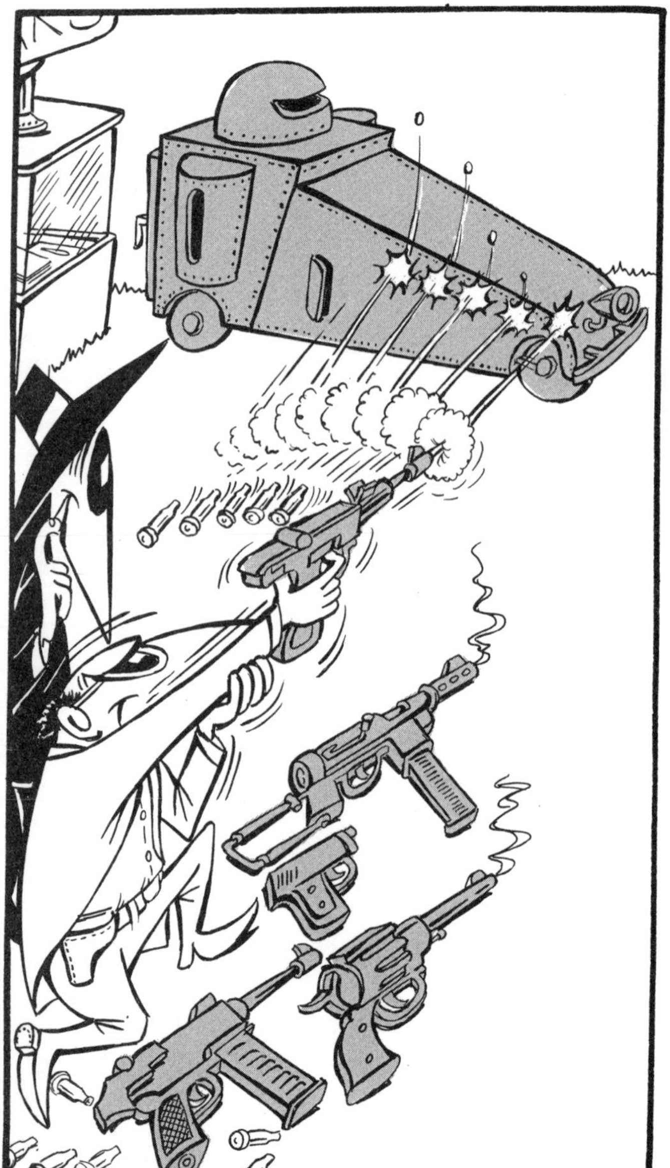

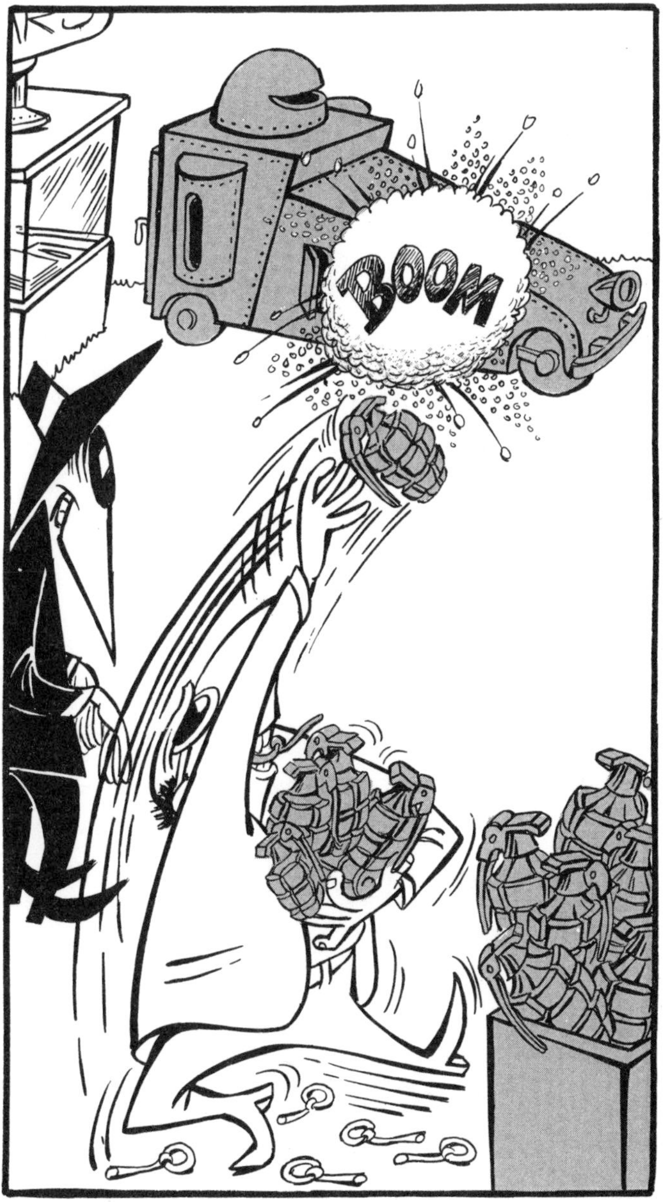
BOOM

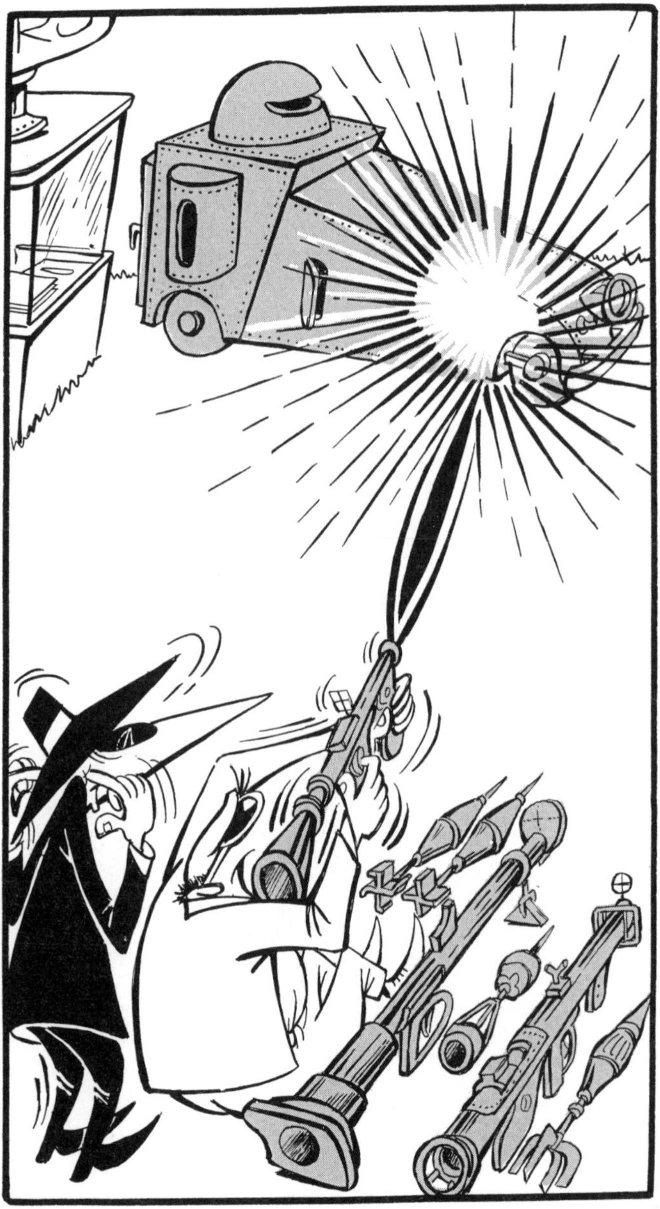

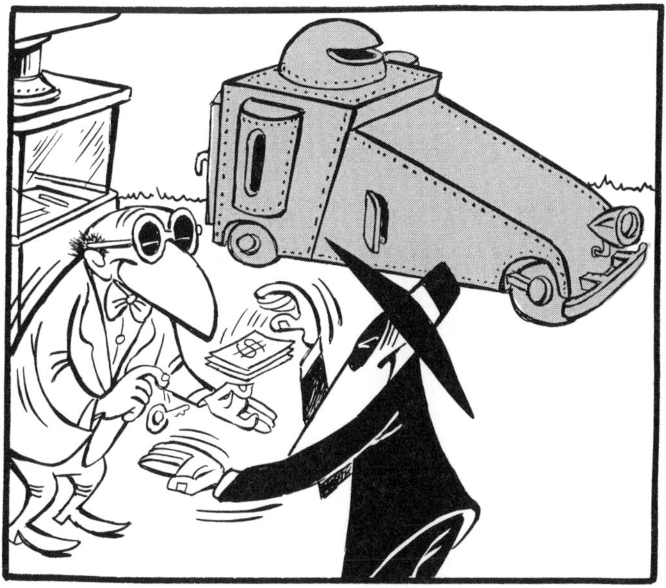

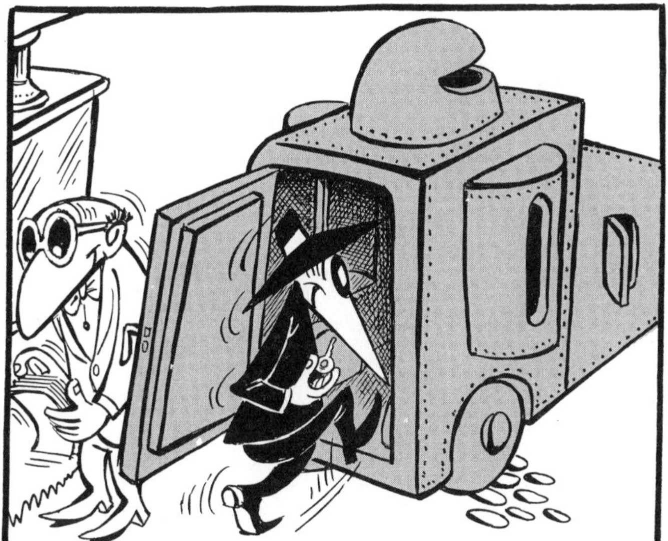

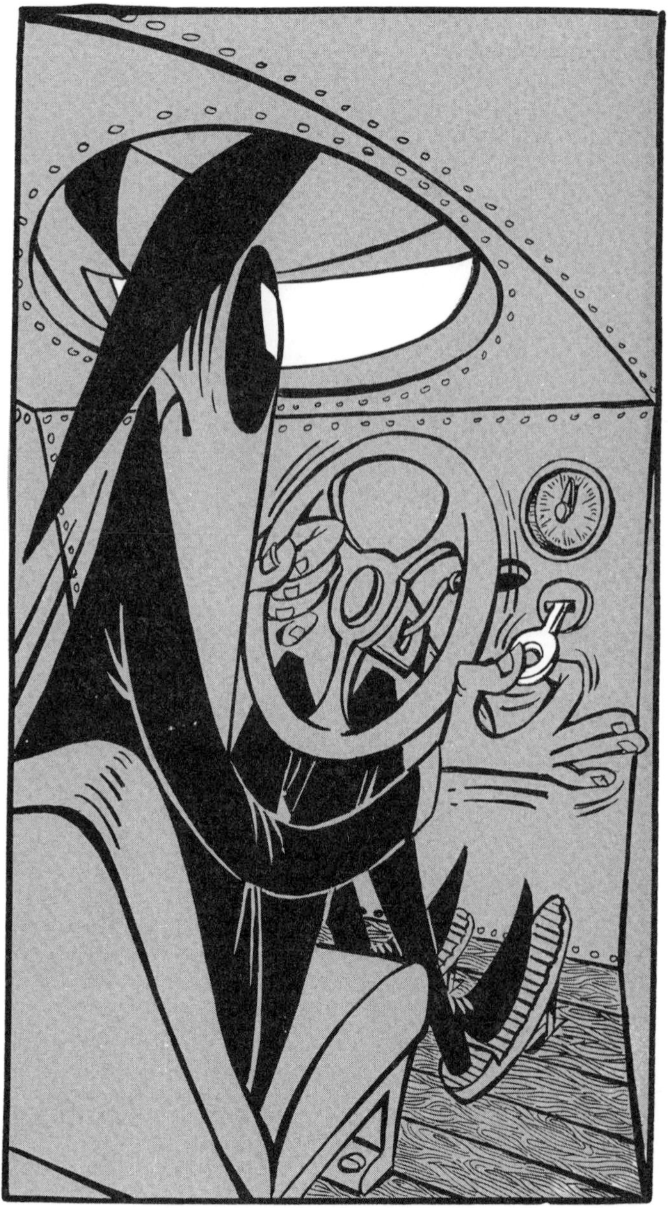

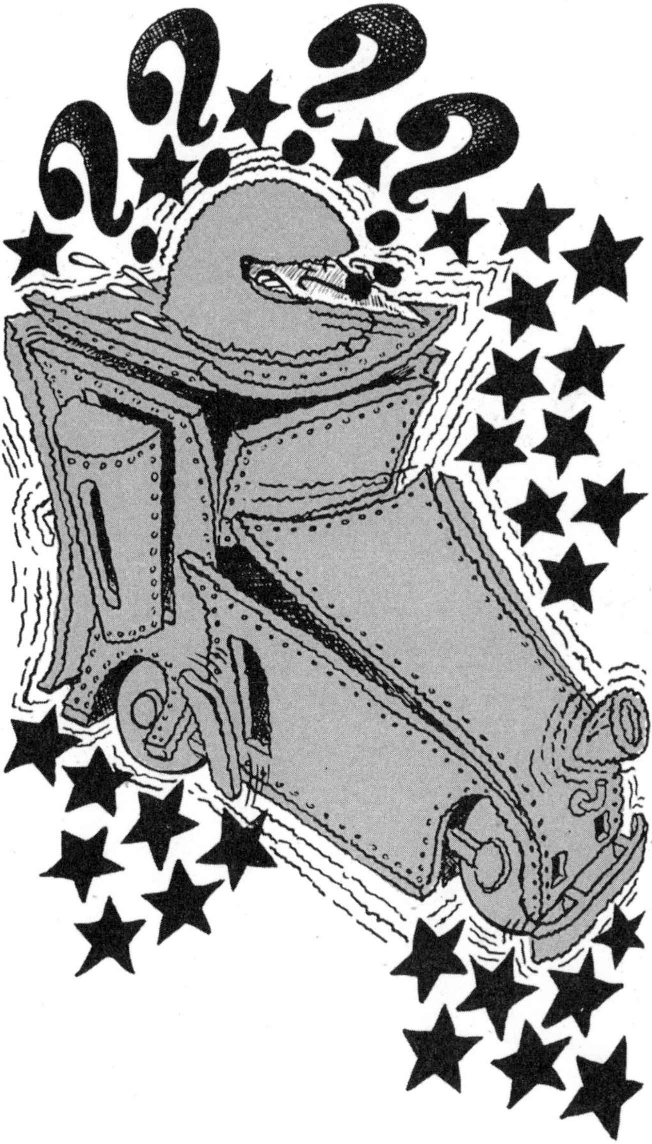

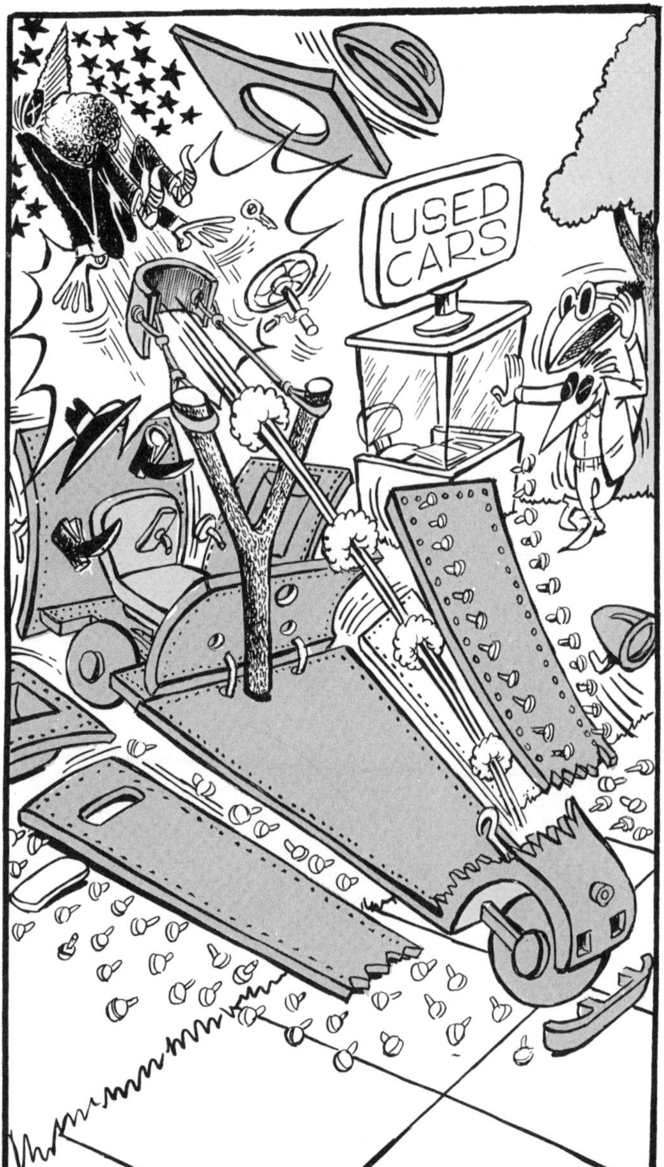
USED CARS

SPY VS SPY

A MINE-BLOWING CAPER

?
TAC
TAC
TAC

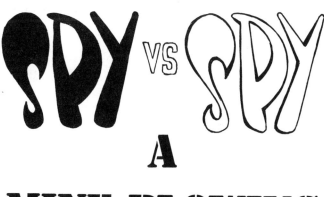

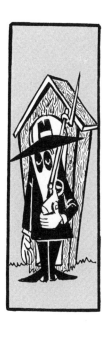

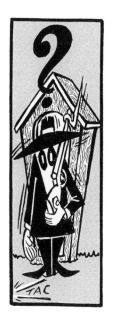

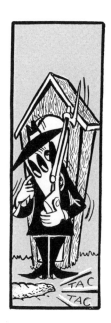

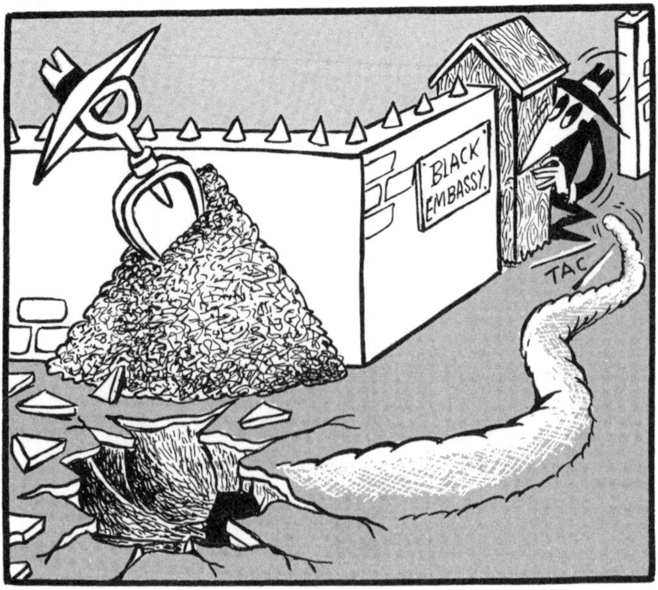
BLACK EMBASSY
TAC

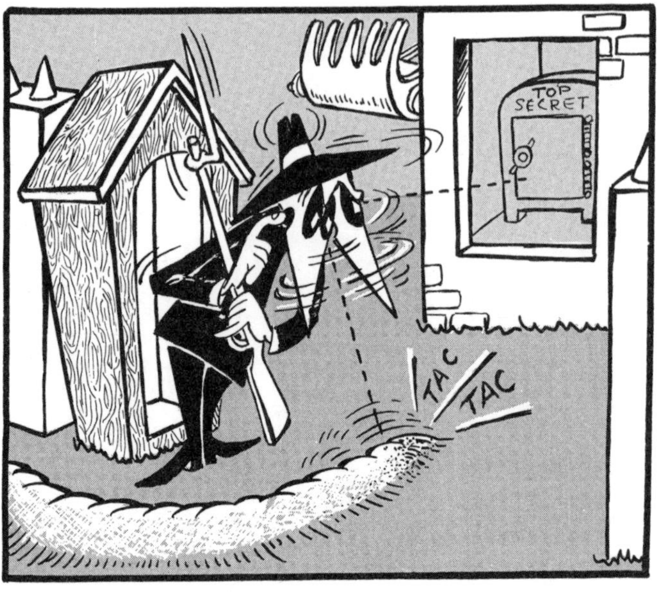
TOP SECRET
TAC
TAC

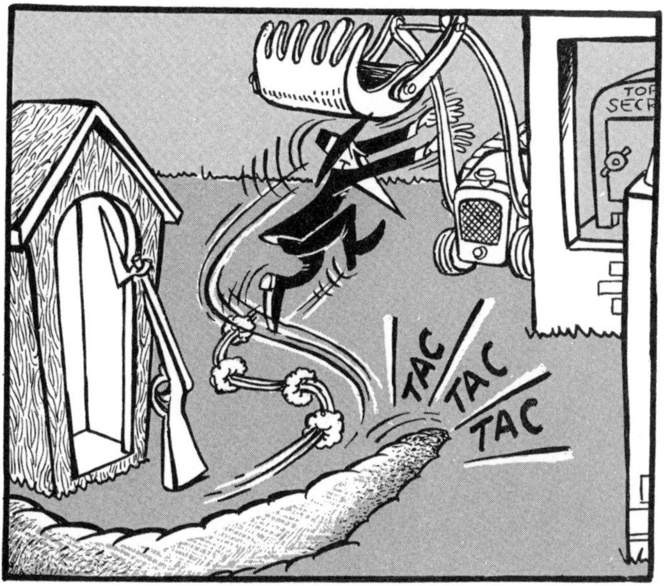
TAC
TAC
TAC

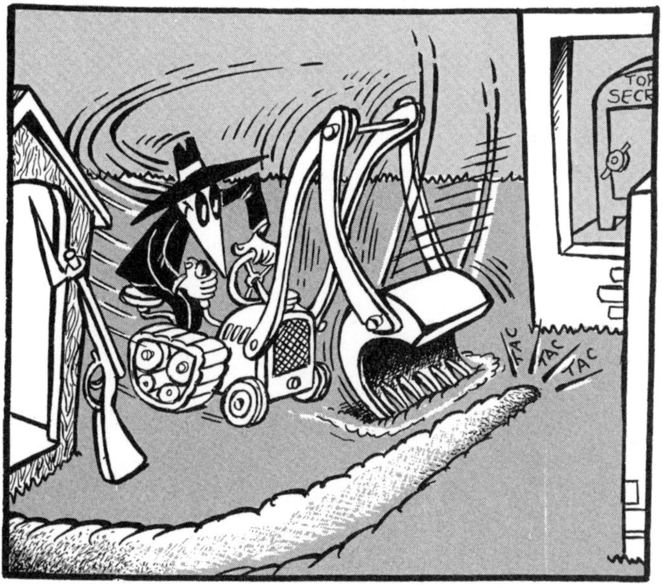
TAC
TAC
TAC

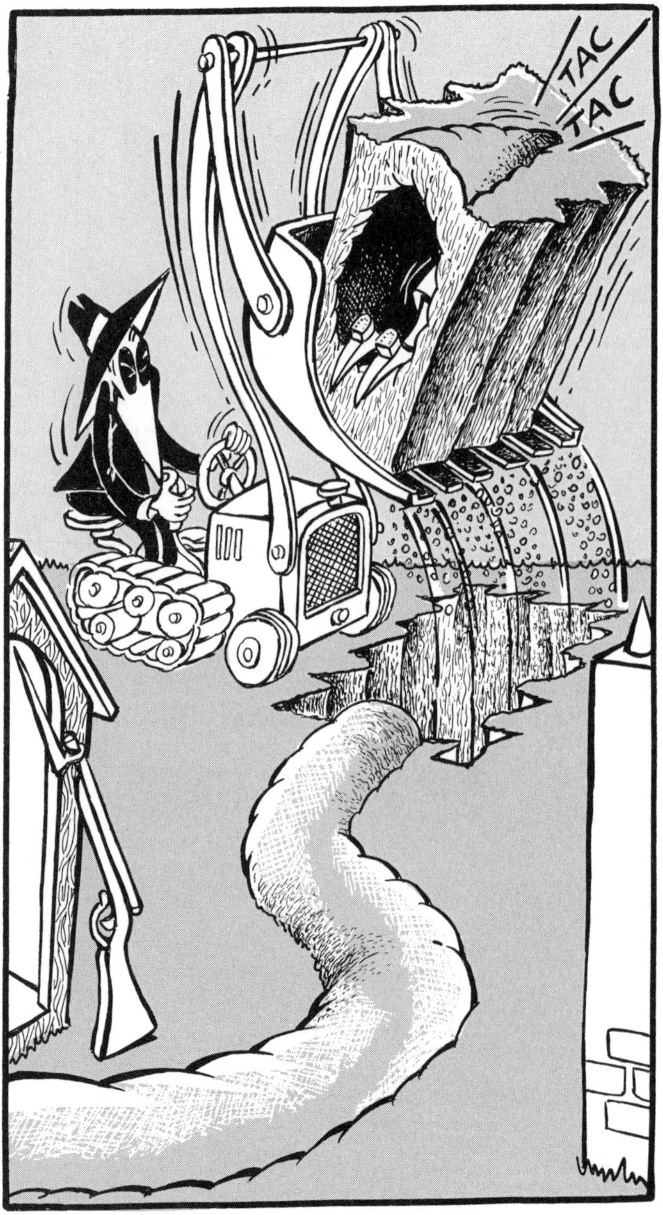
TAC
TAC

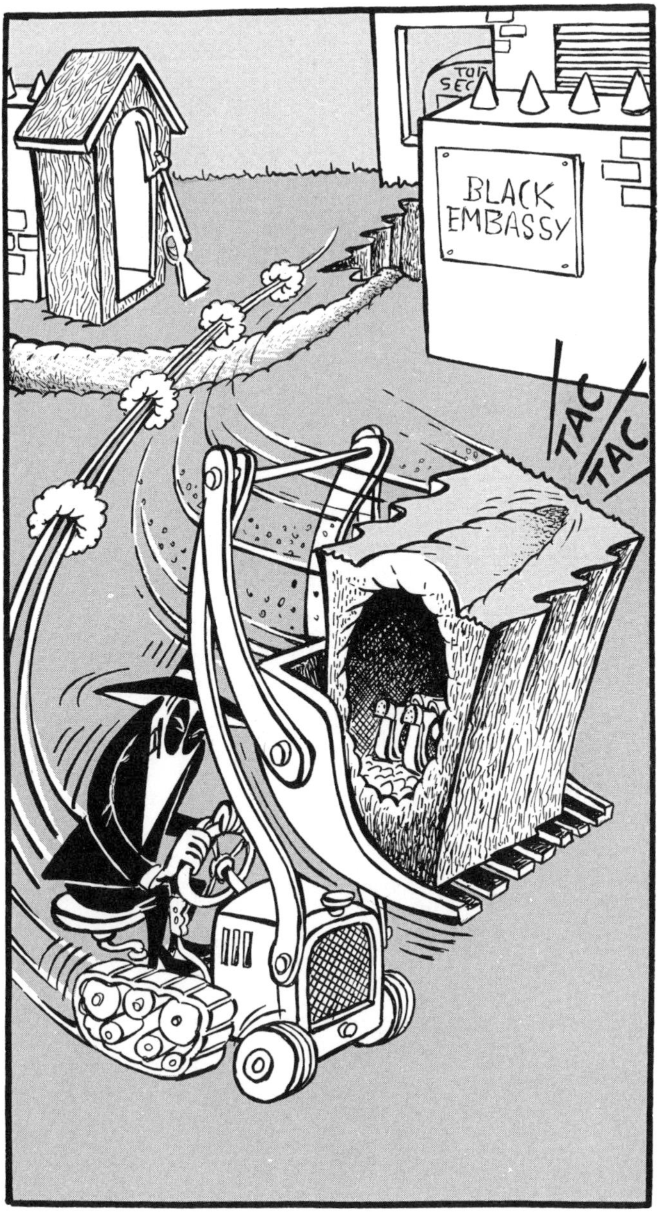
BLACK EMBASSY
TAC
TAC

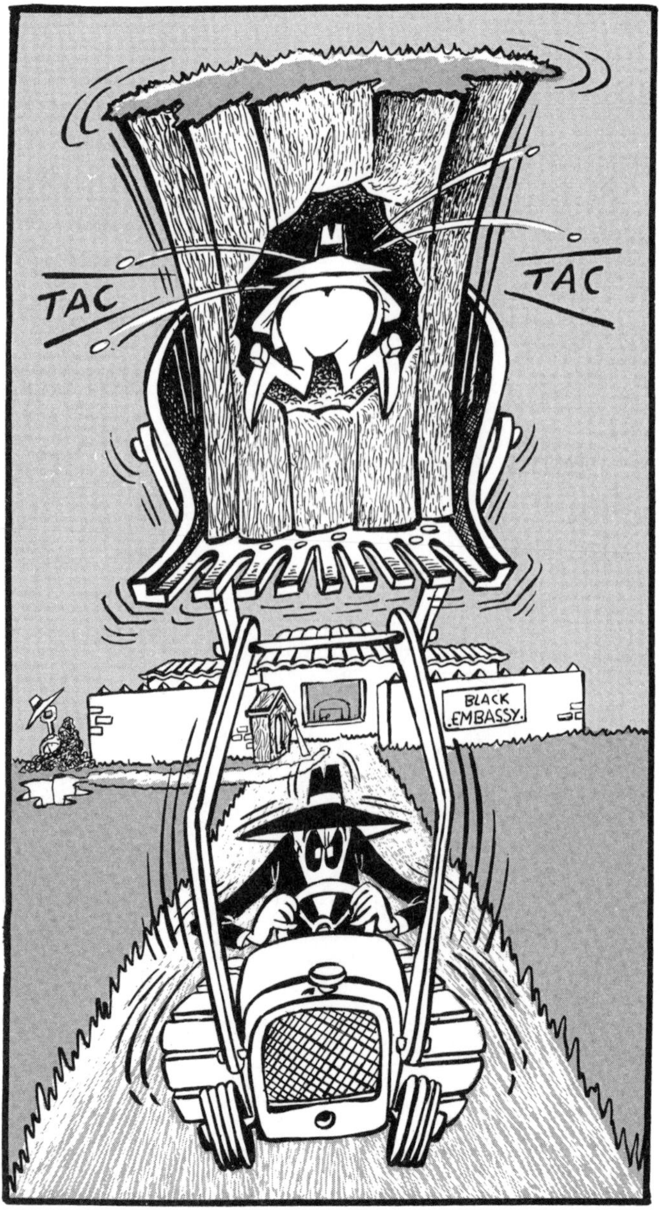
TAC
TAC
BLACK
EMBASSY.

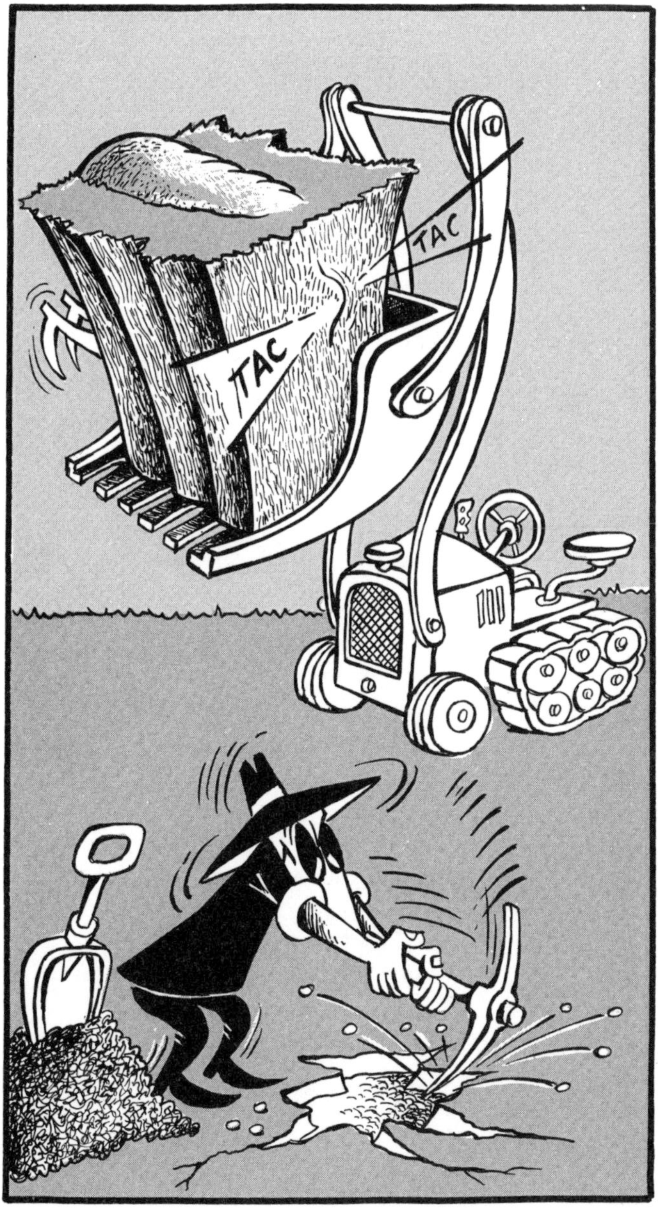
TAC
TAC

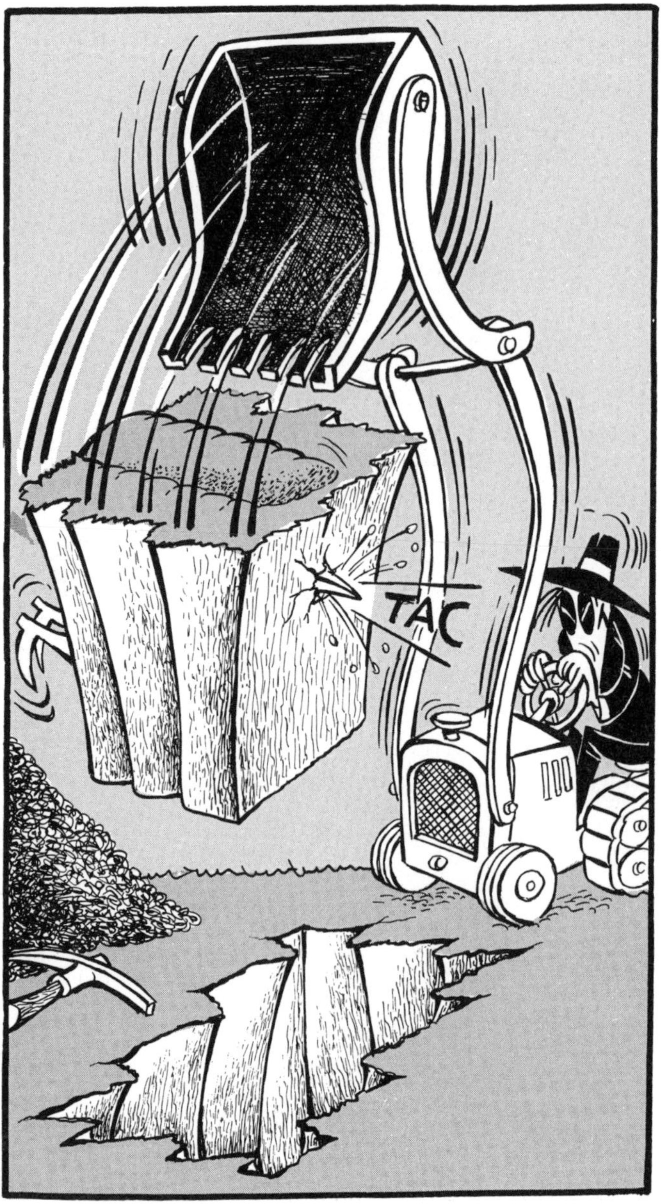
TAC

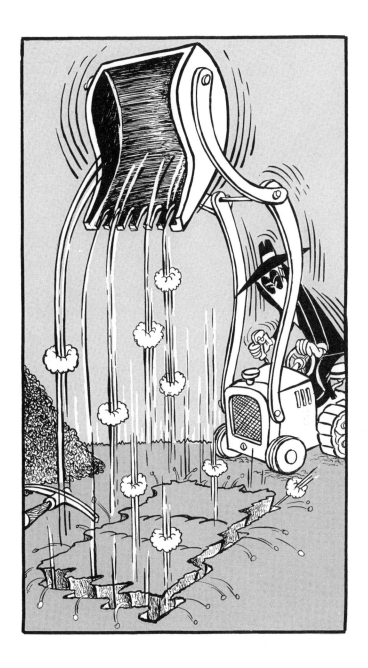

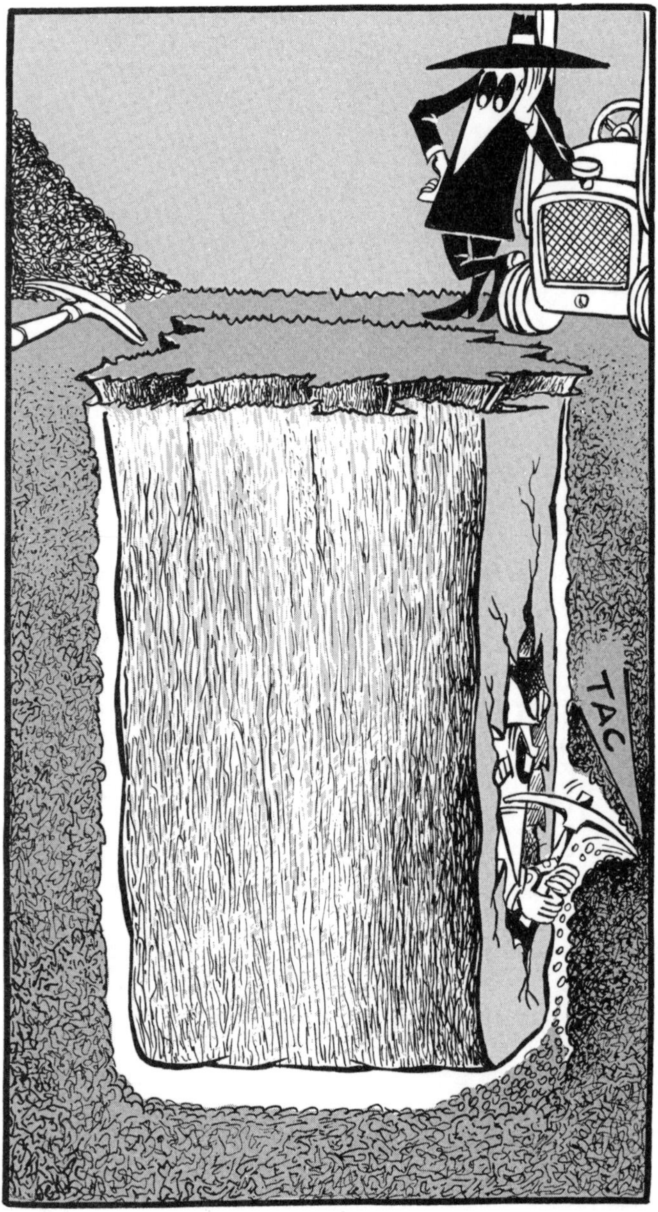
TAC

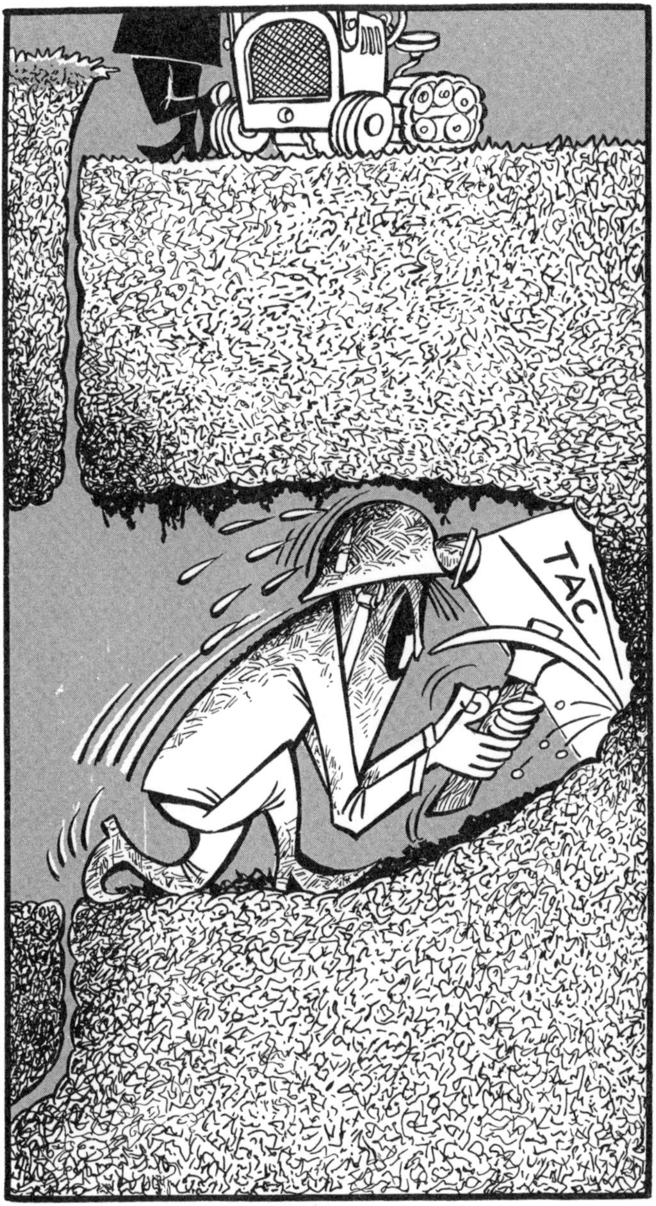
TAC

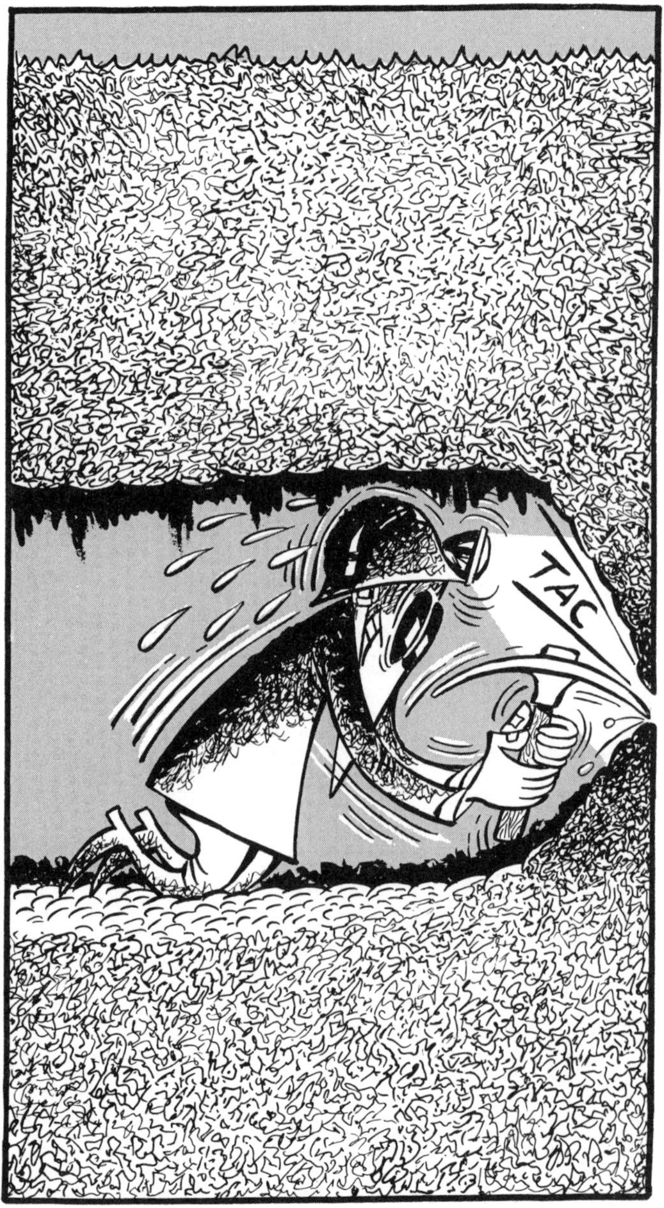
TAC

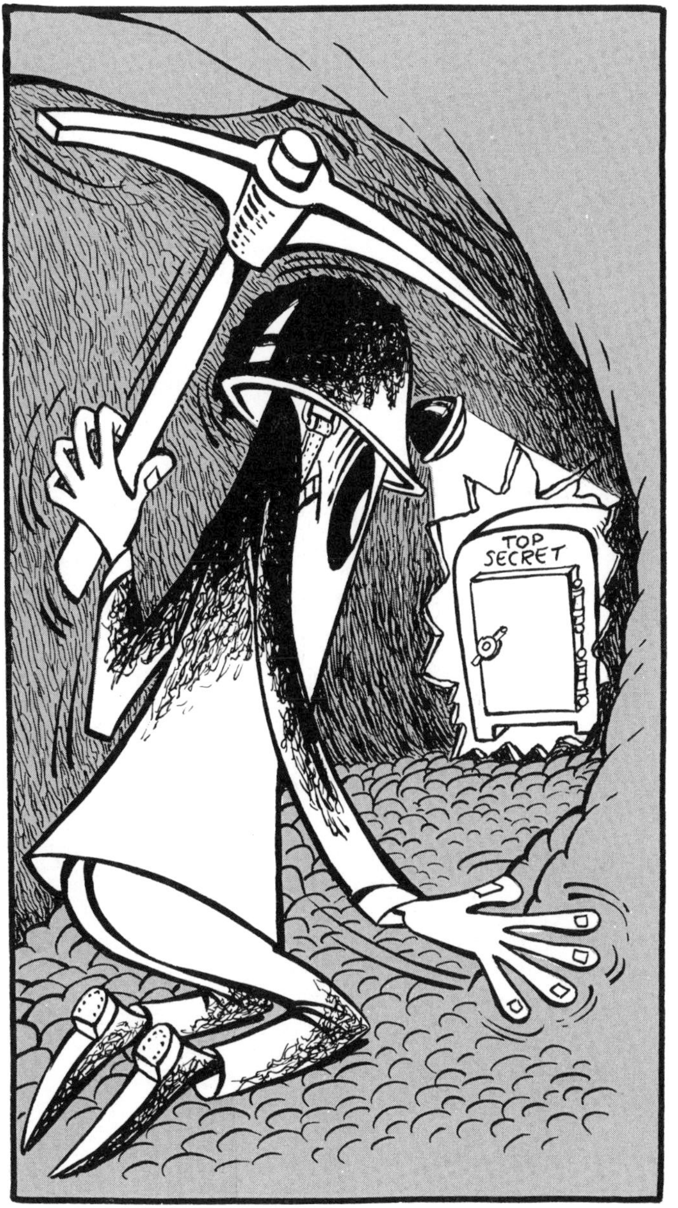
TOP
SECRET

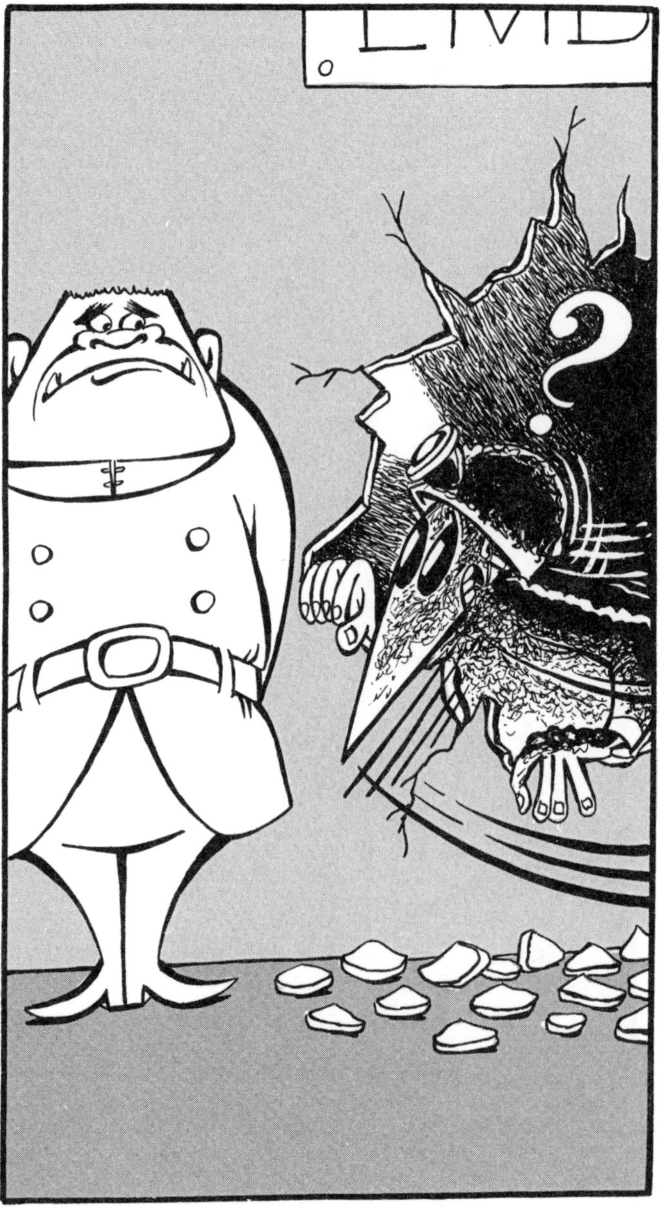

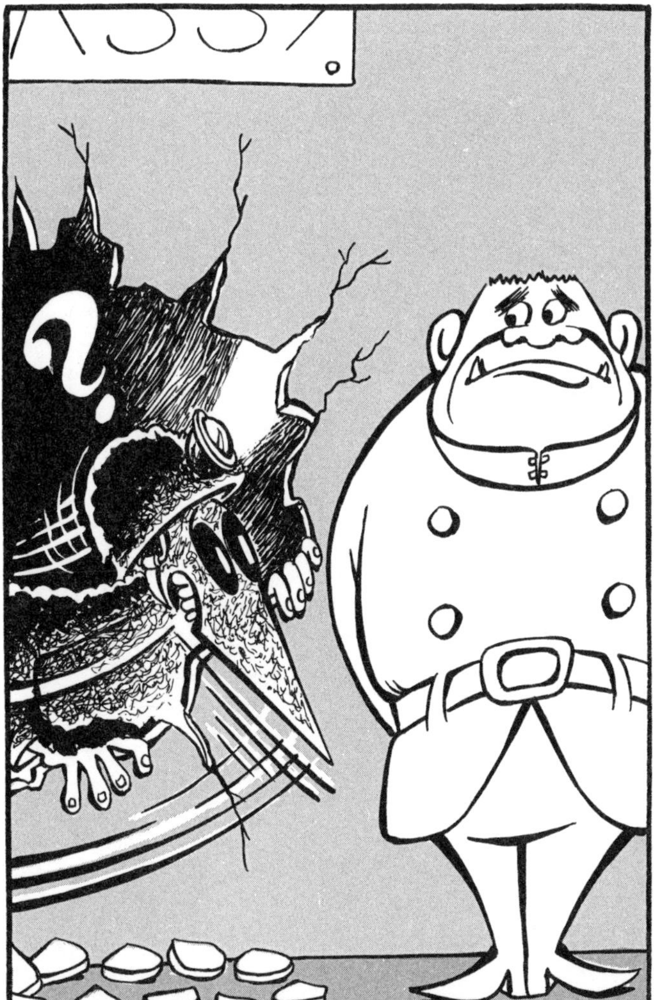

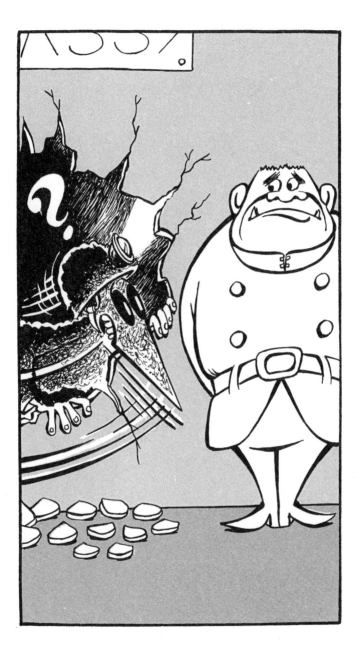

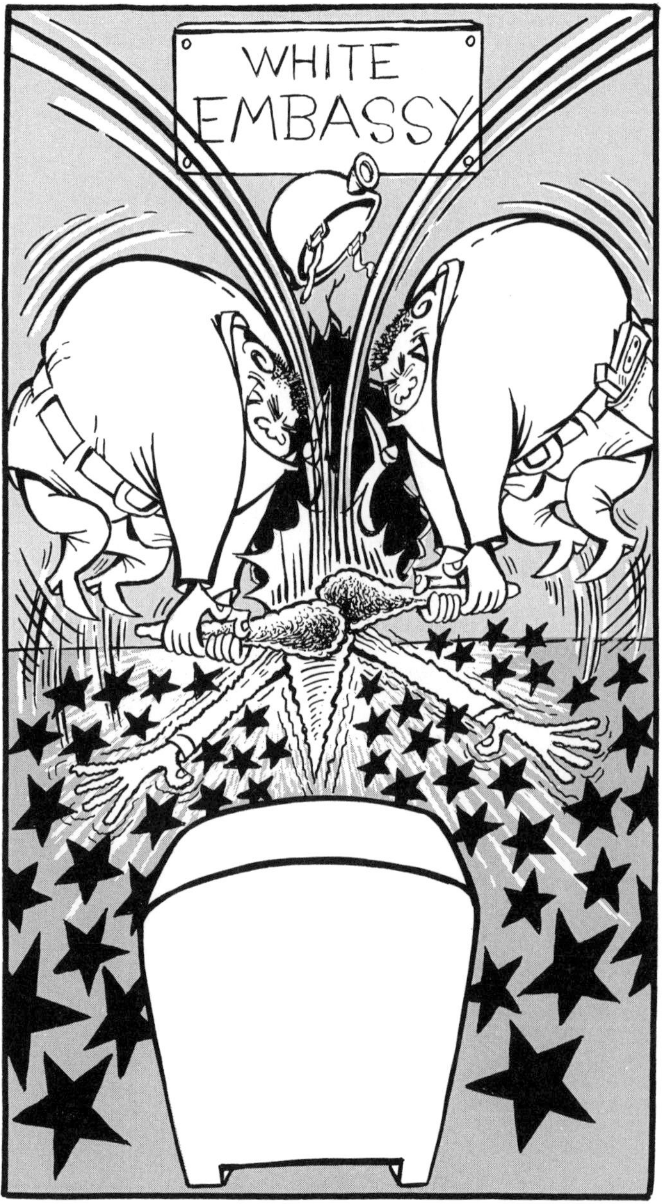
WHITE EMBASSY

SPY vs SPY

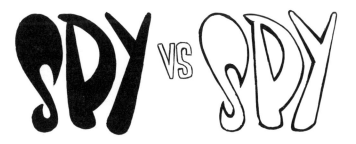

DROLL OUT THE BARREL

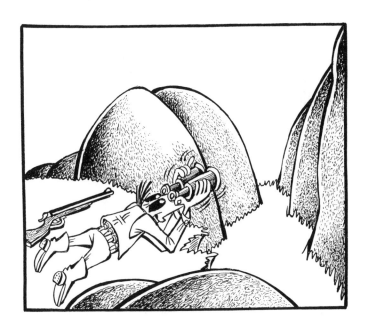

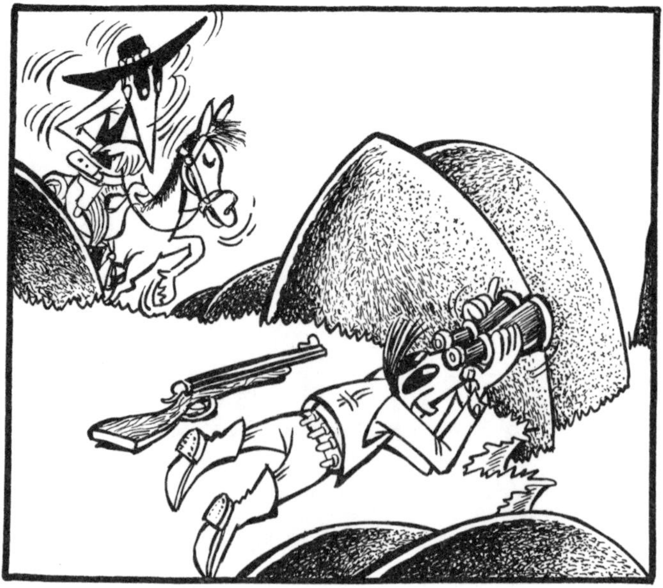
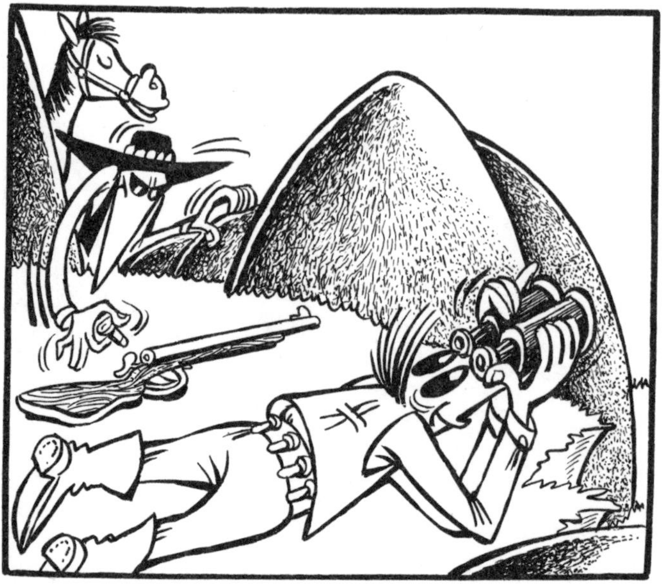

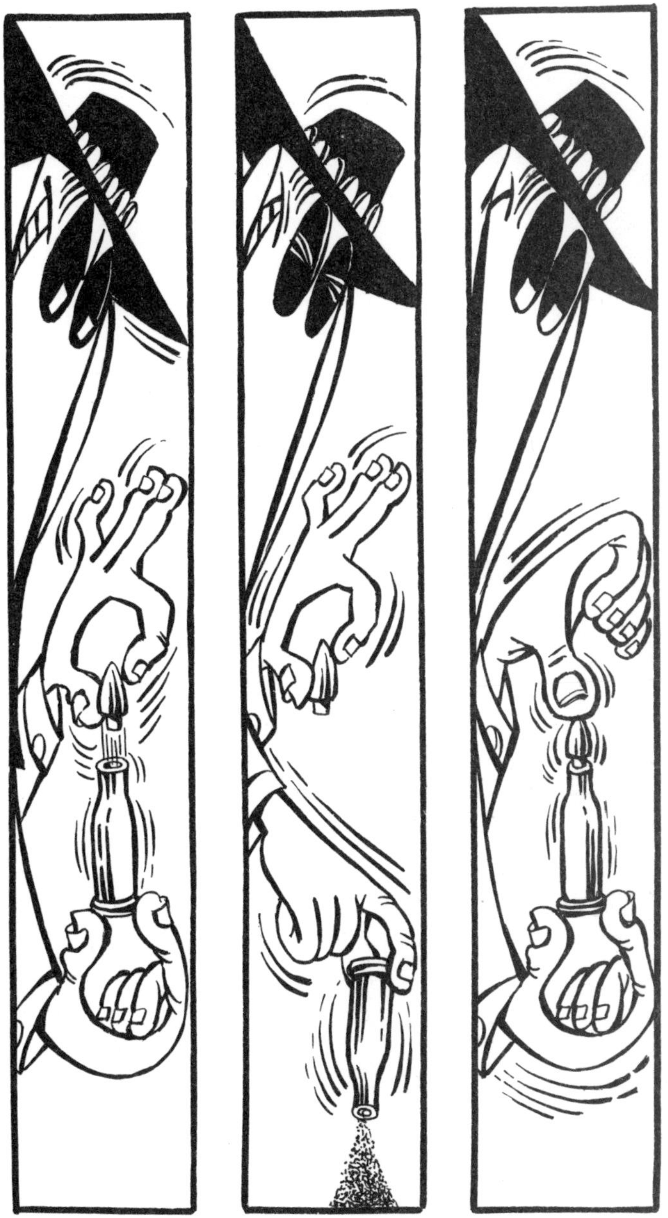

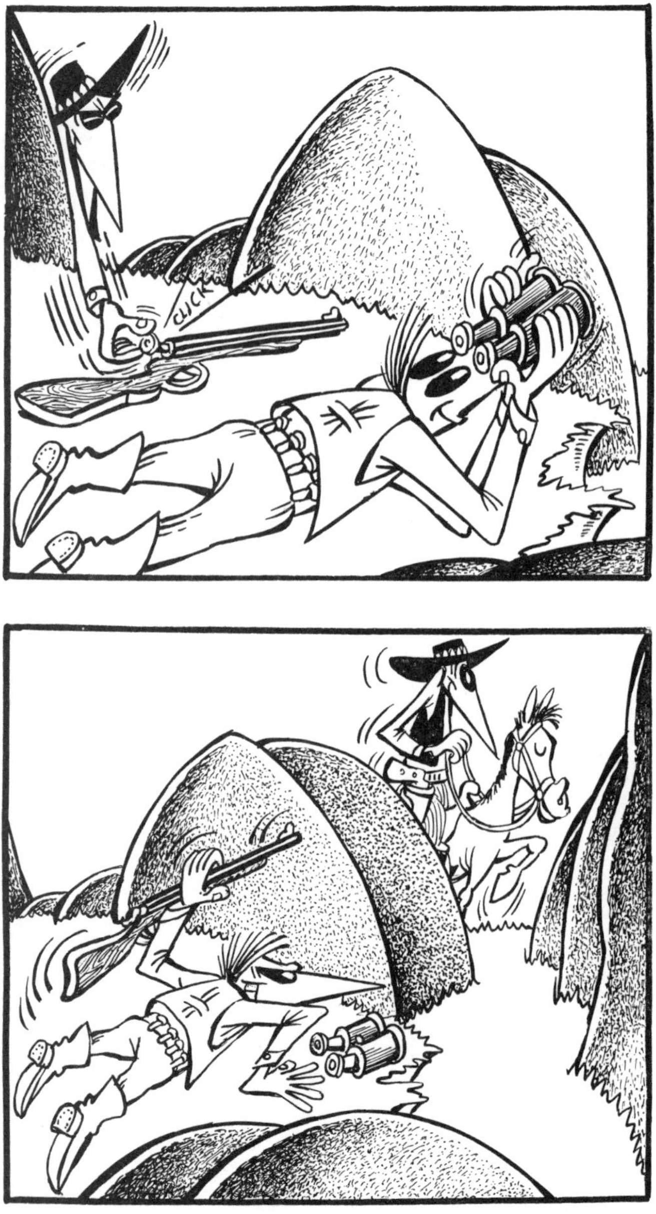
CLICK

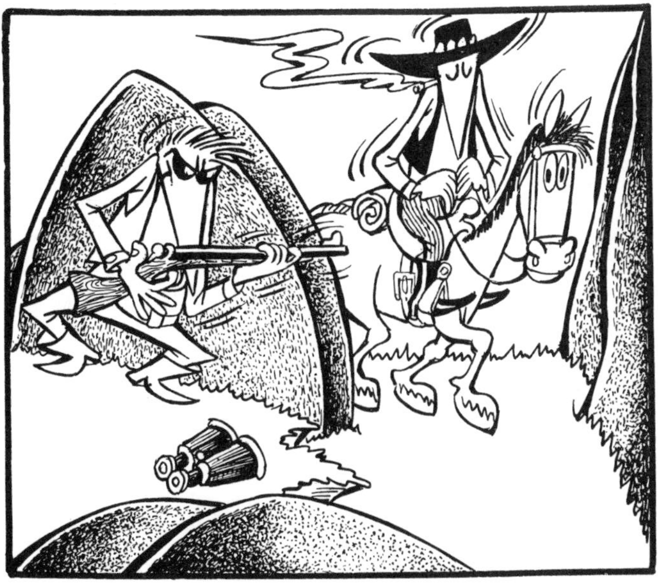

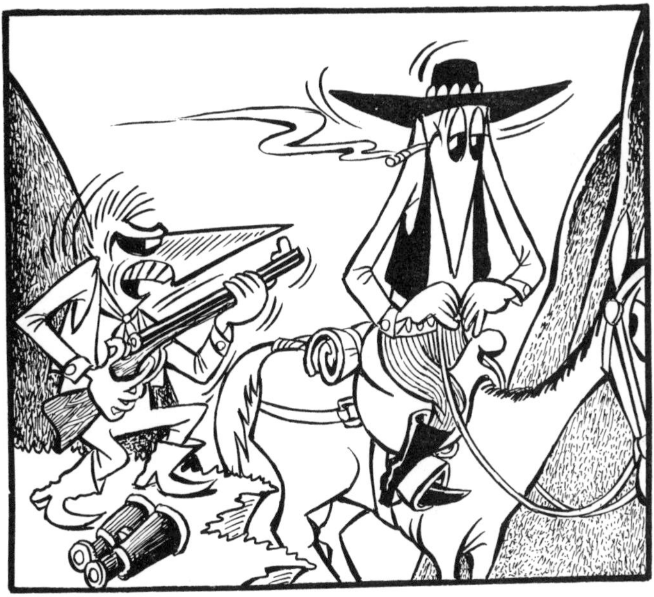

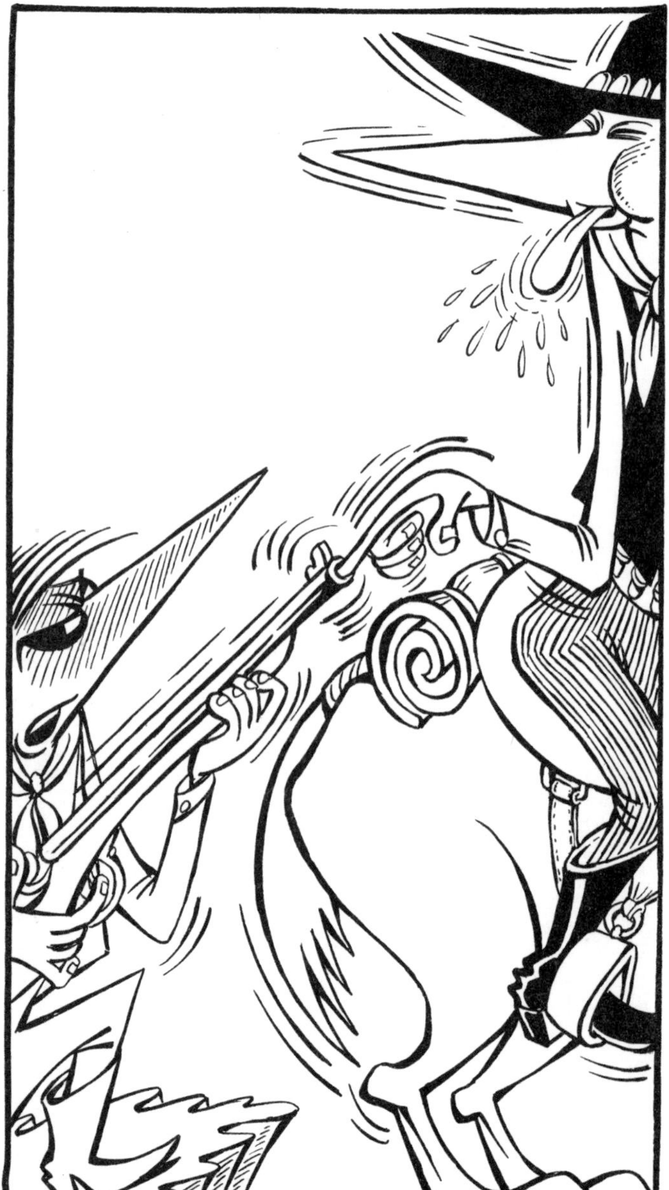

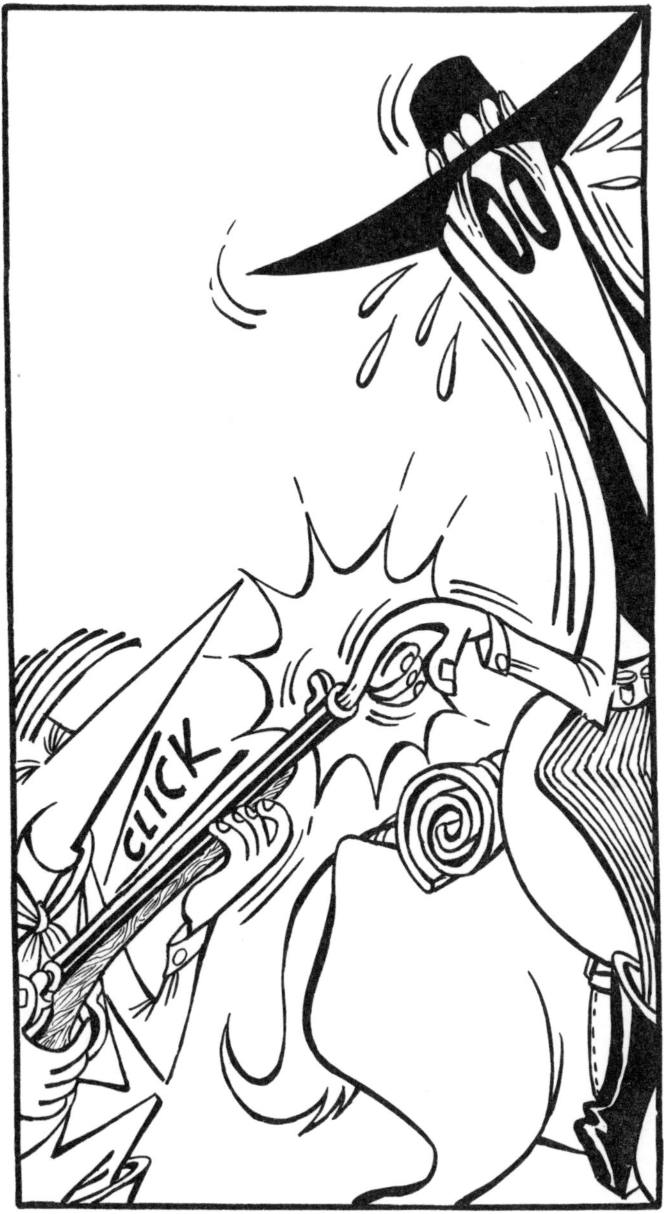
CLICK

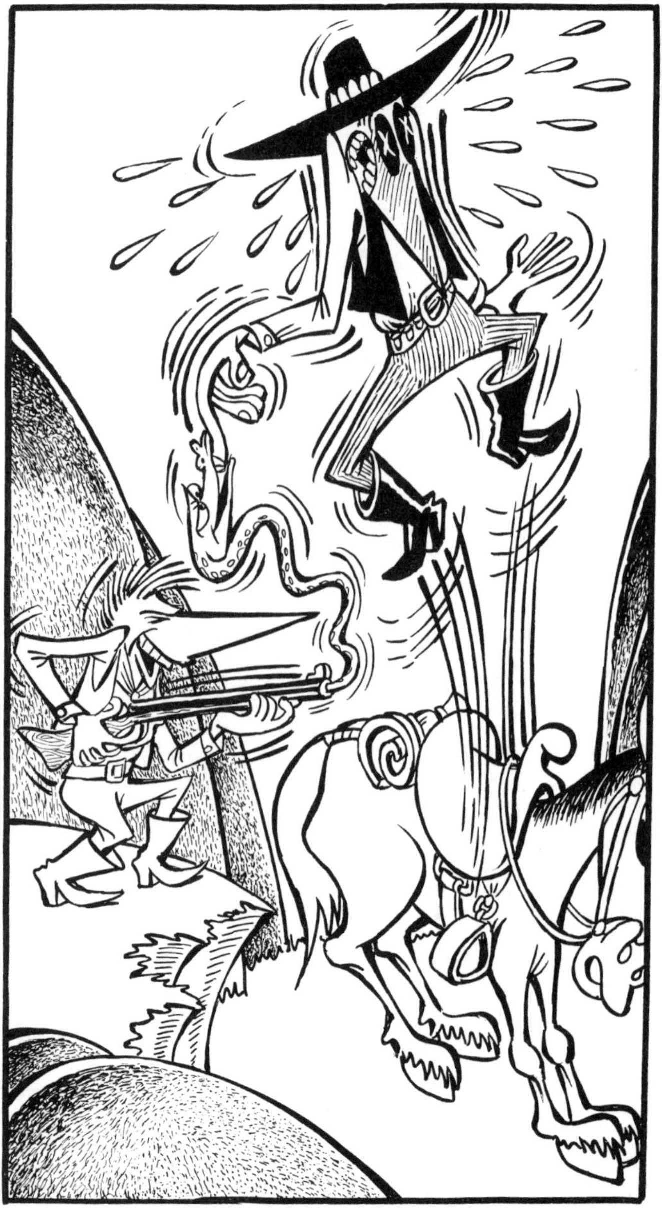

SPY vs SPY

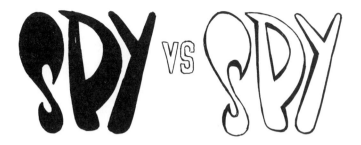

PEARL-1
HIT-2

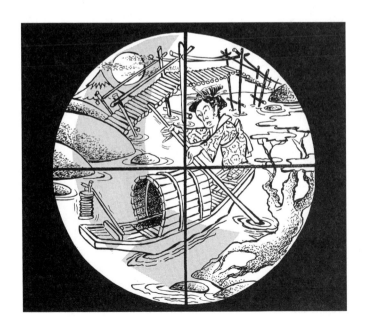

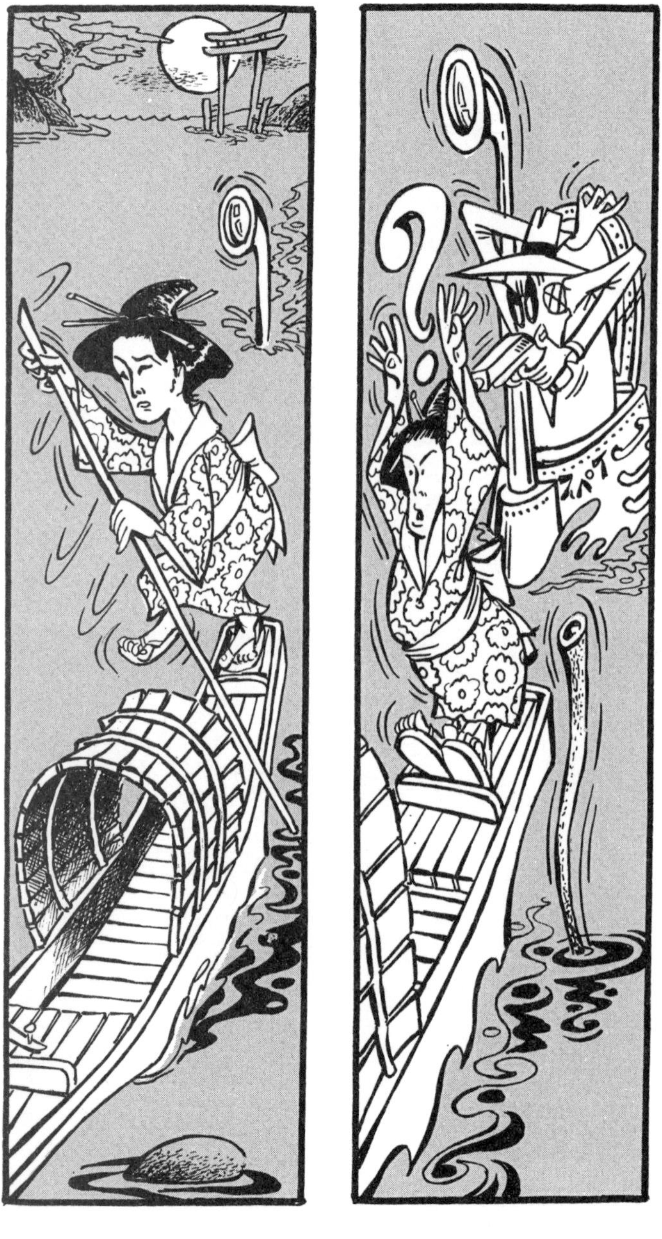
スパイ

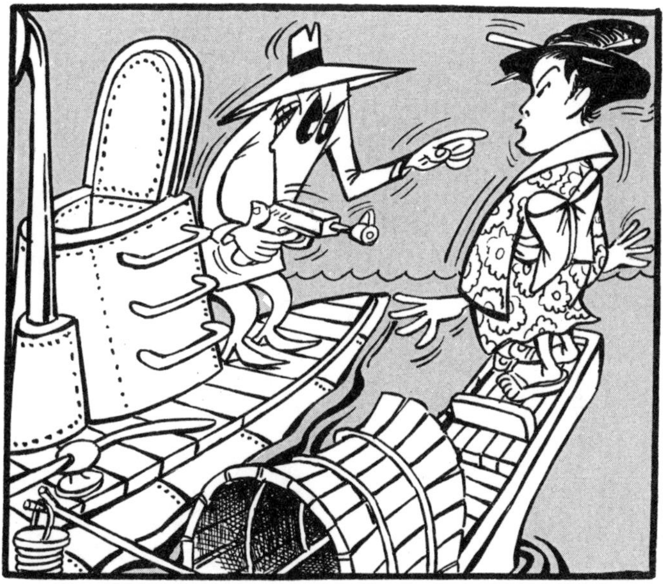

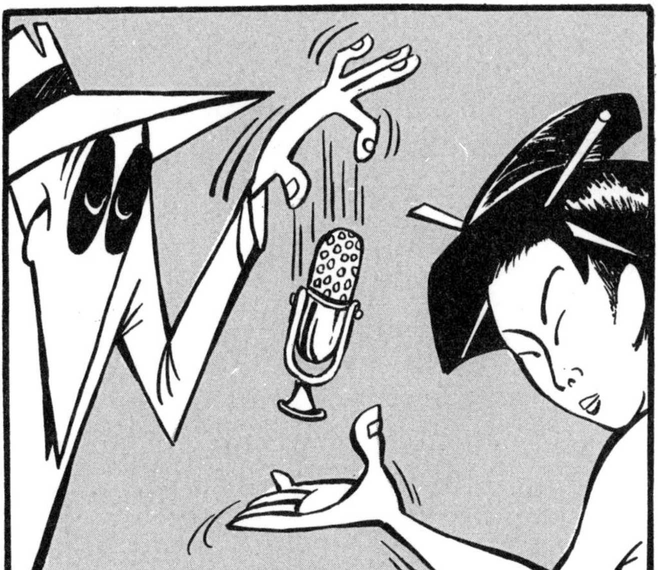

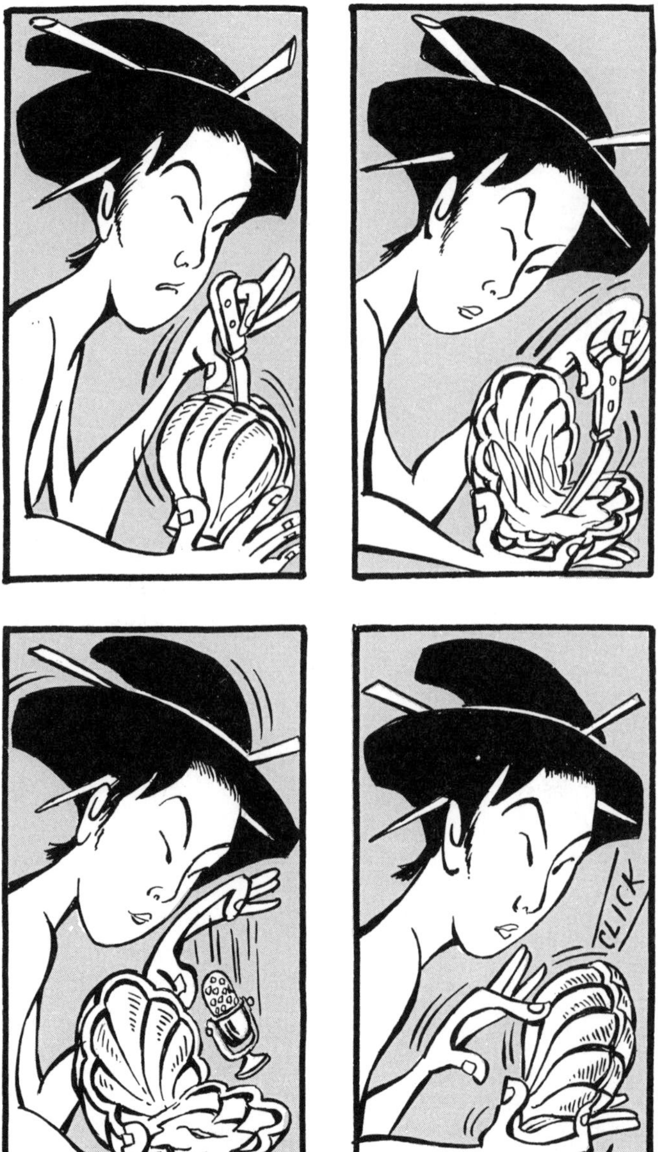
CLICK

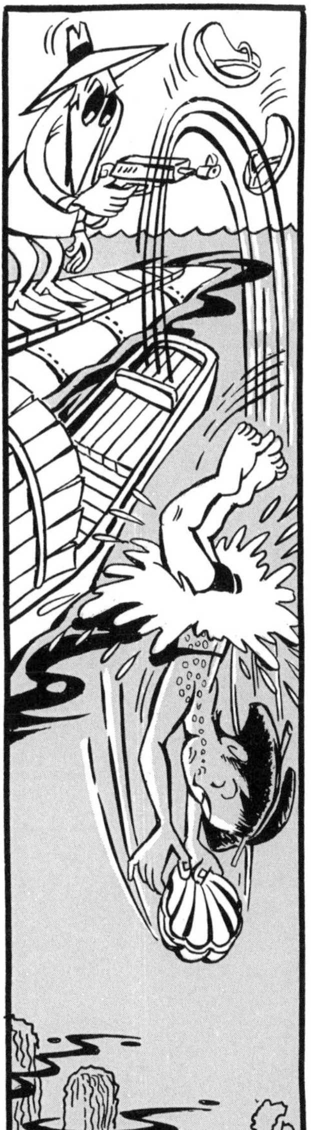
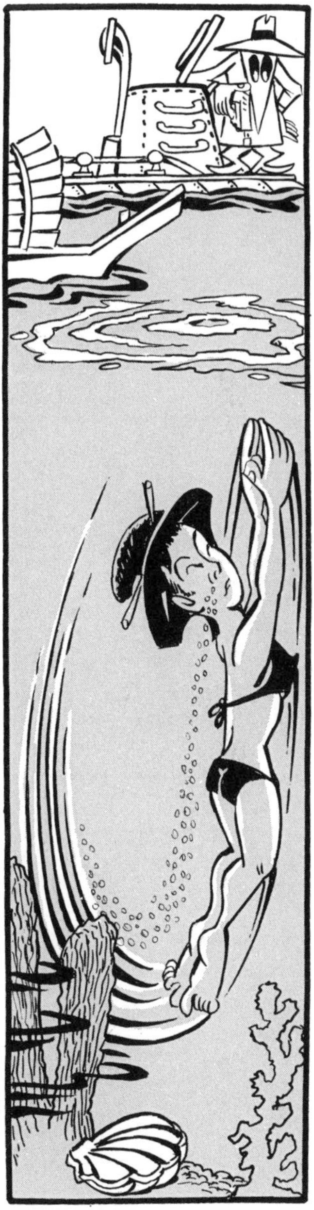

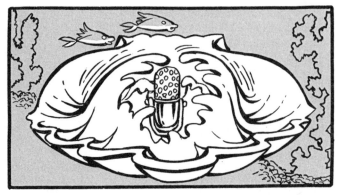

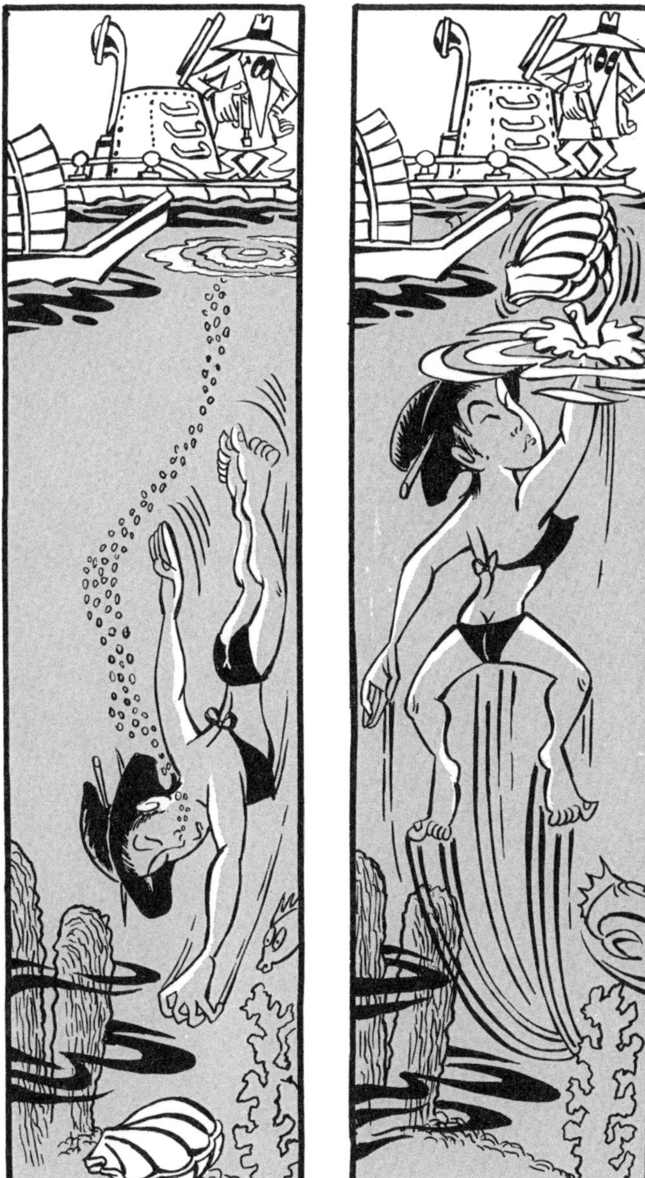

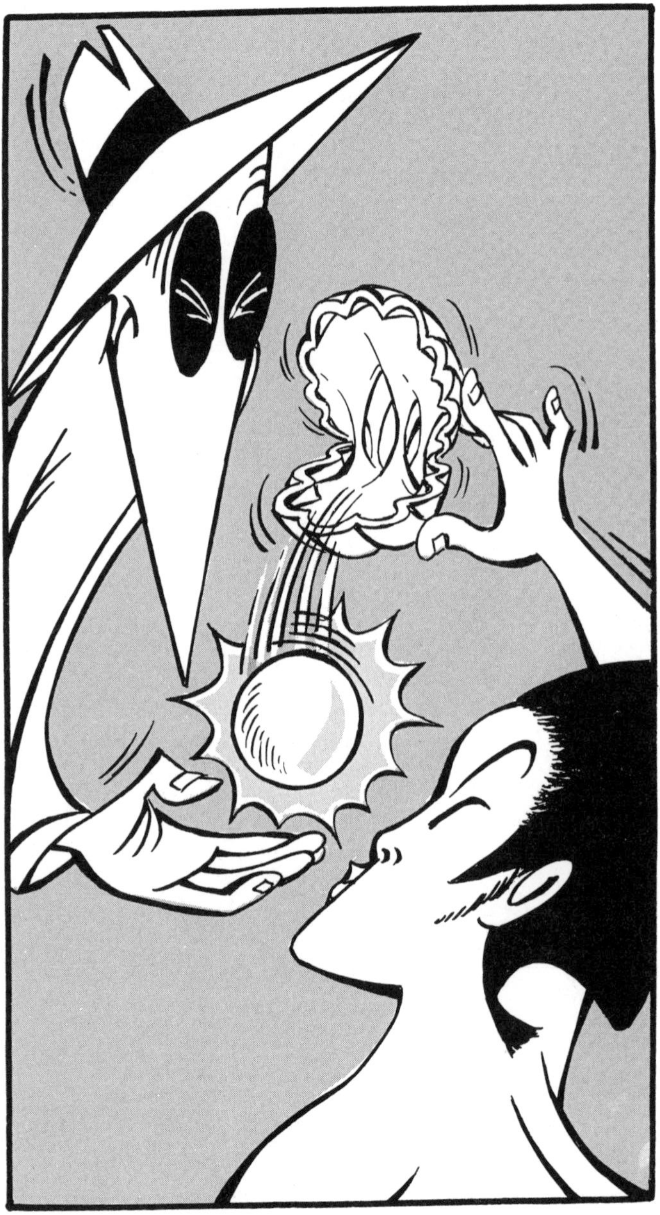

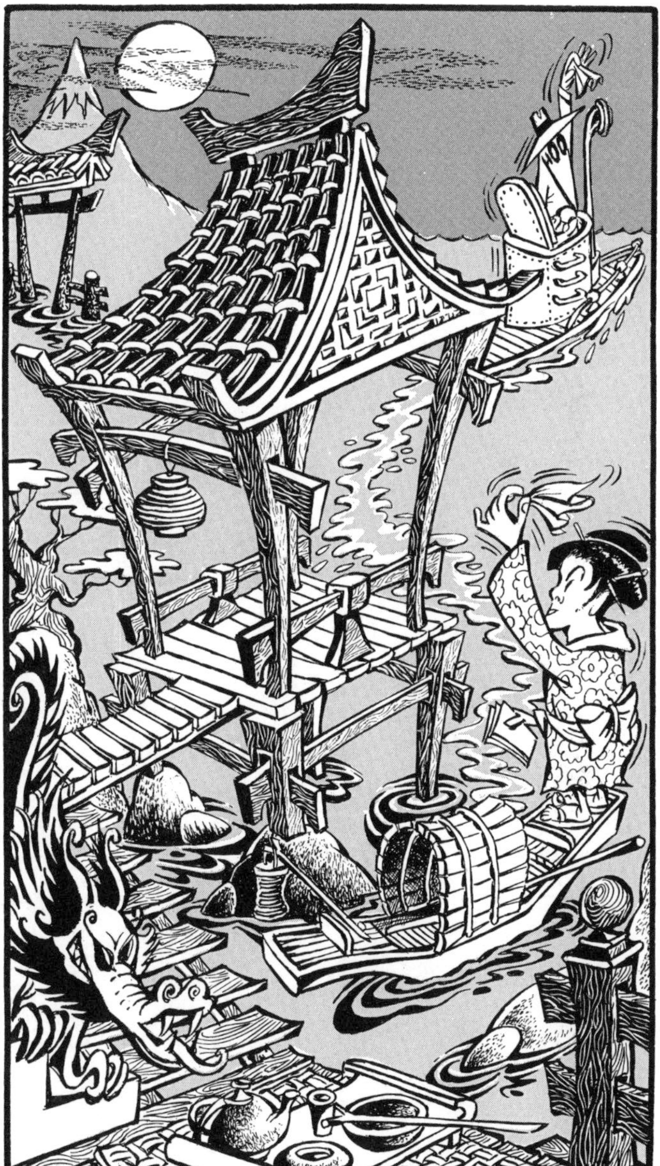

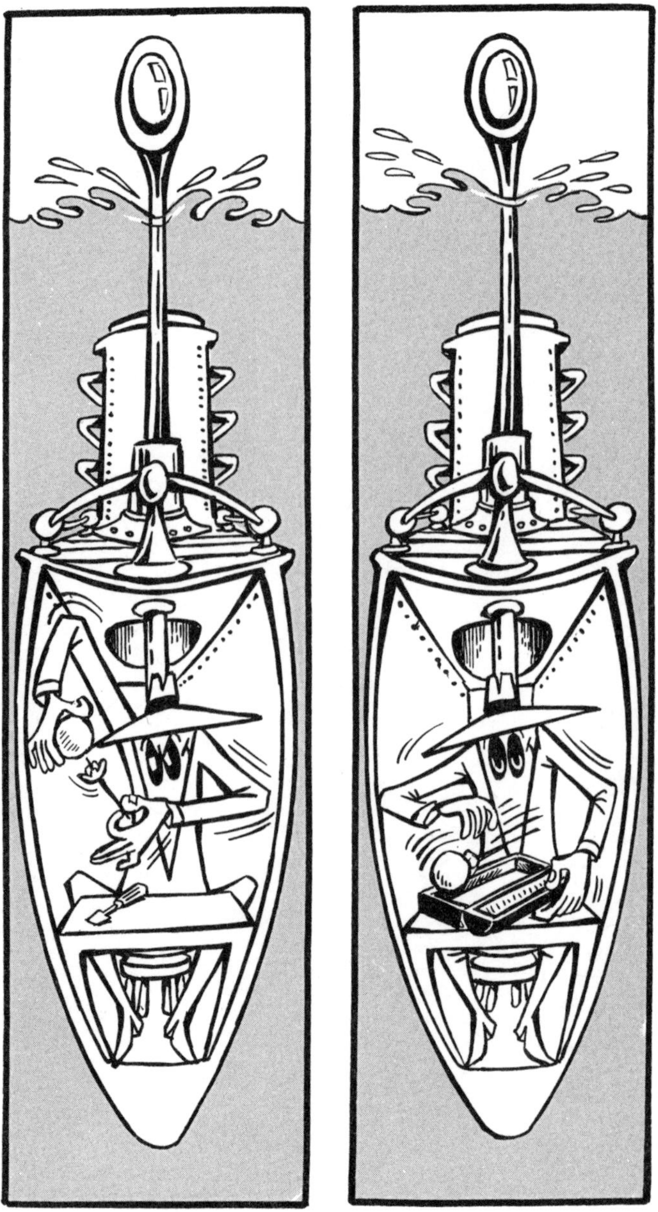

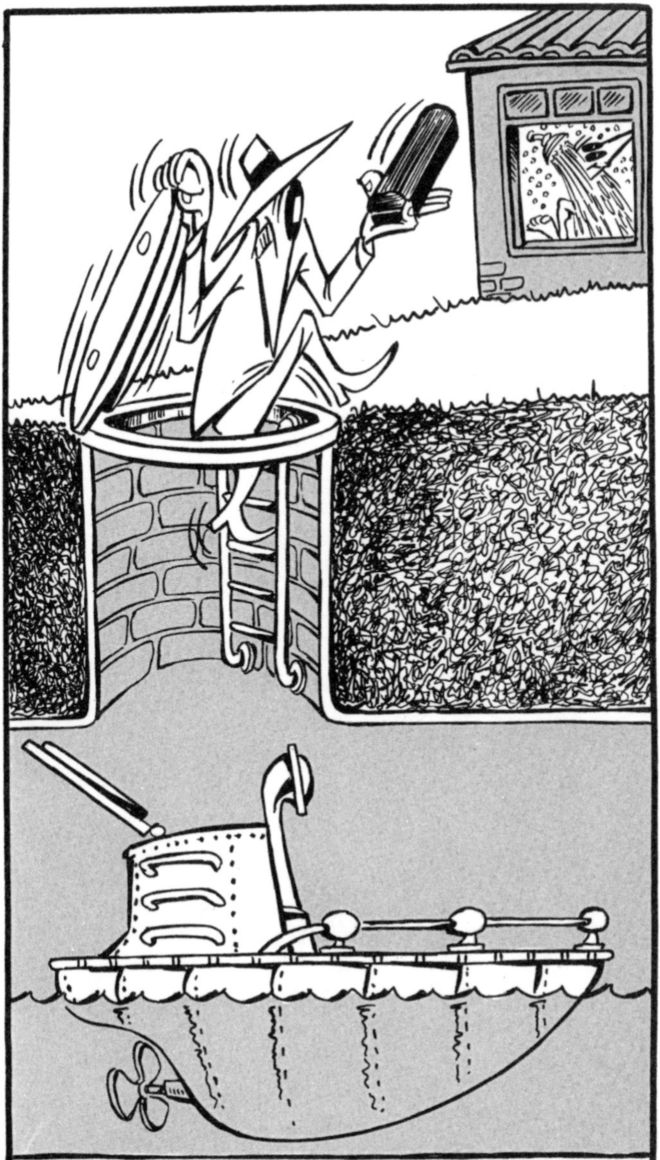

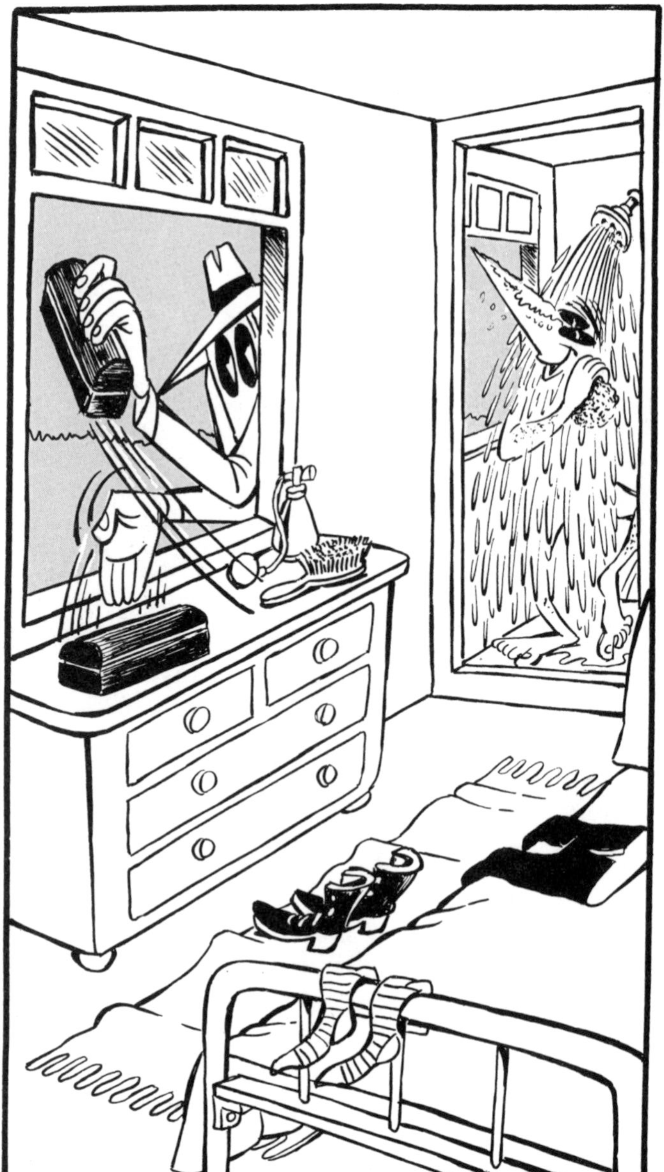

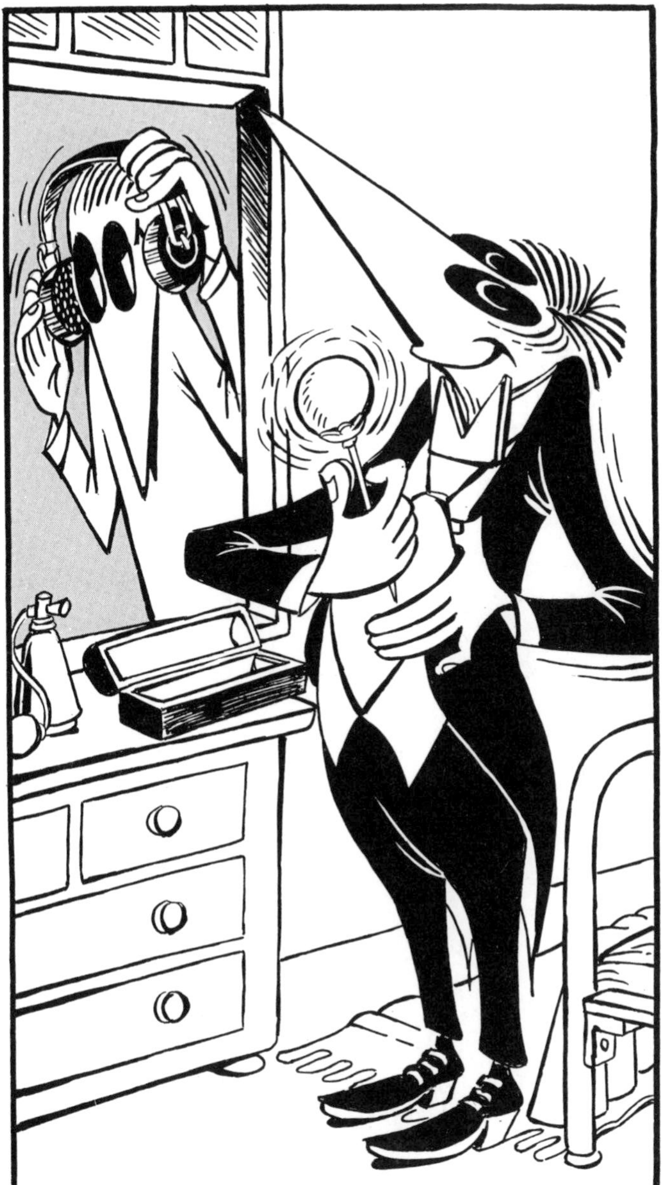

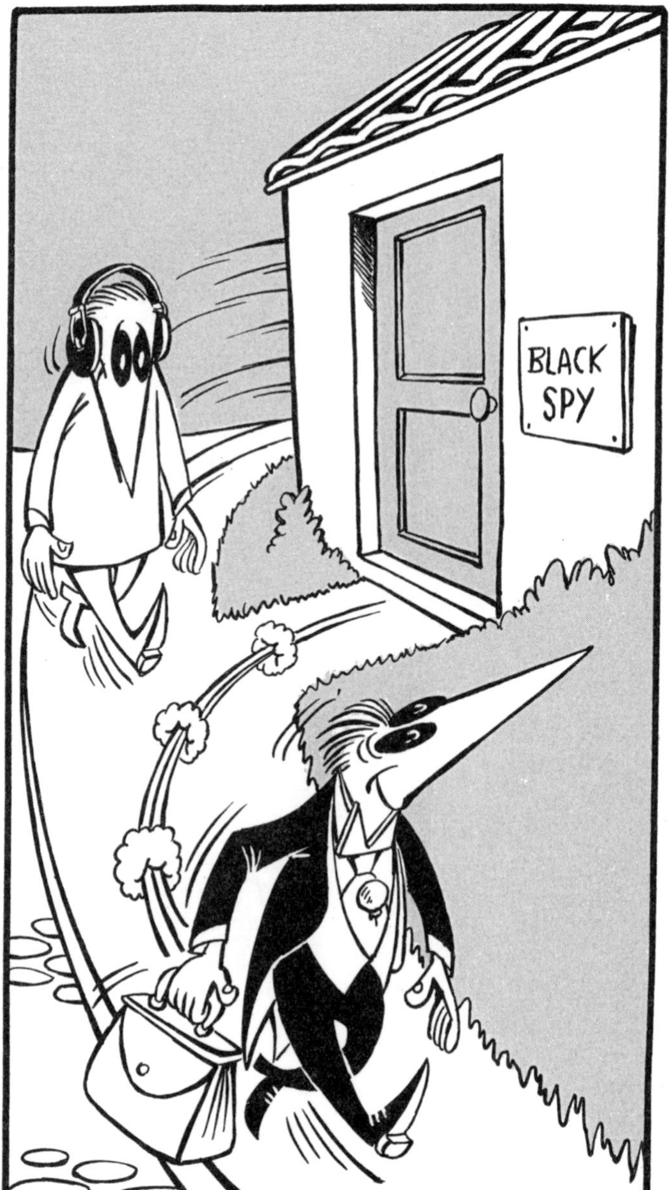
BLACK SPY

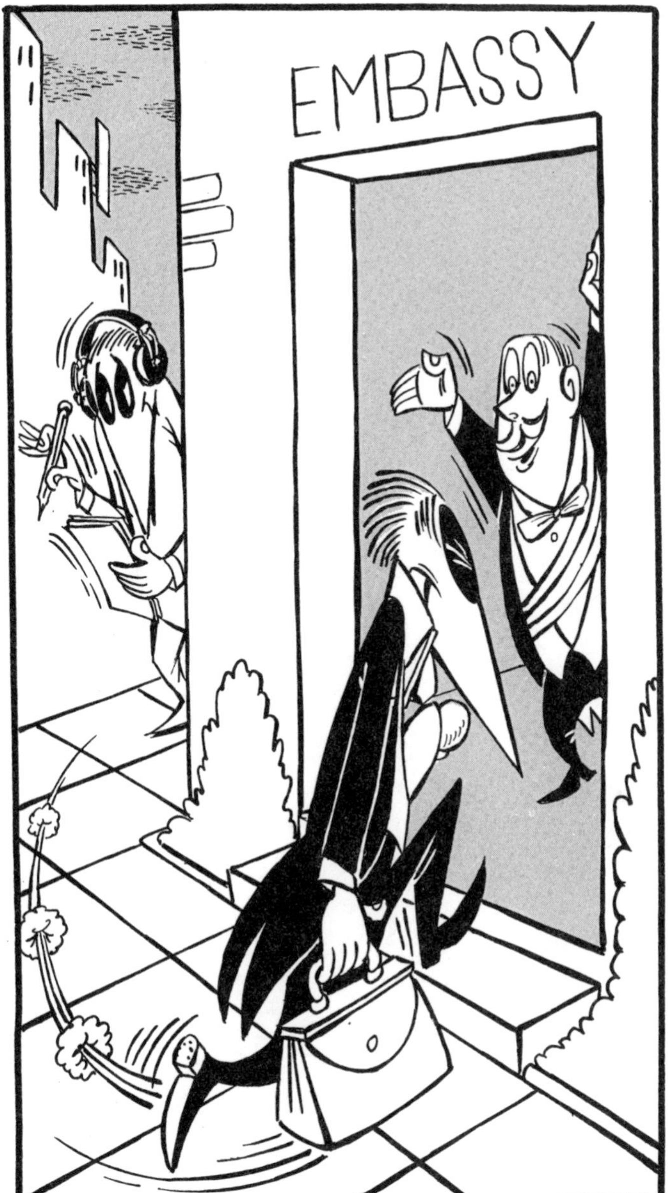
EMBASSY

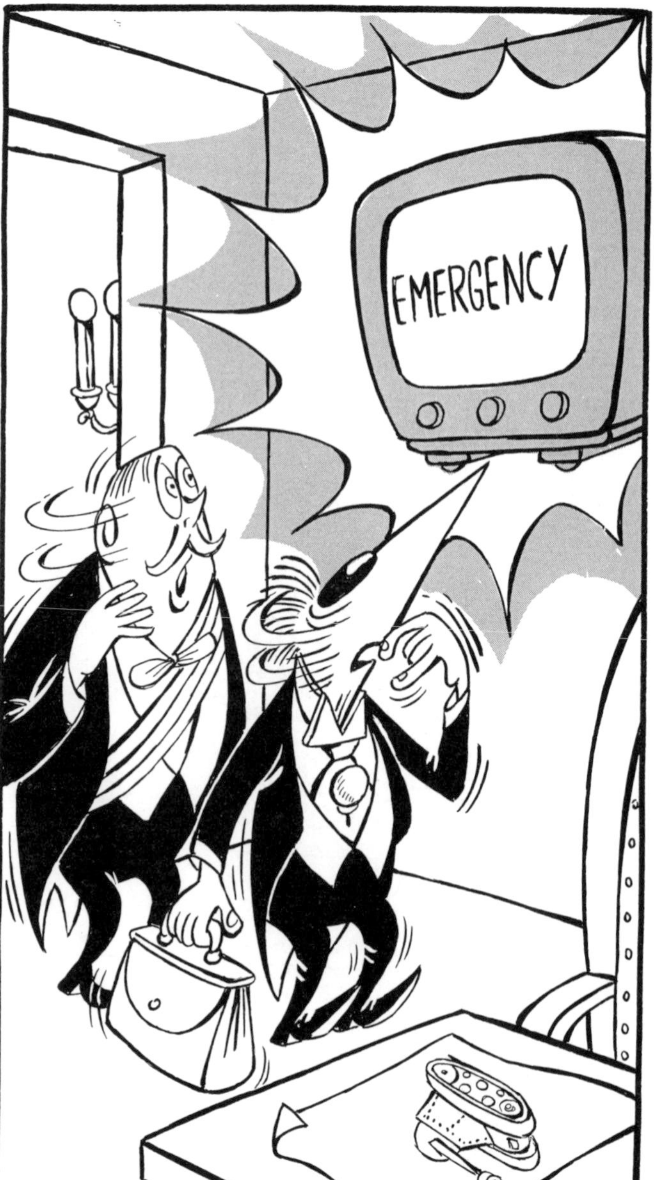
EMERGENCY

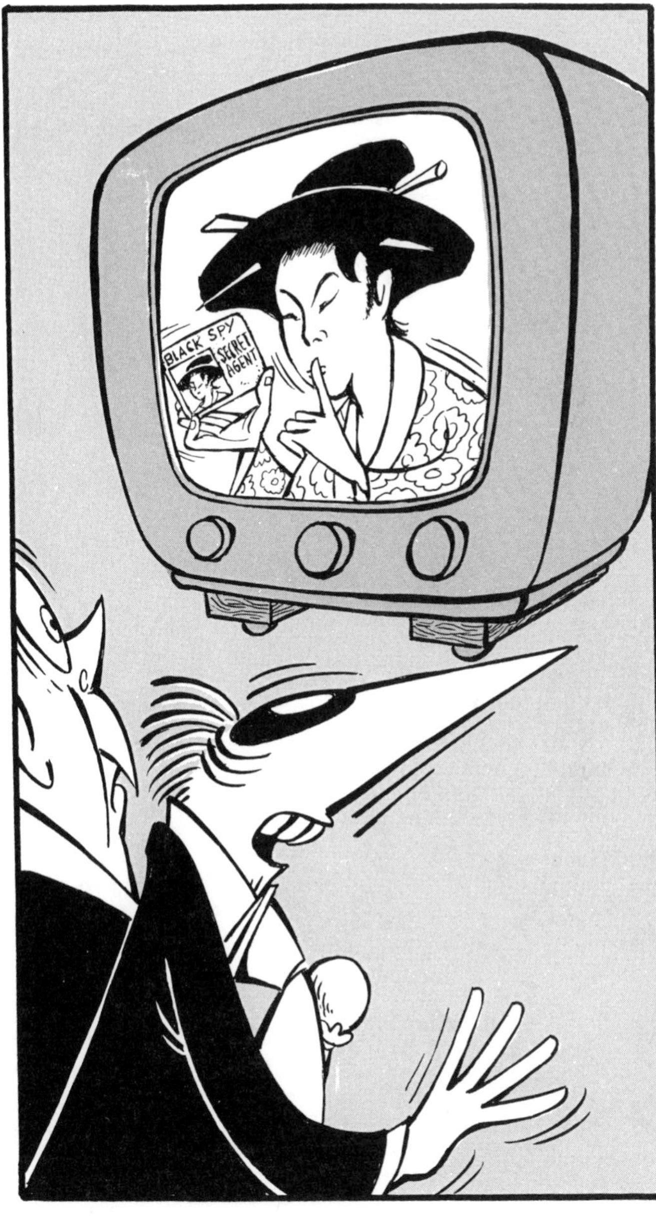
BLACK SPY
SECRET AGENT

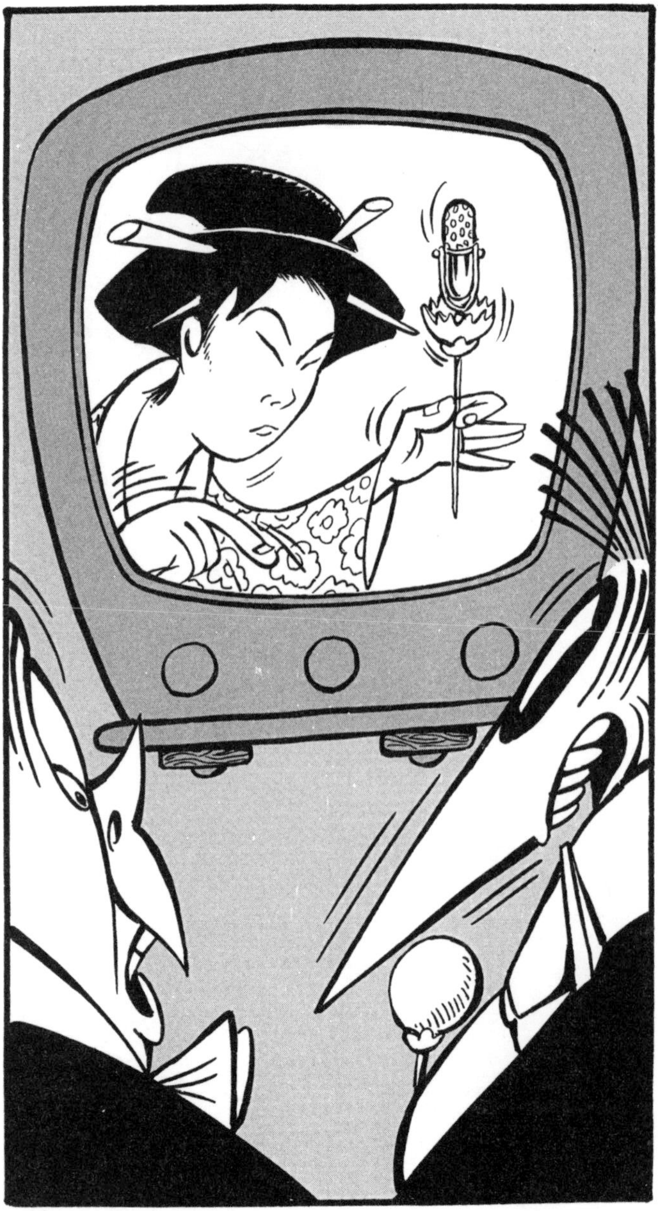

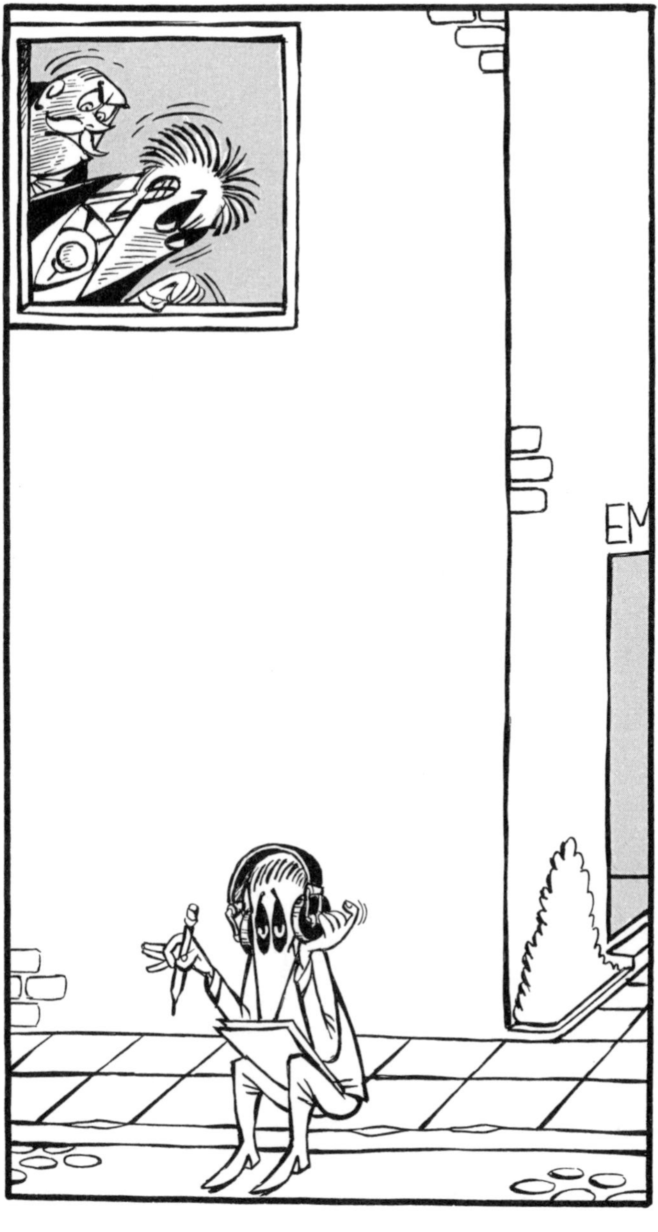
EM

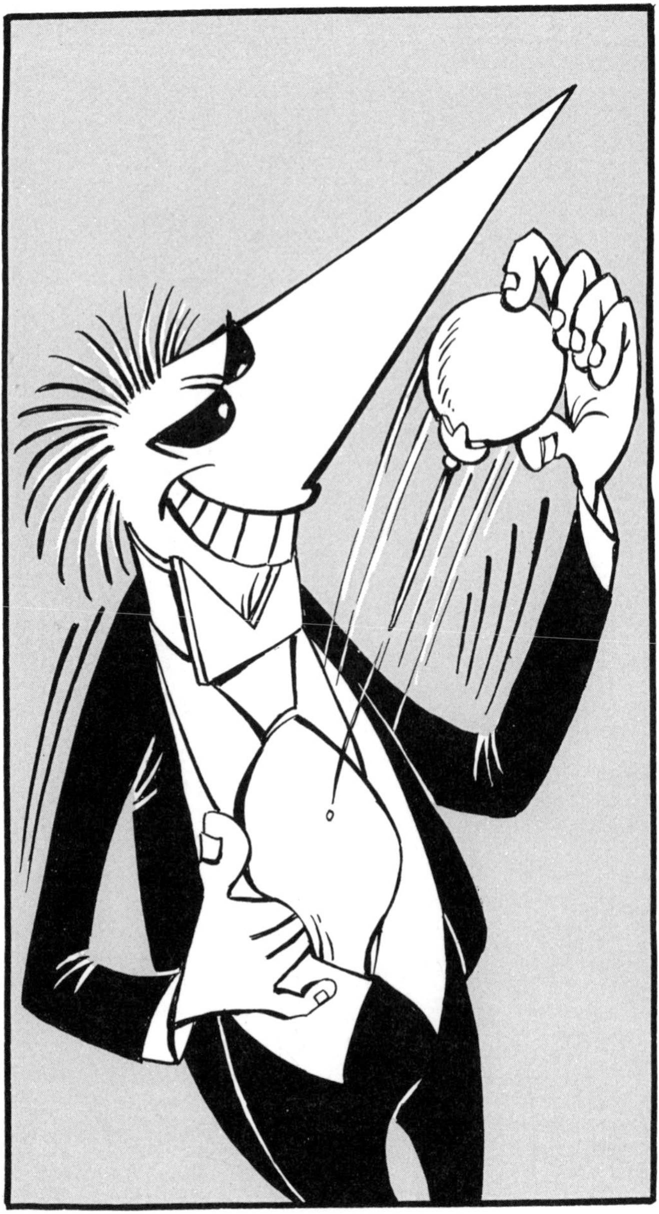

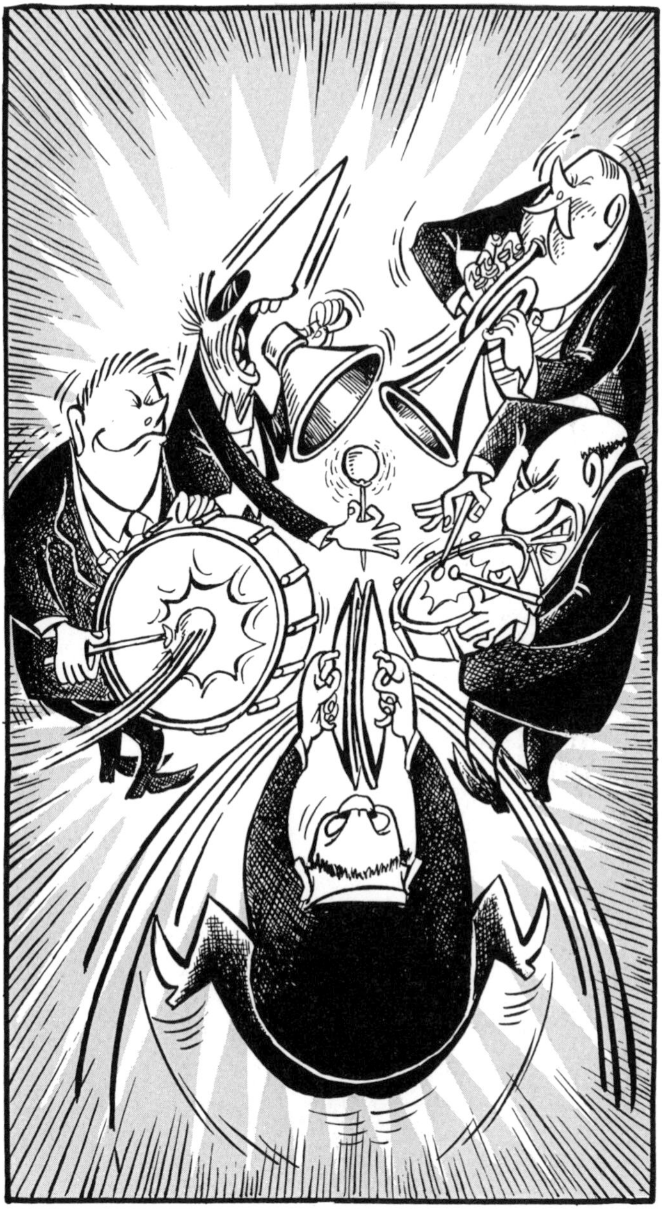

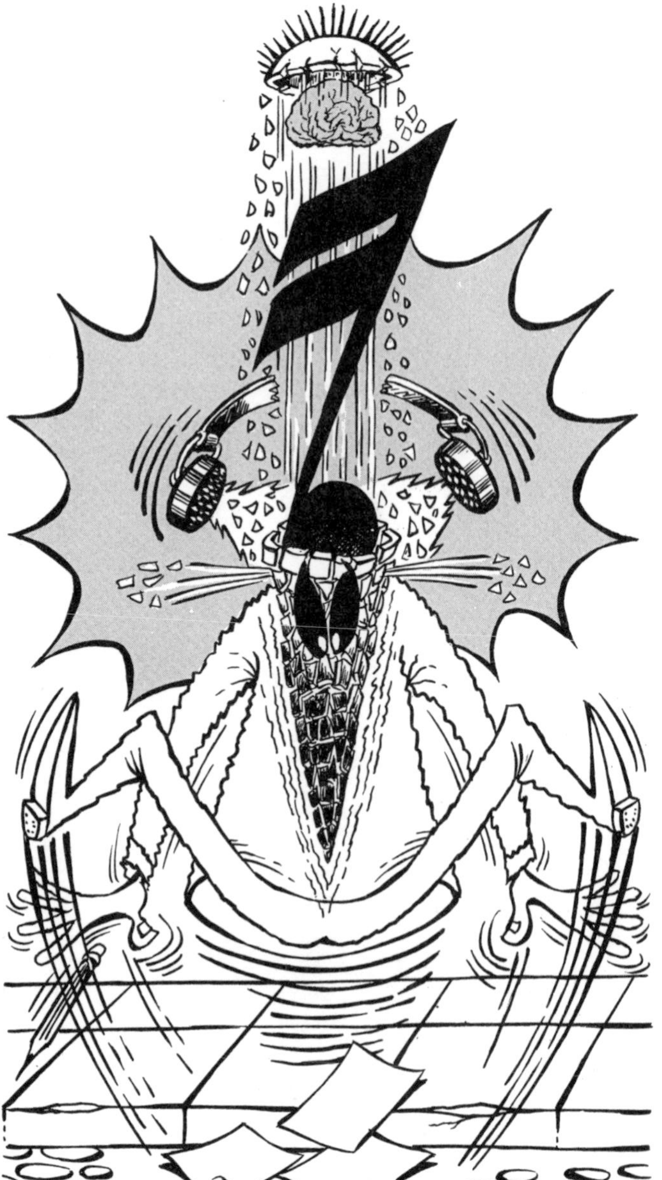

SPY vs SPY

SPIN-OFF

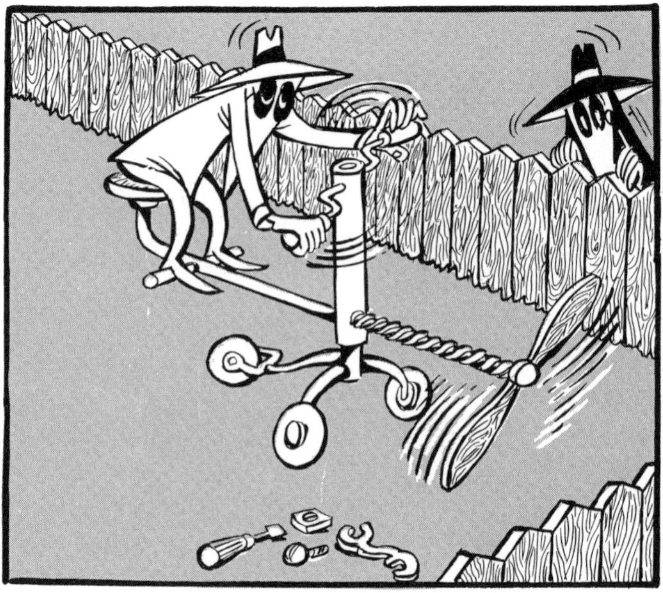

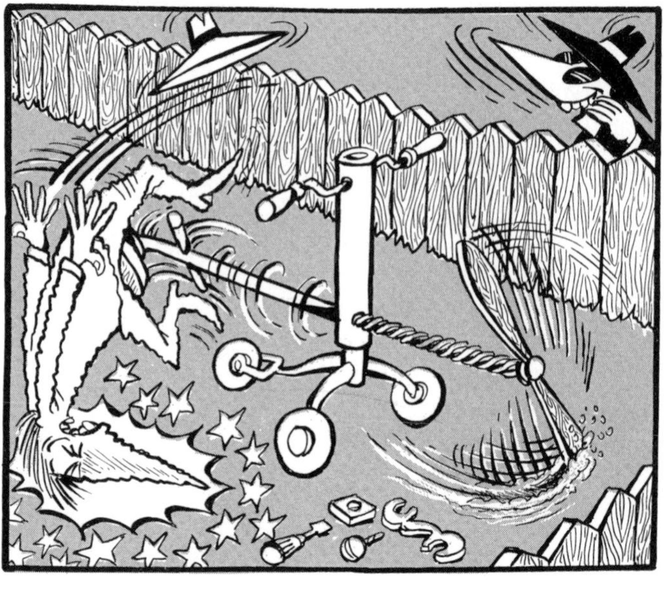

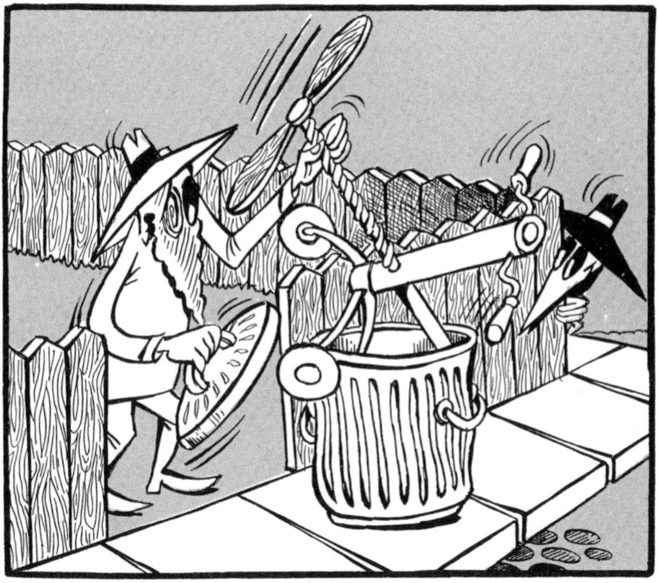

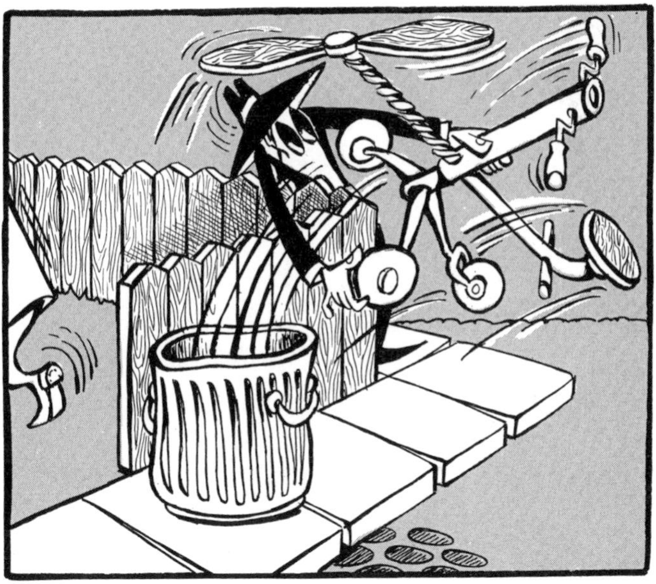

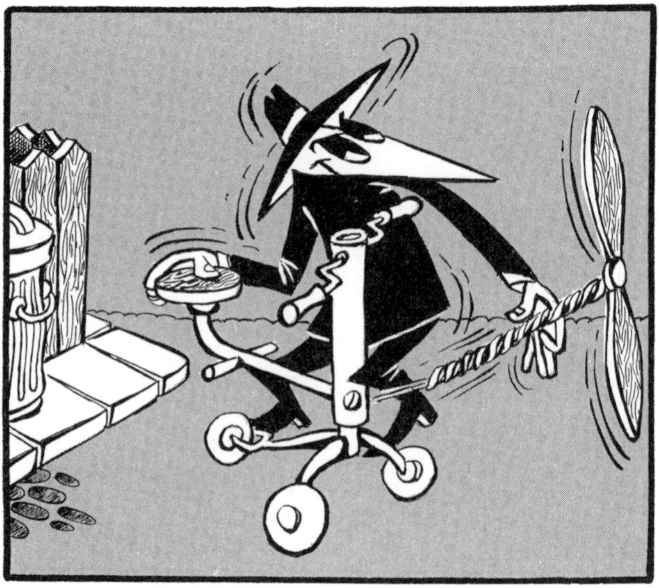

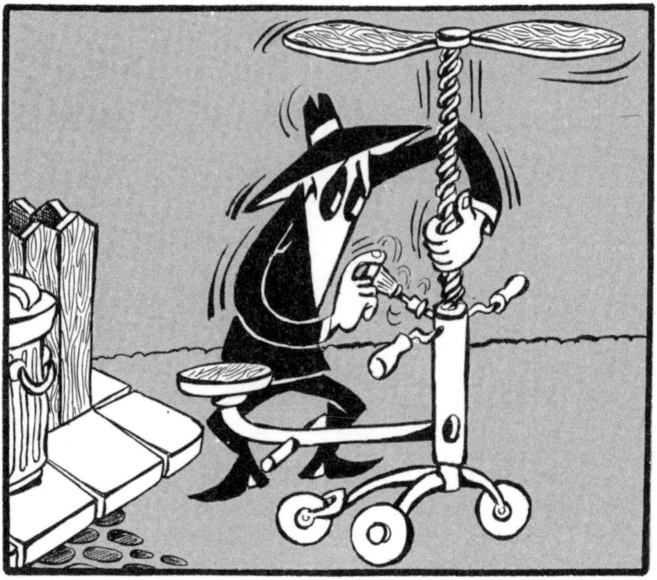

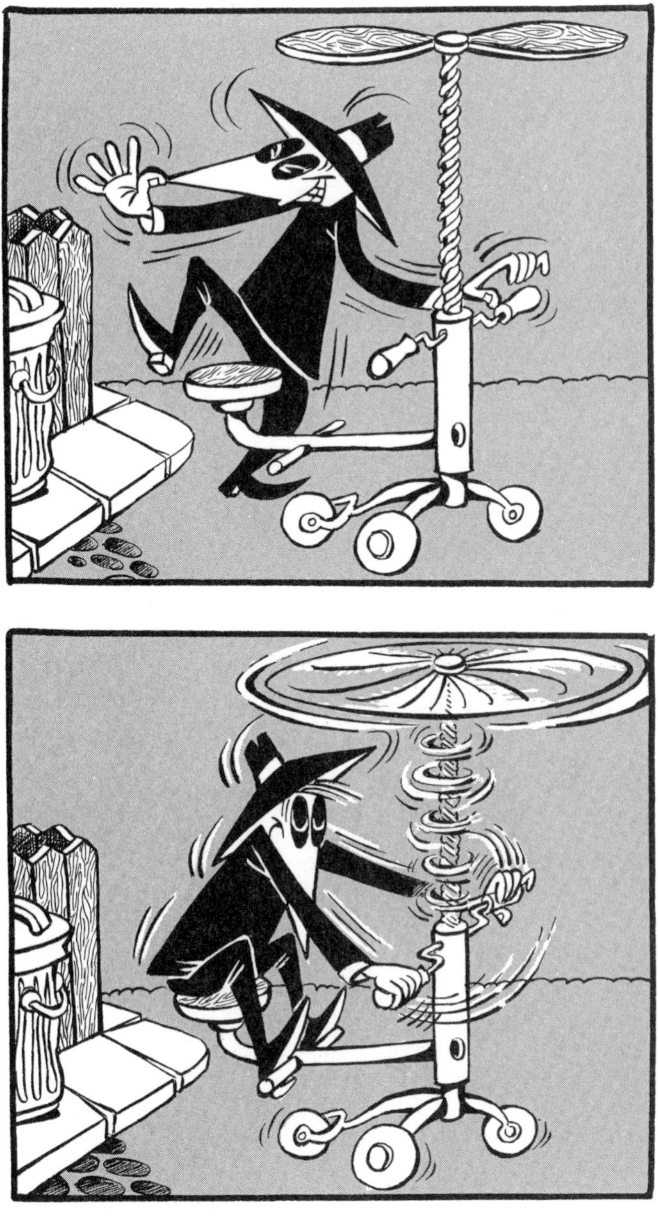

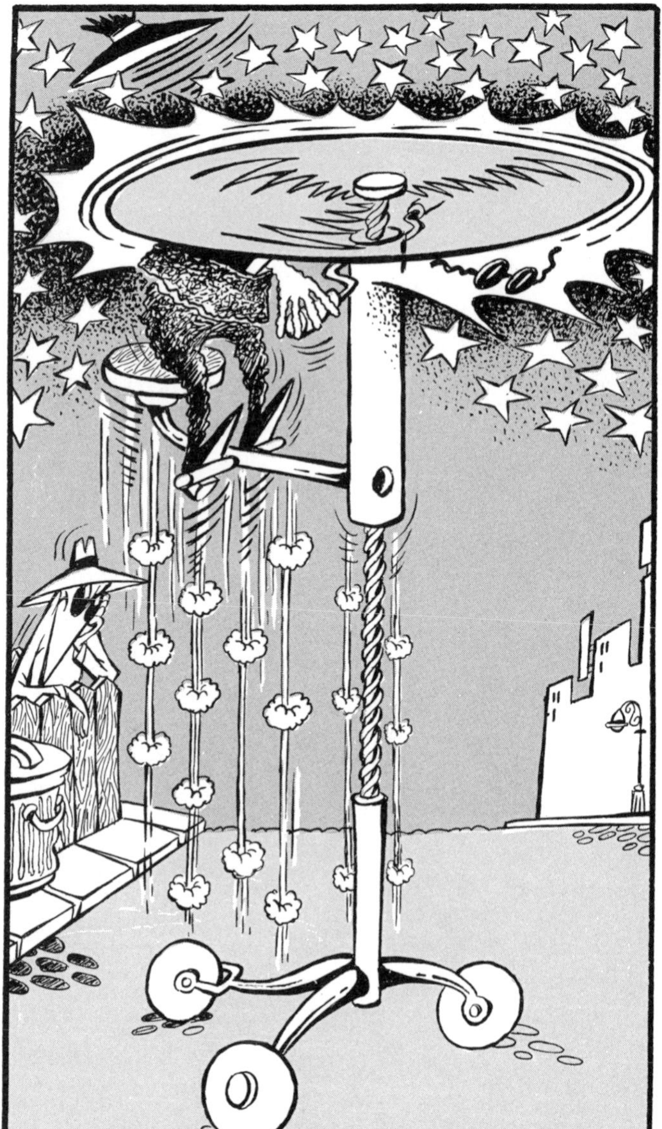

SPY vs SPY

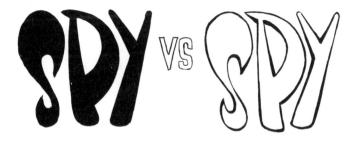

BOULDER-DASH!

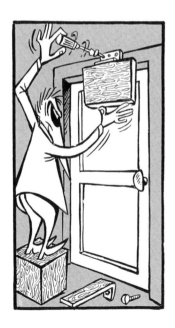

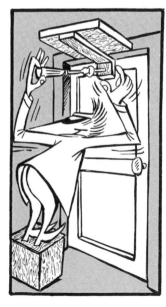

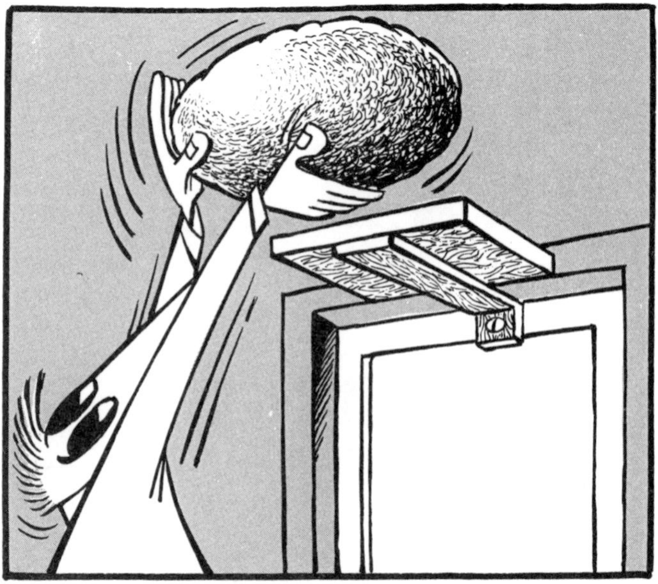

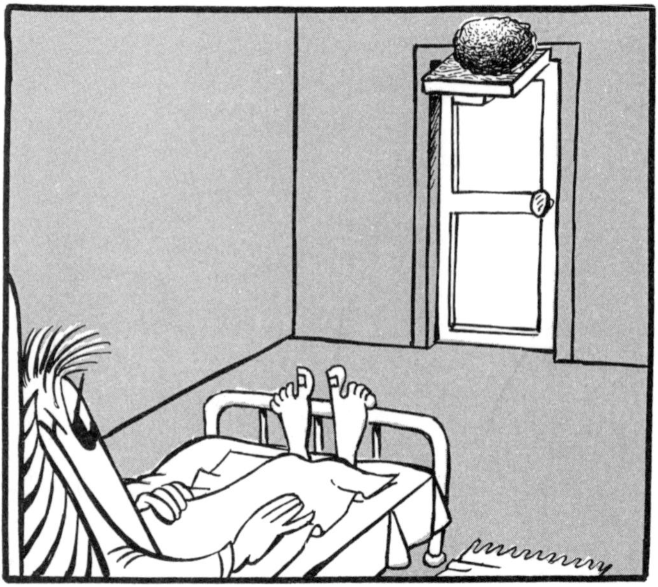

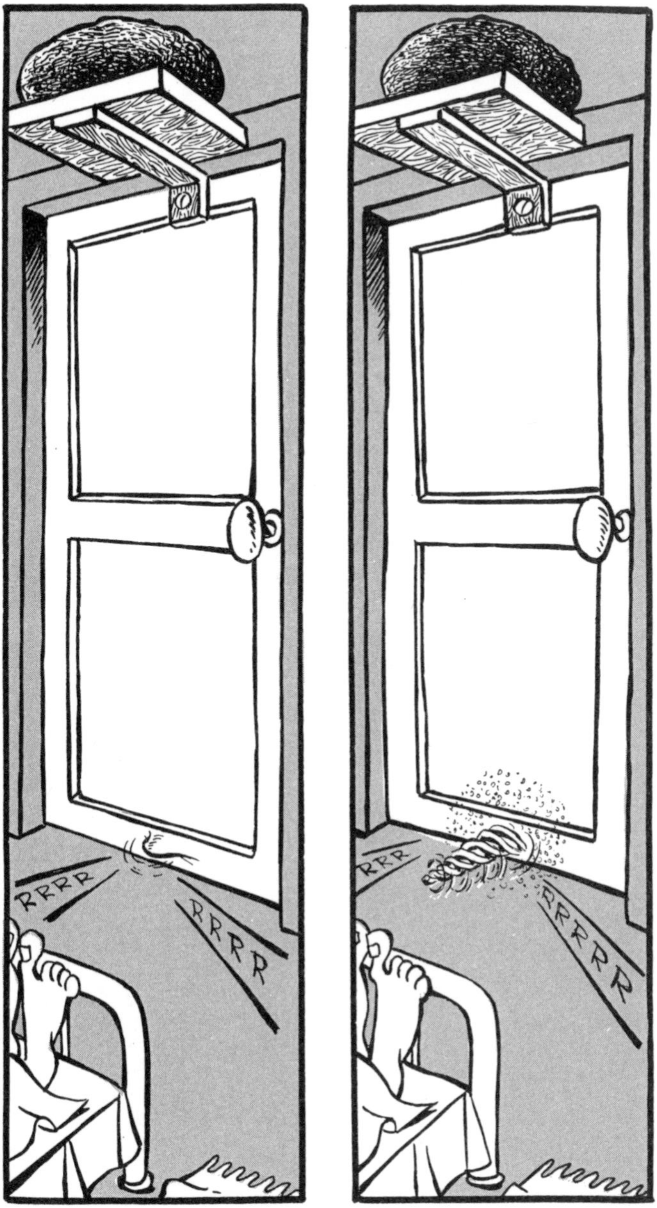
RRRR
RRRR
RRR
RRRRR

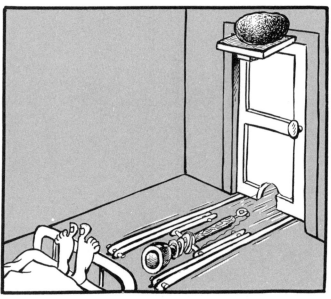

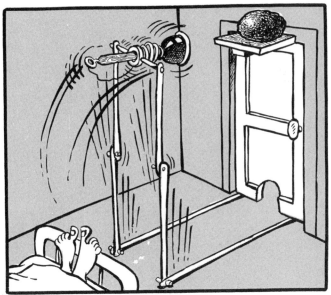

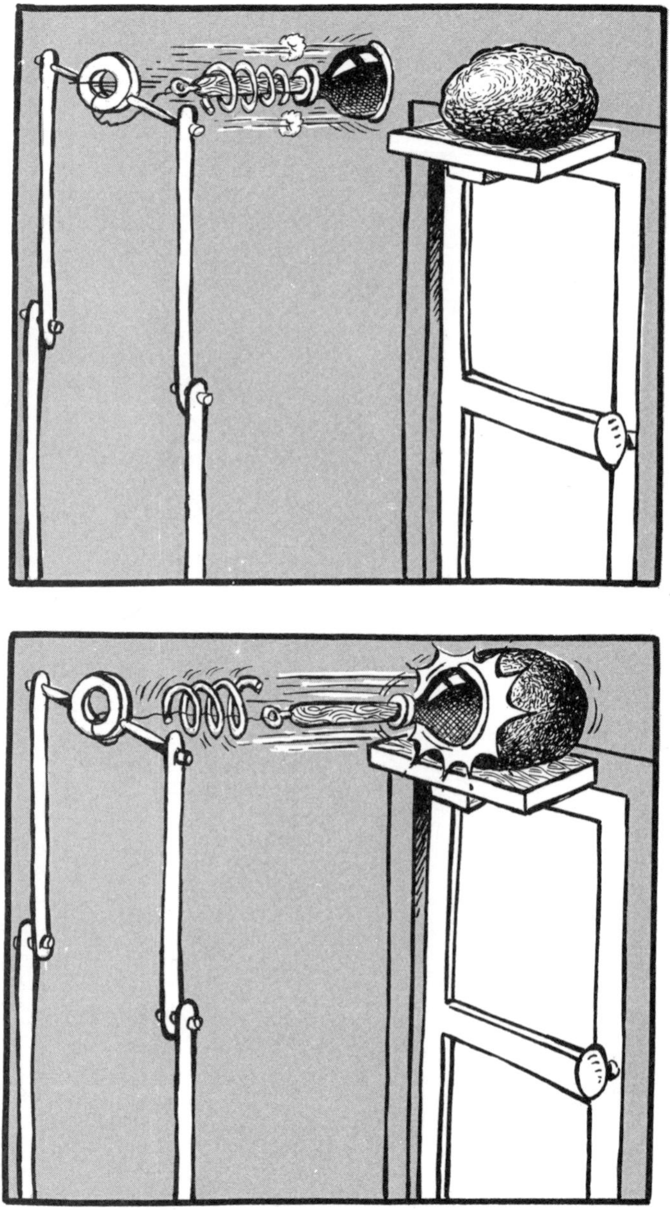

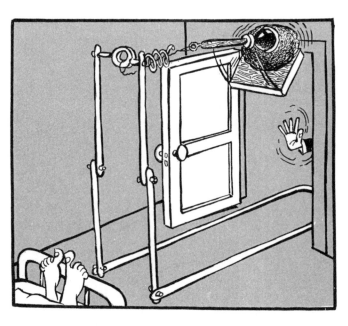

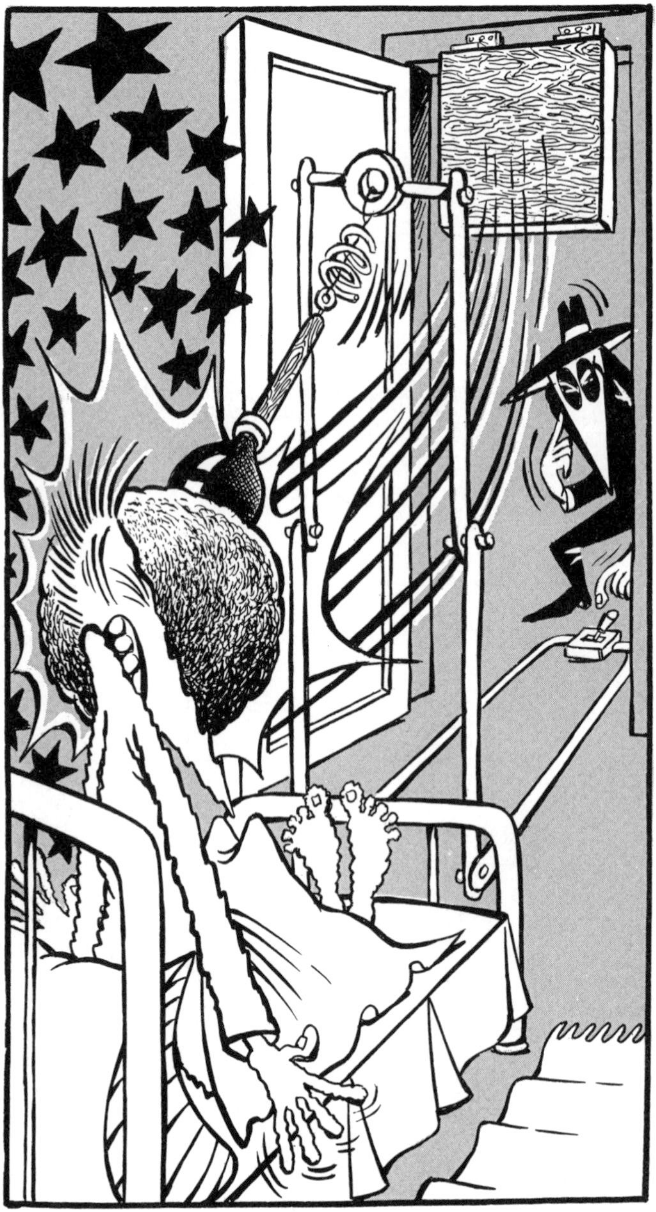

SPY vs SPY

A CUCKOO PLOT

T.N.T.

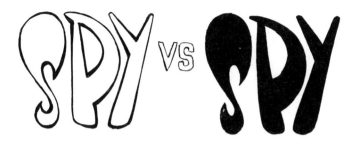

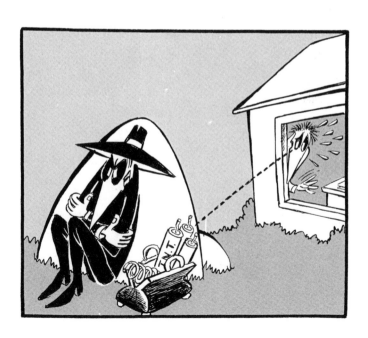

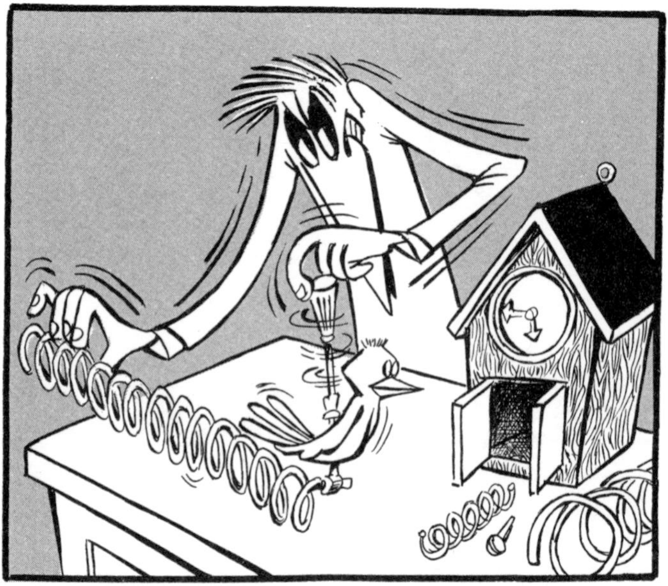

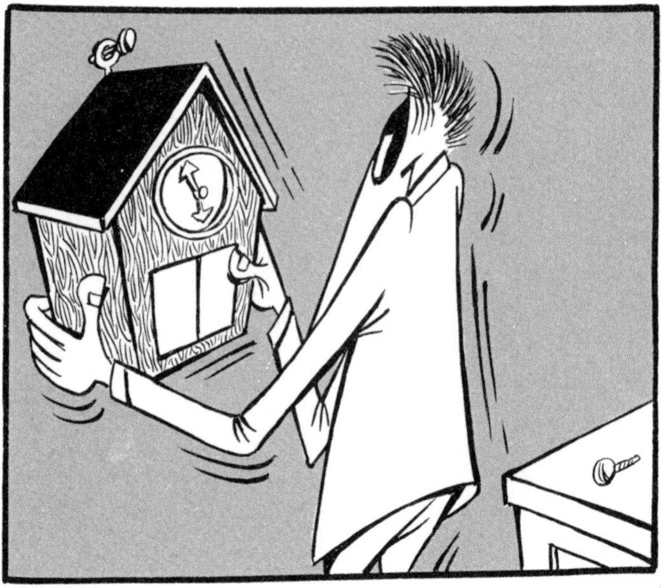

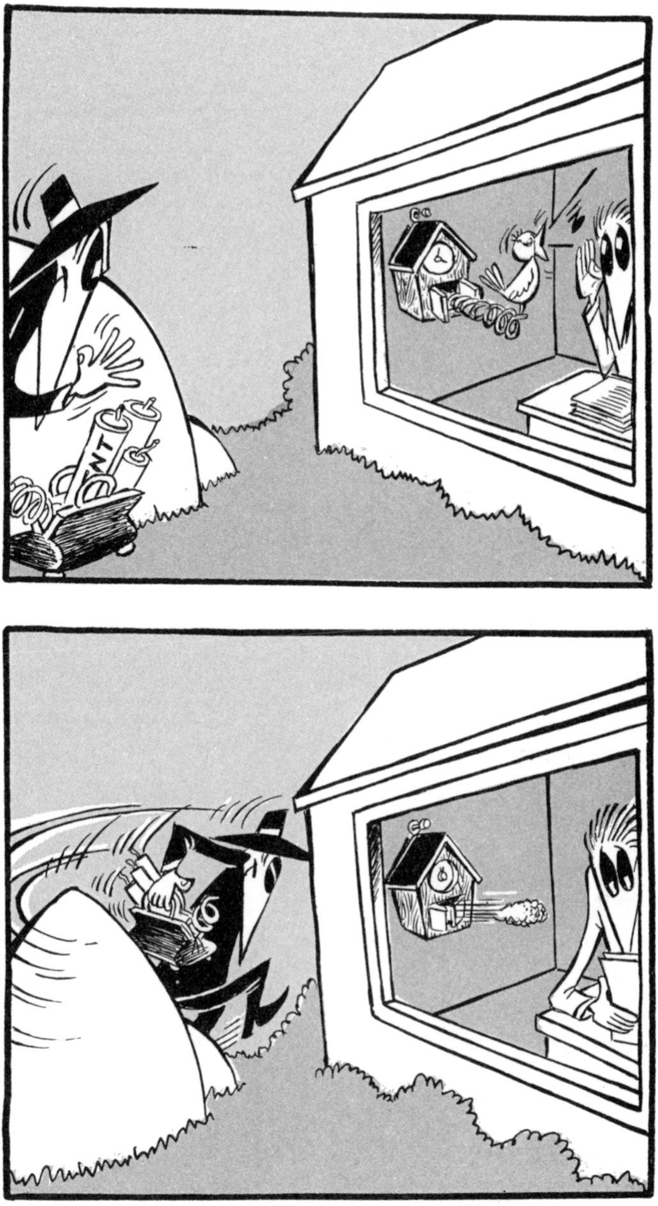

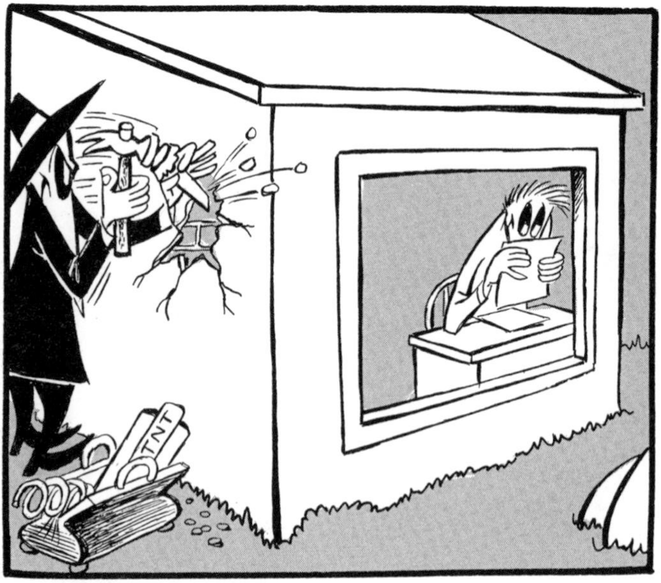
TNT

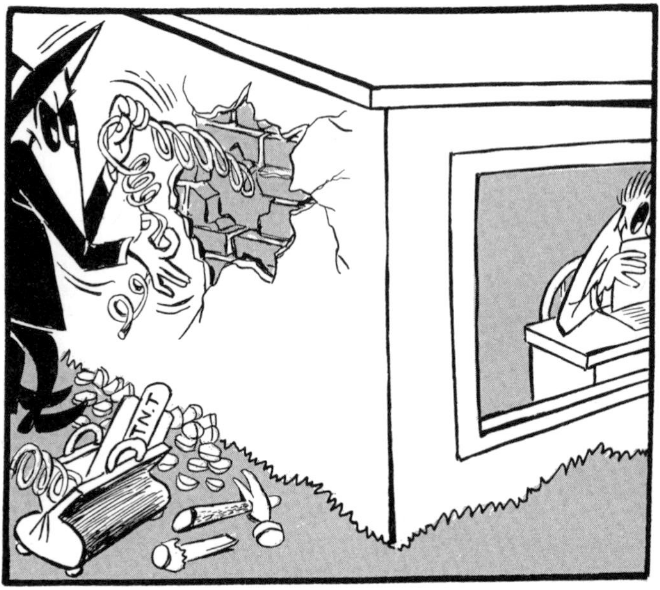
TN.T

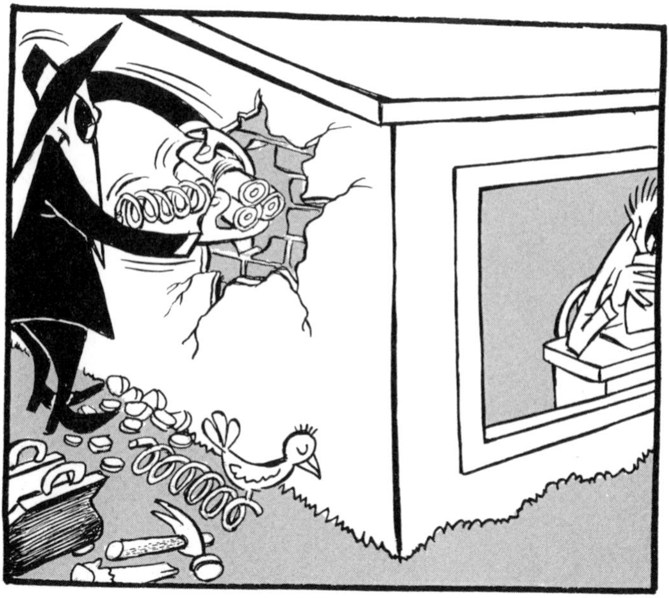

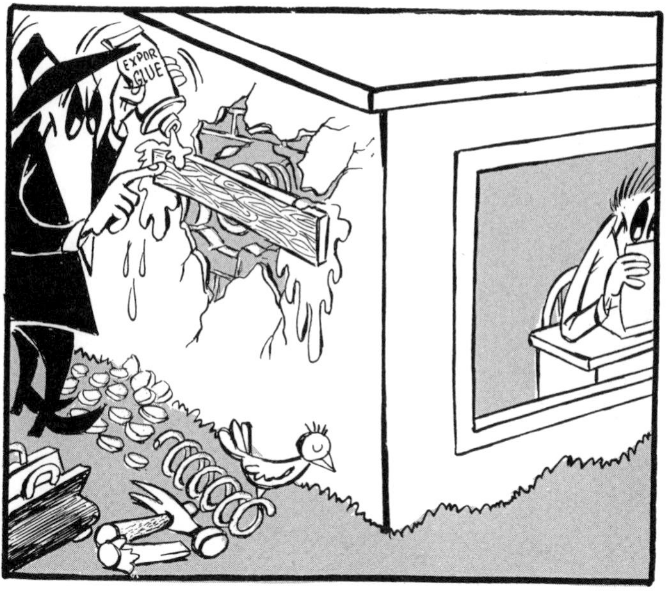
EXPOR
GLUE

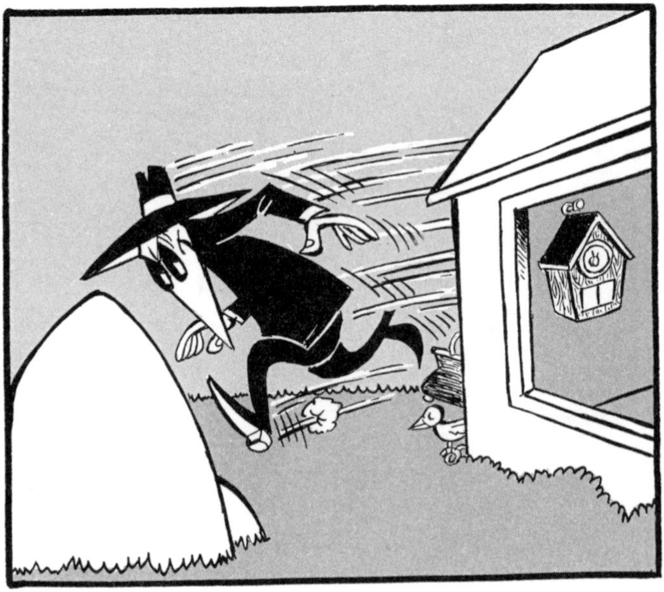

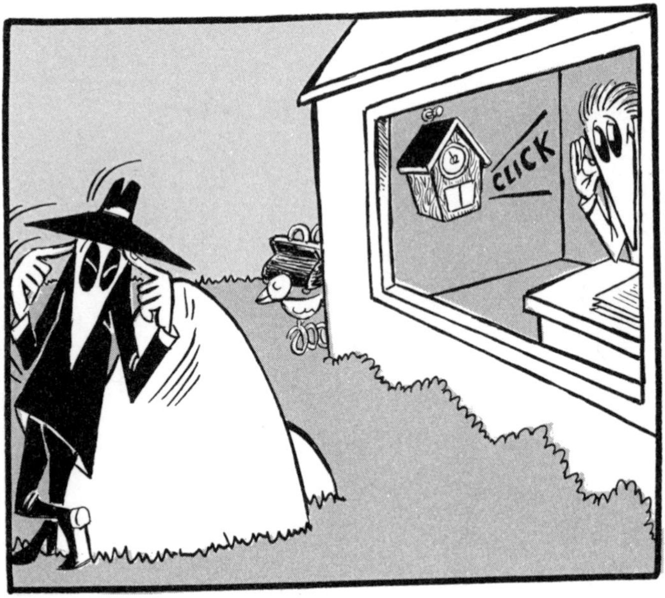
CLICK

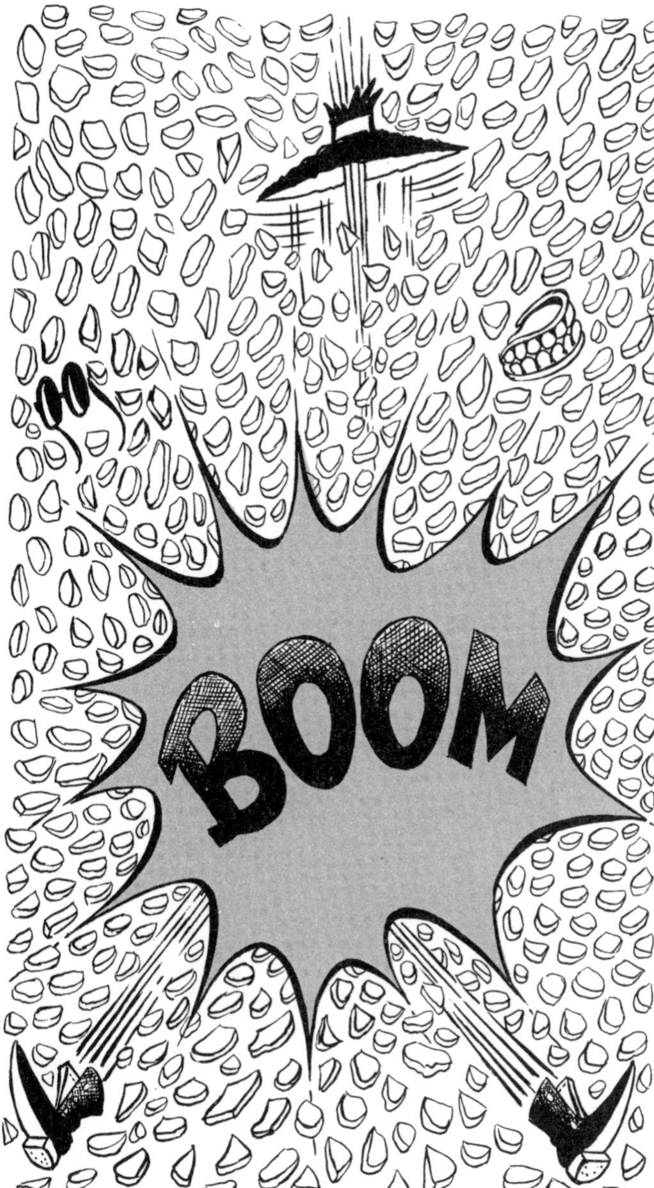
BOOM

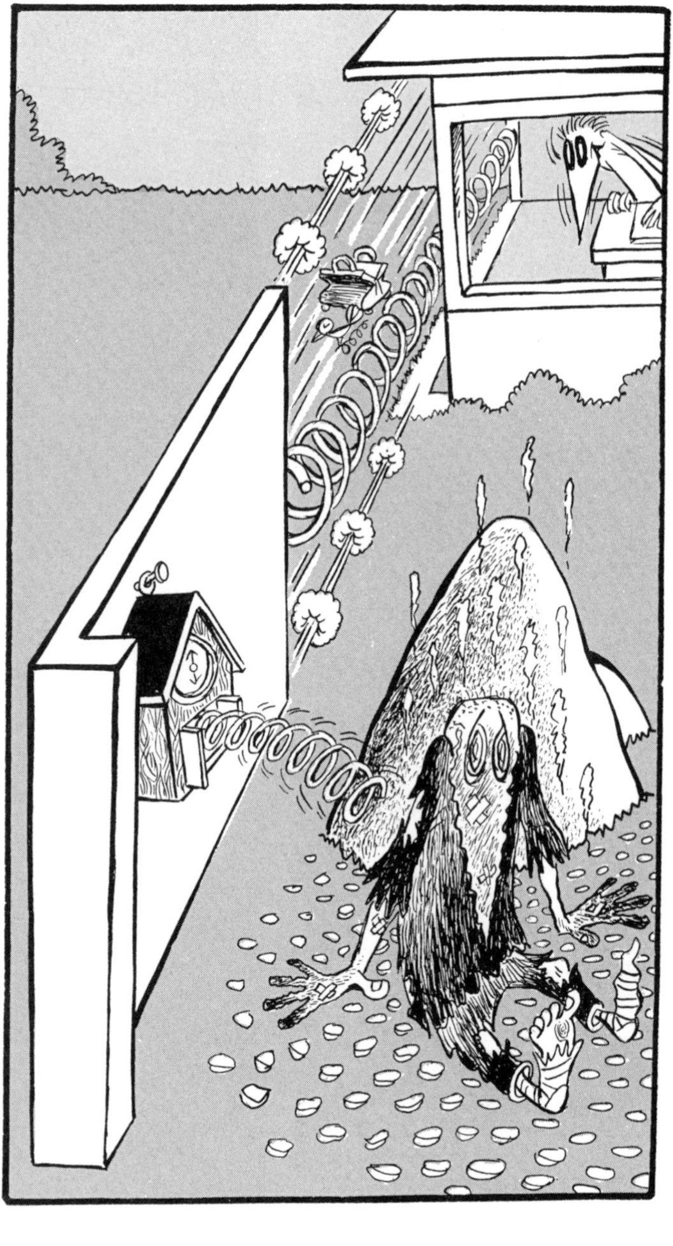

SPY vs SPY

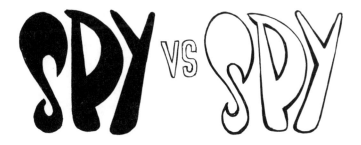

THE IRON DOUBLE-CROSS

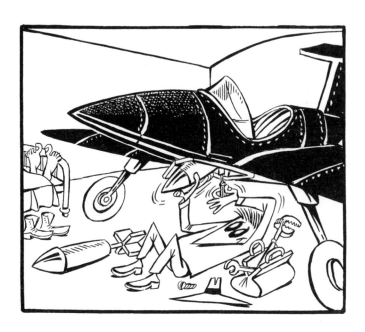

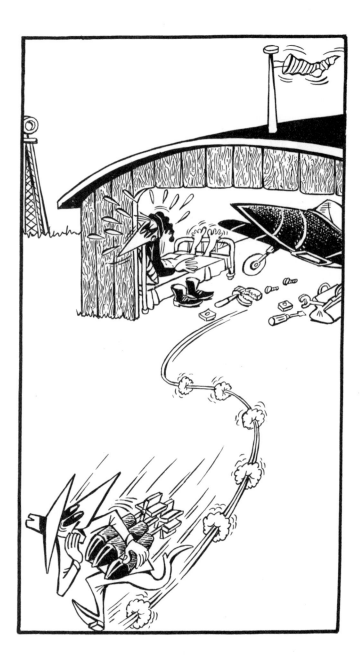

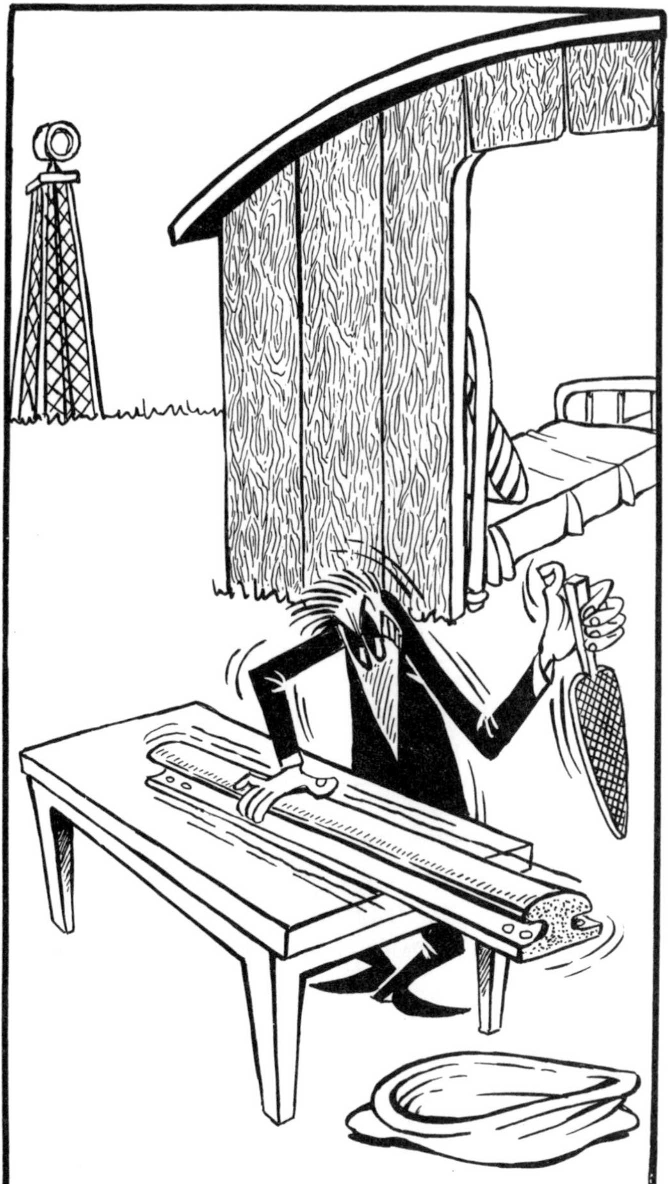

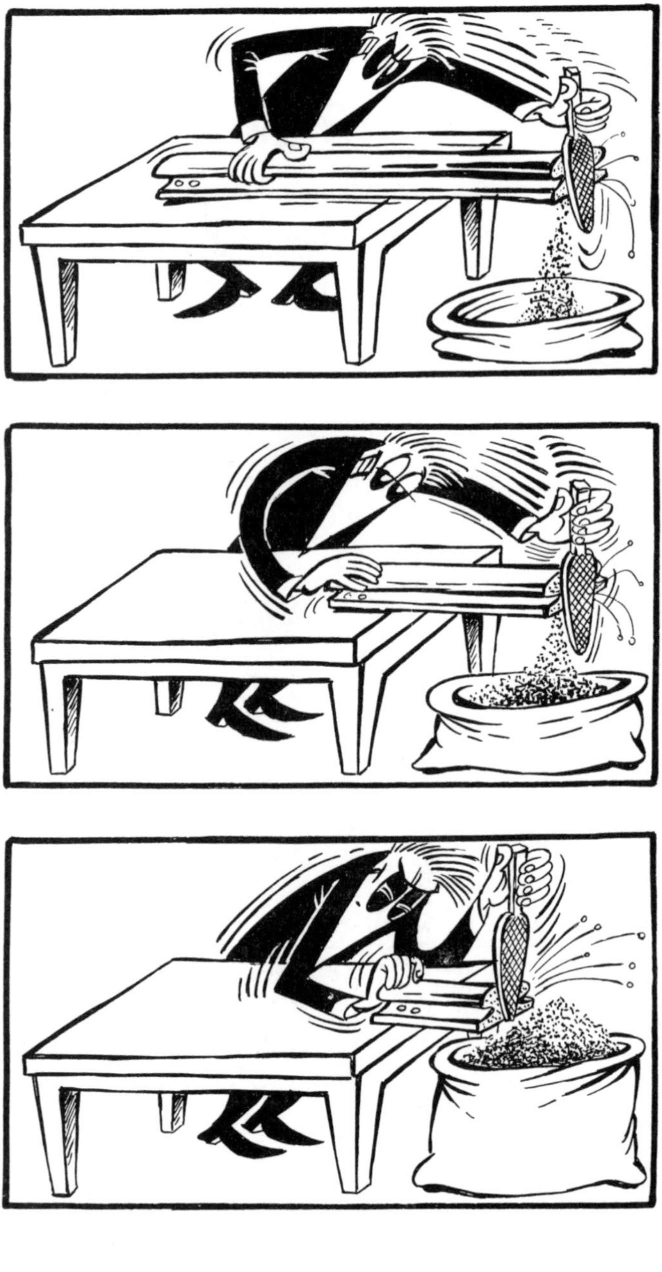

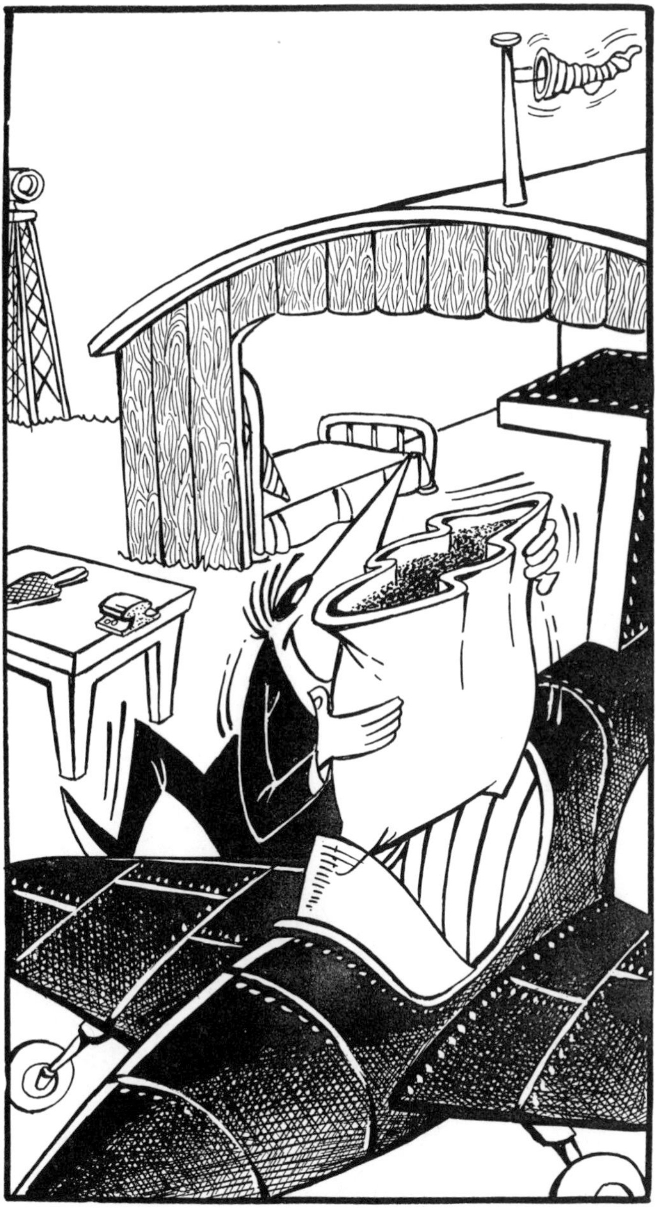

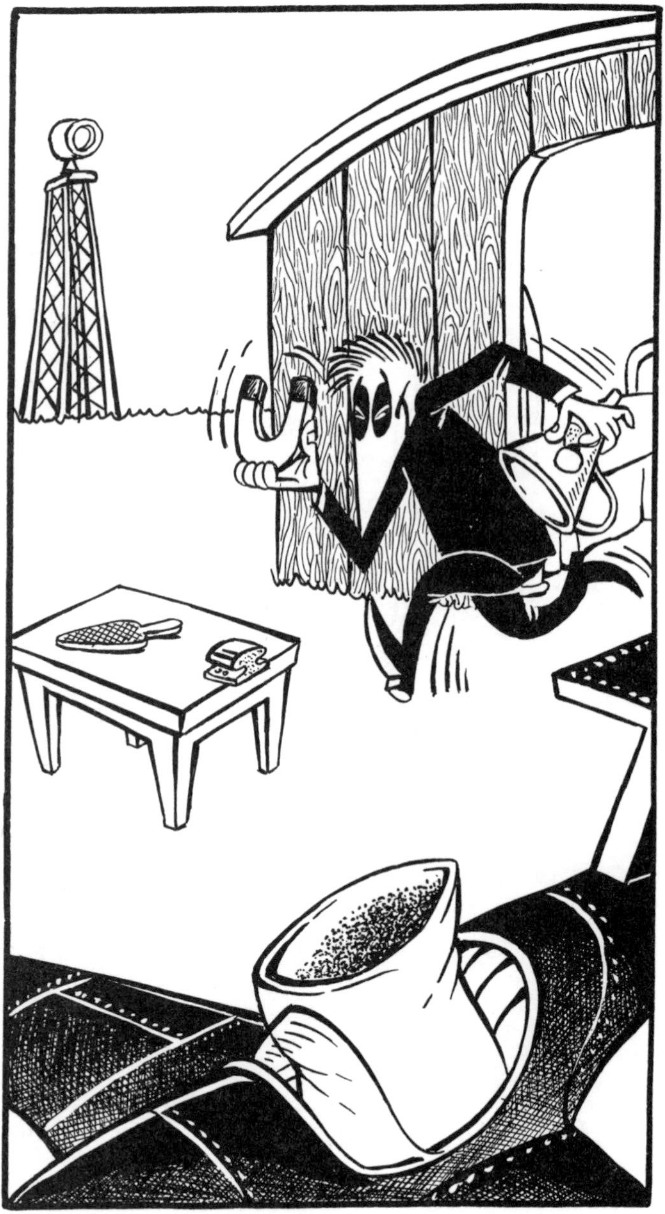

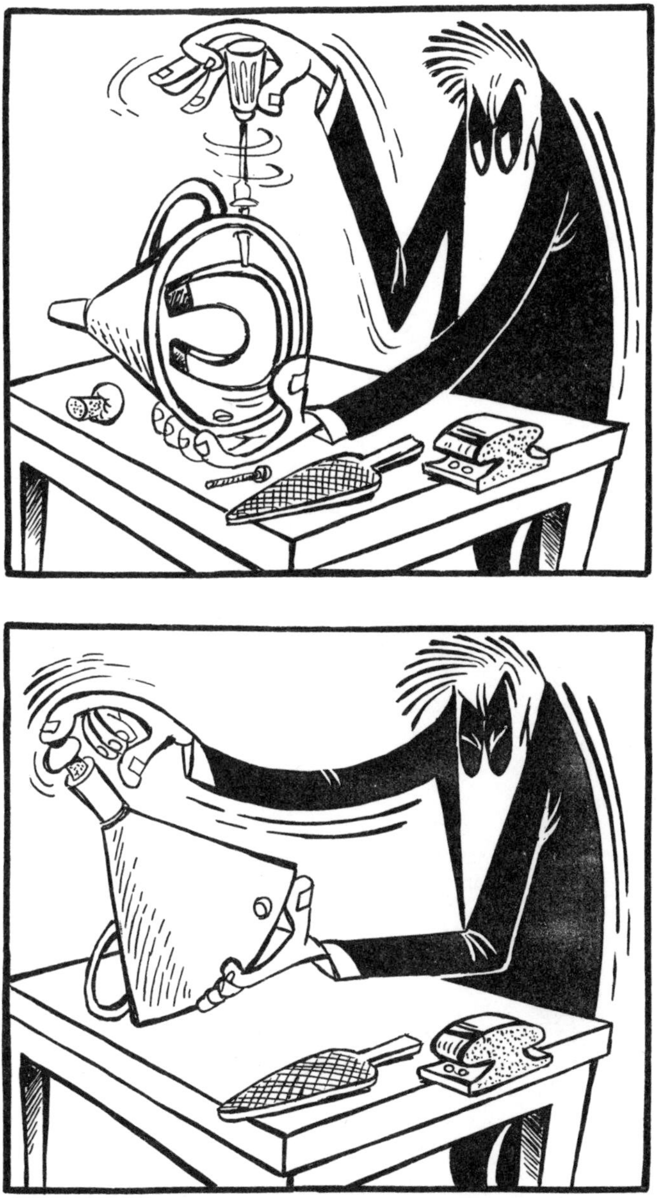

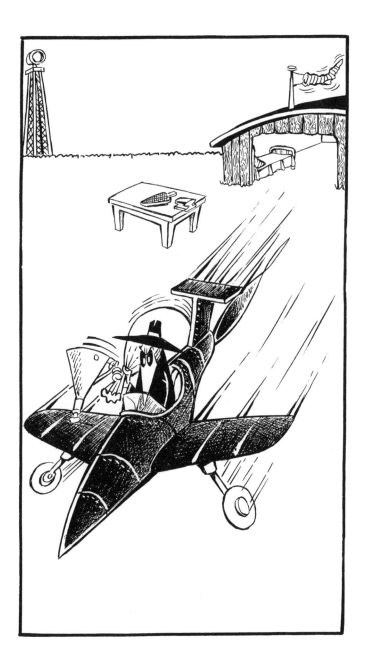

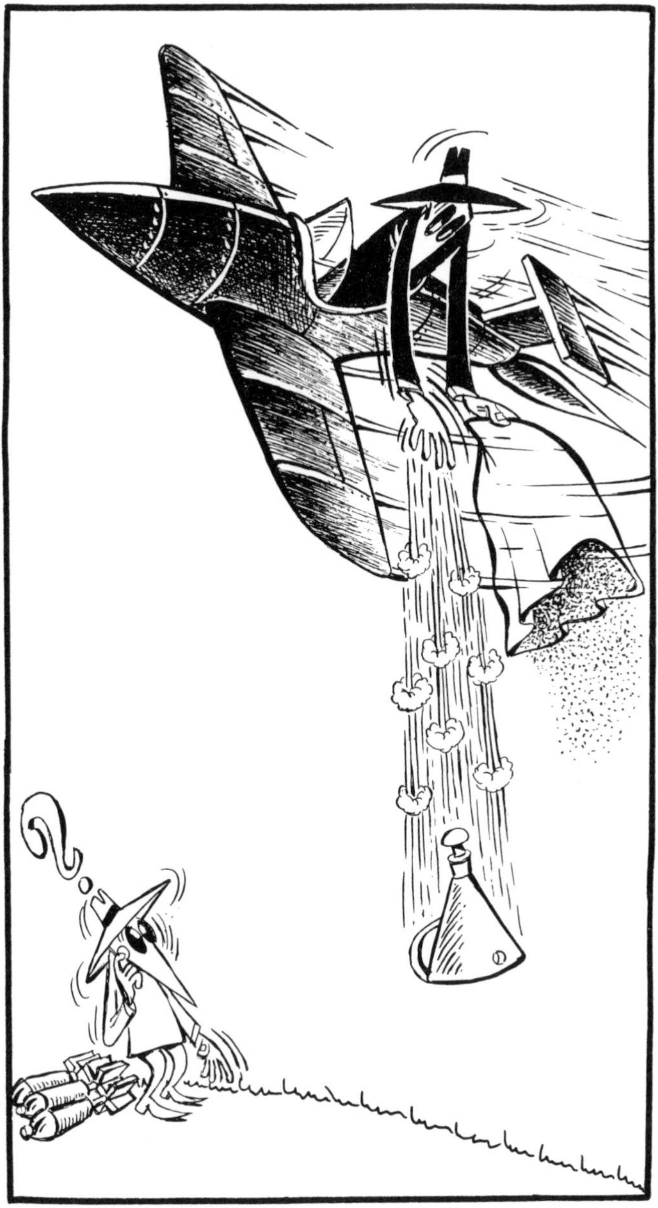

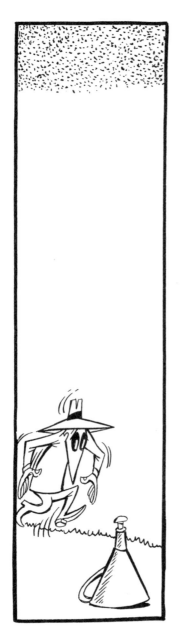

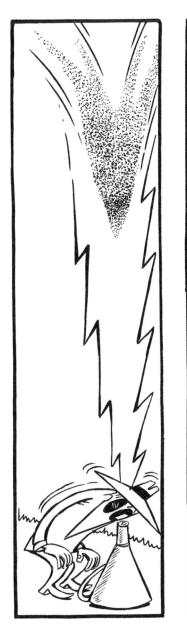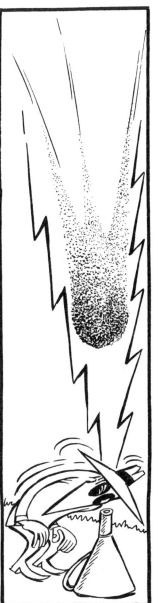

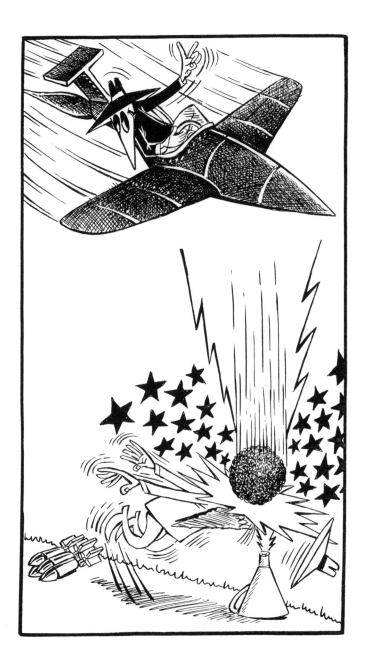

SPY vs SPY

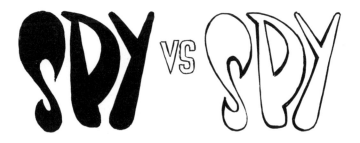

DOGGIE BAGGED

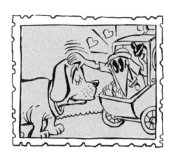

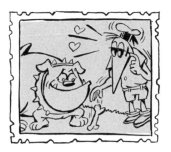

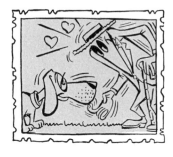

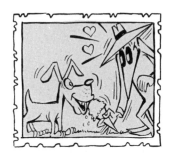

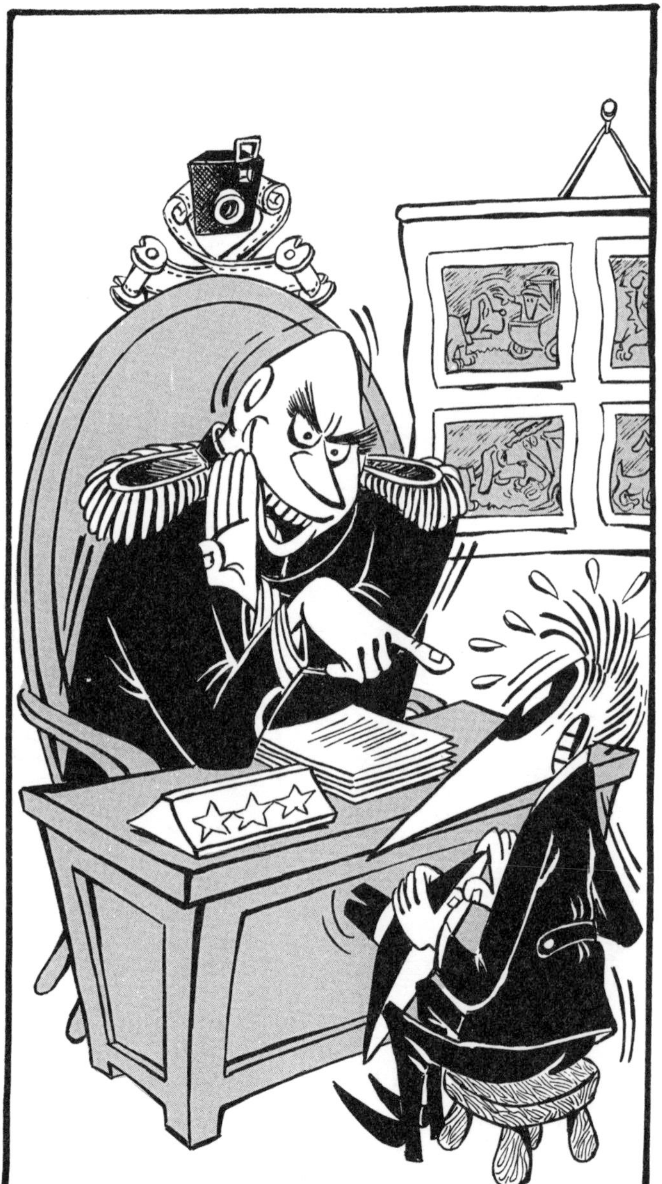

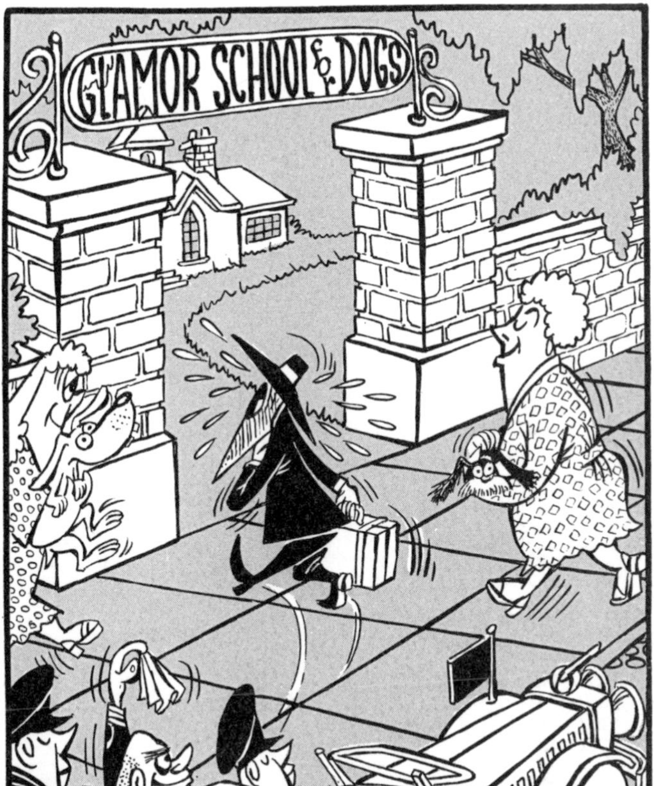
GLAMOR SCHOOL for DOGS
DIPLOMATIC

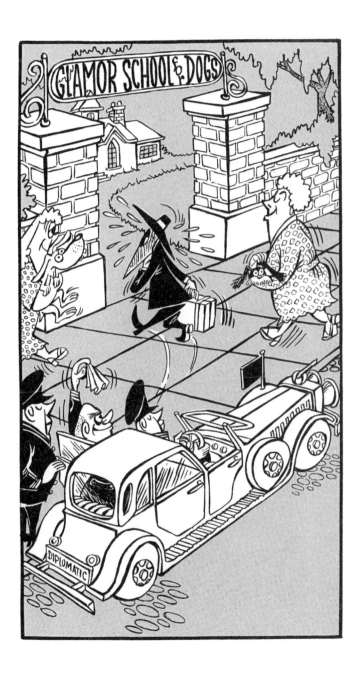

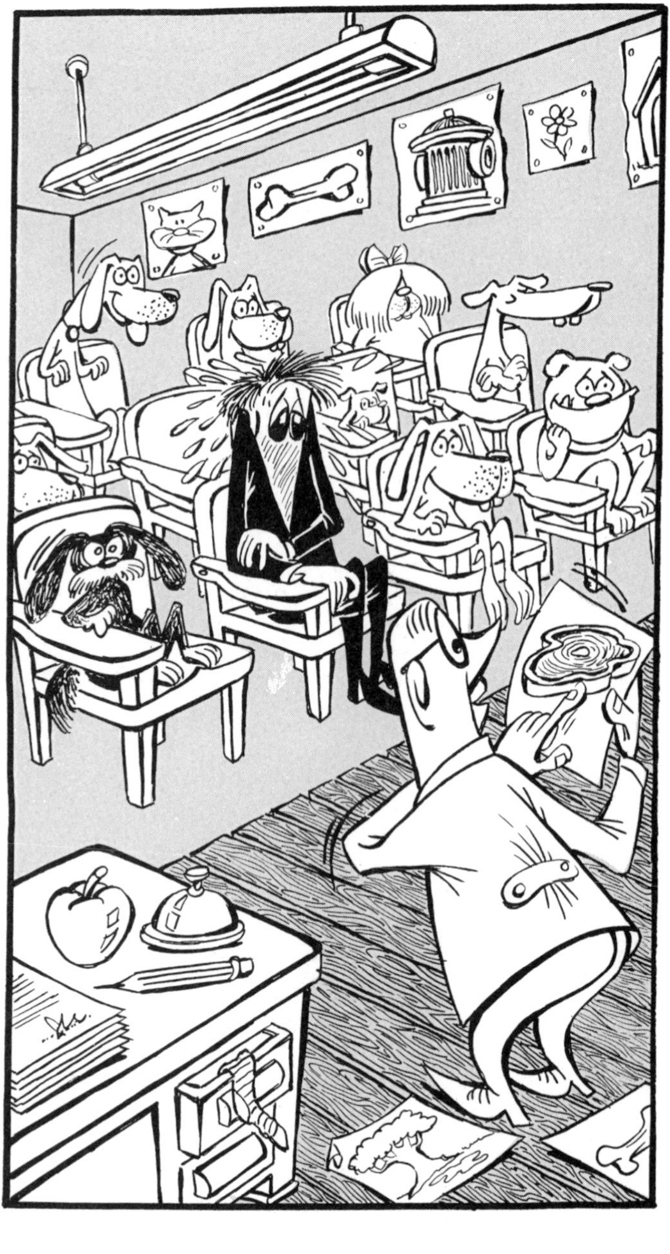

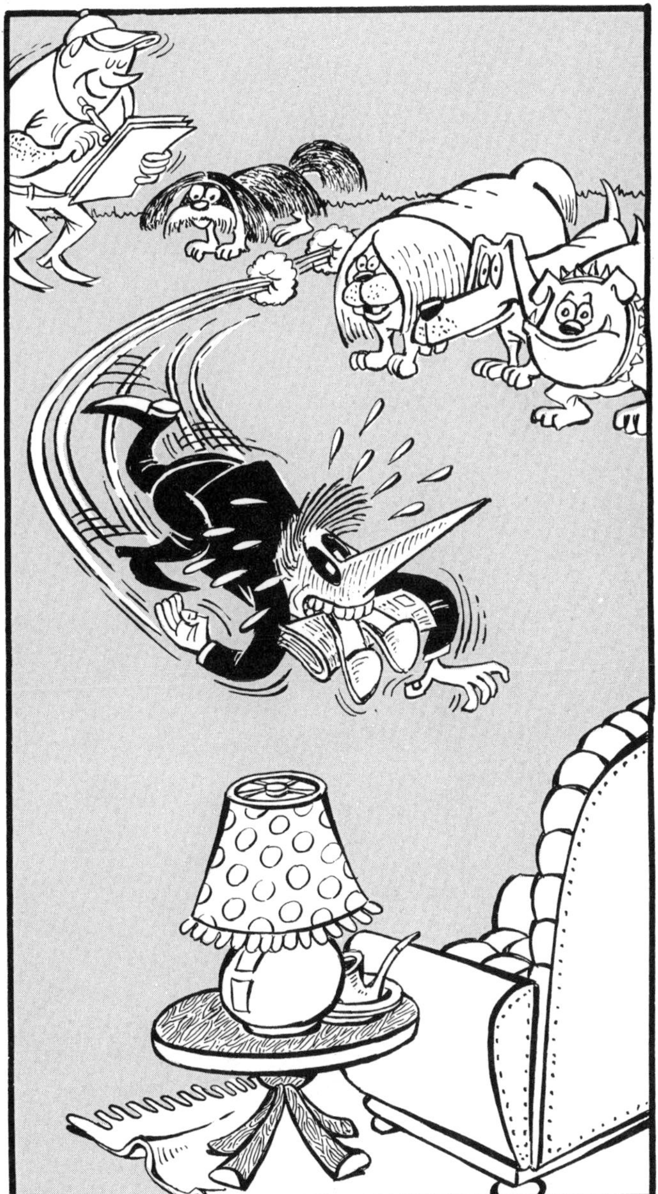

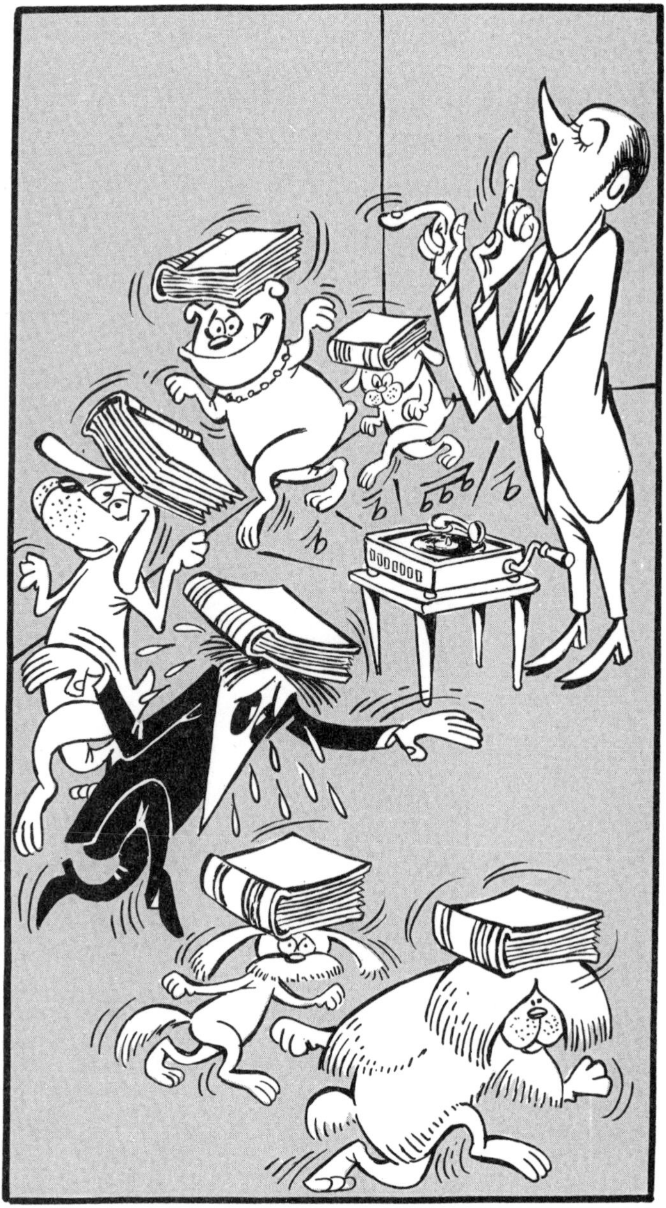

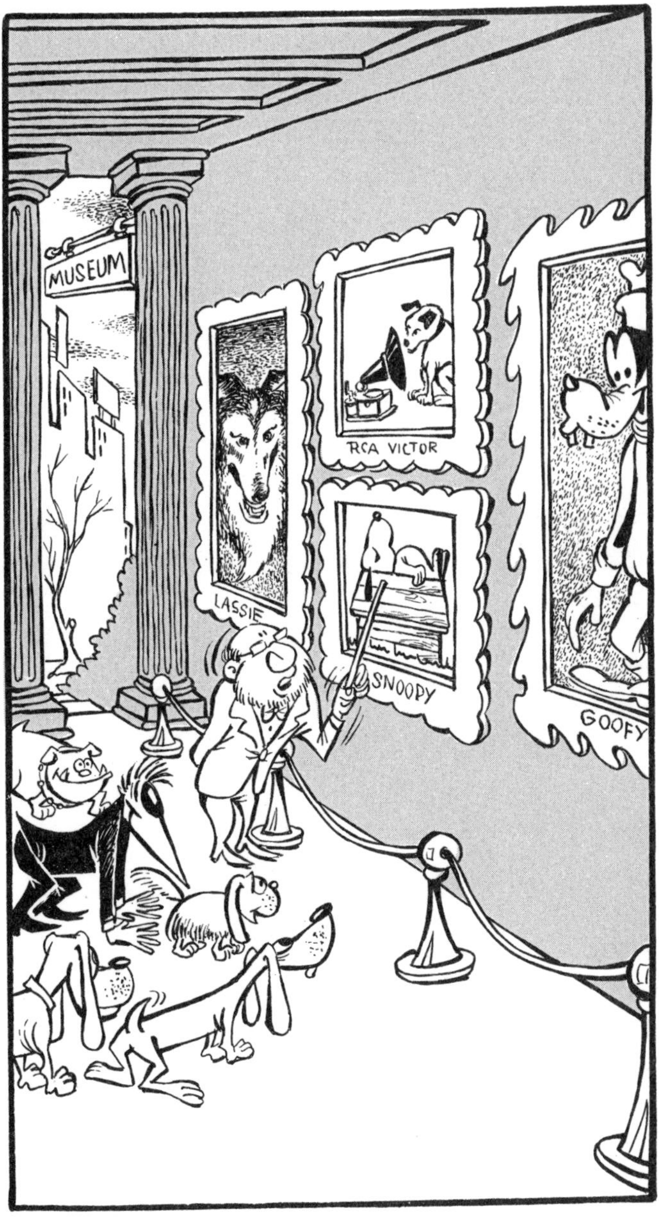
MUSEUM
LASSIE
RCA VICTOR
SNOOPY
GOOFY

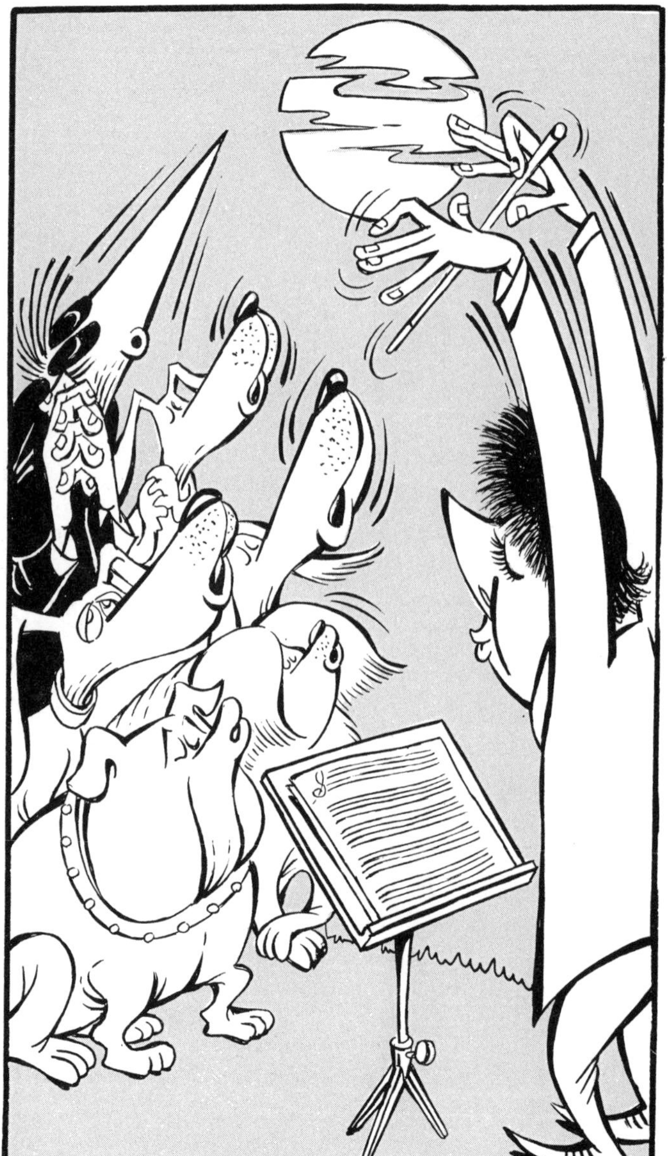

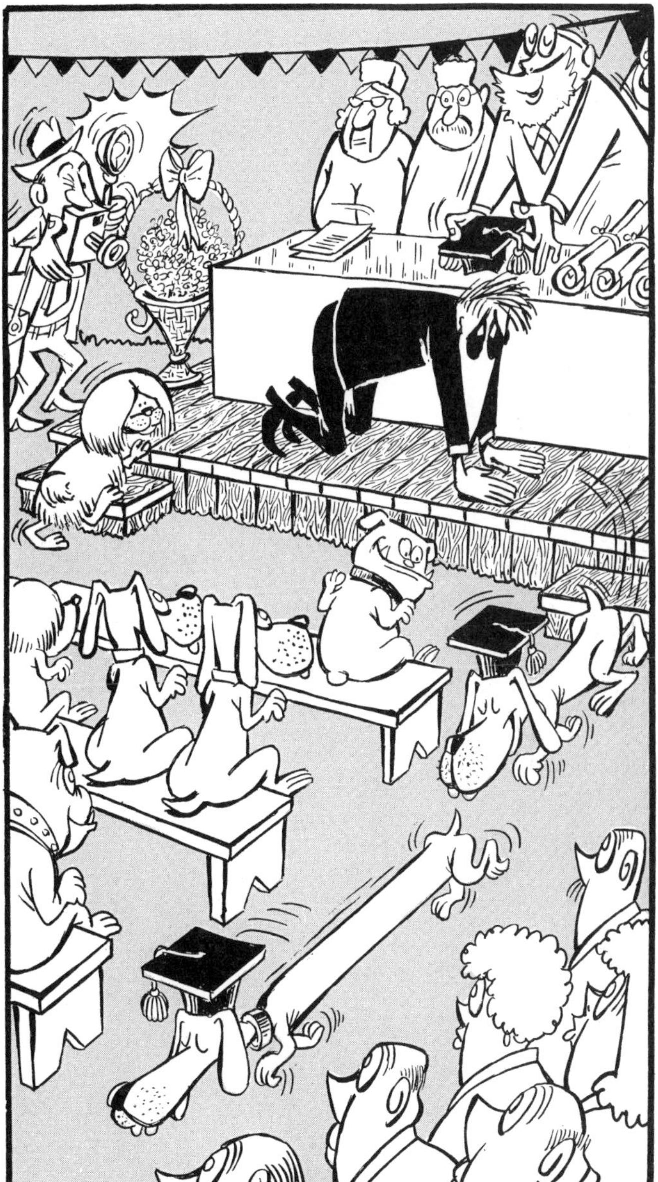

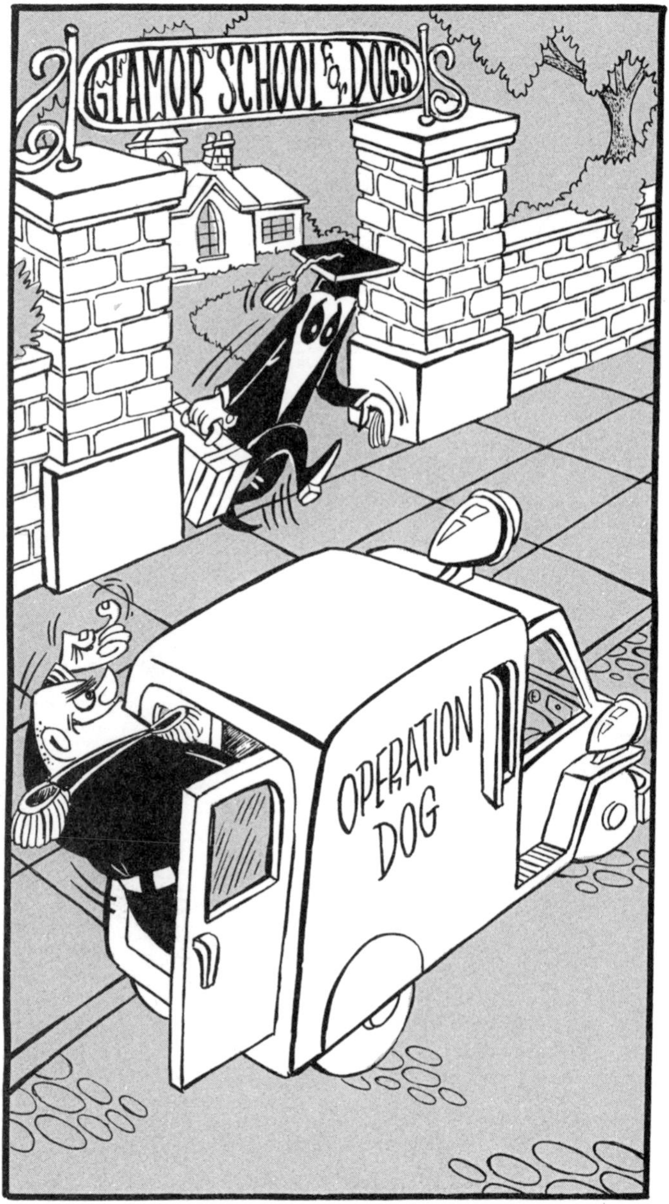
GLAMOR SCHOOL FOR DOGS
OPERATION DOG

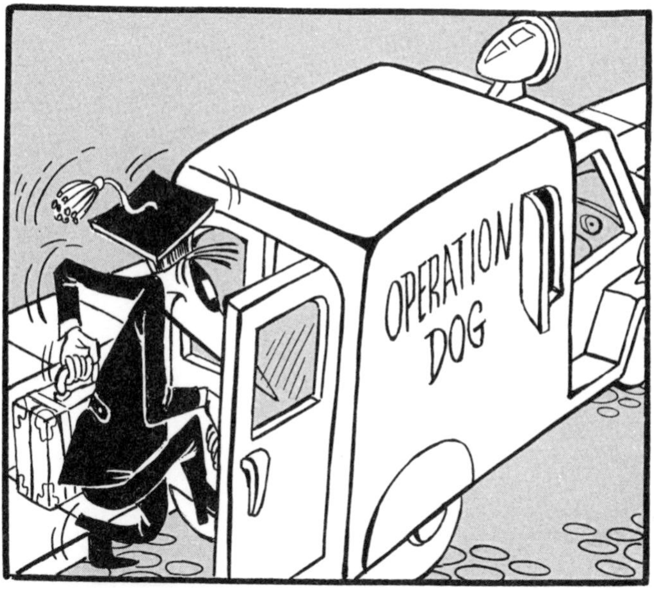
OPERATION DOG

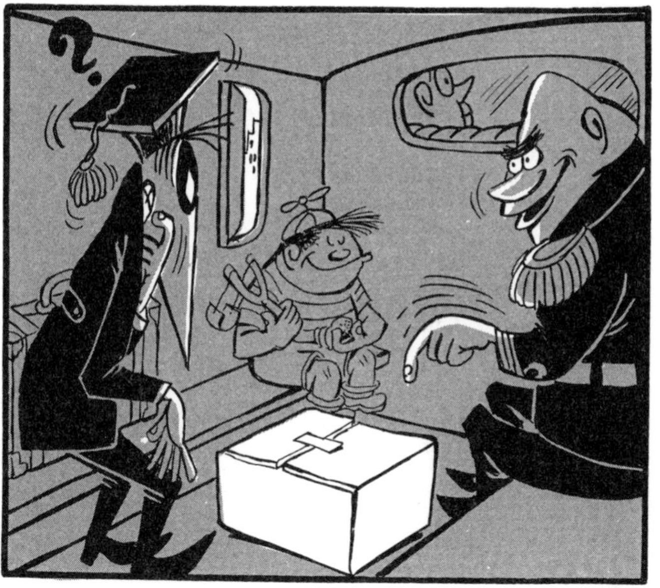

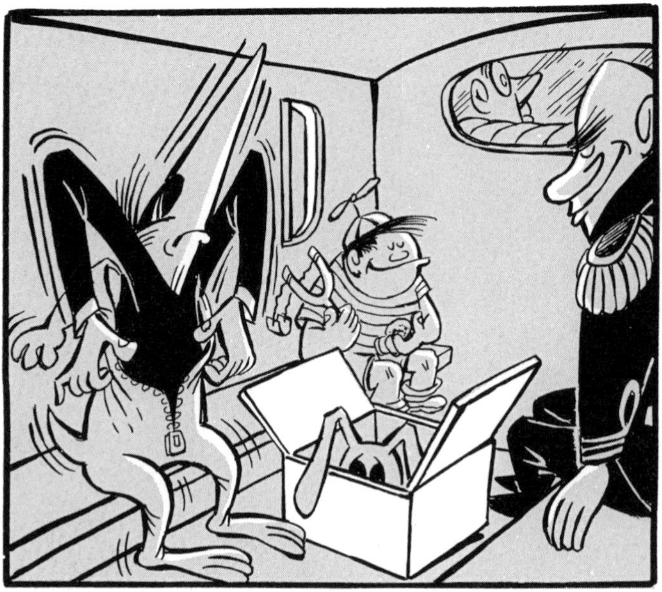

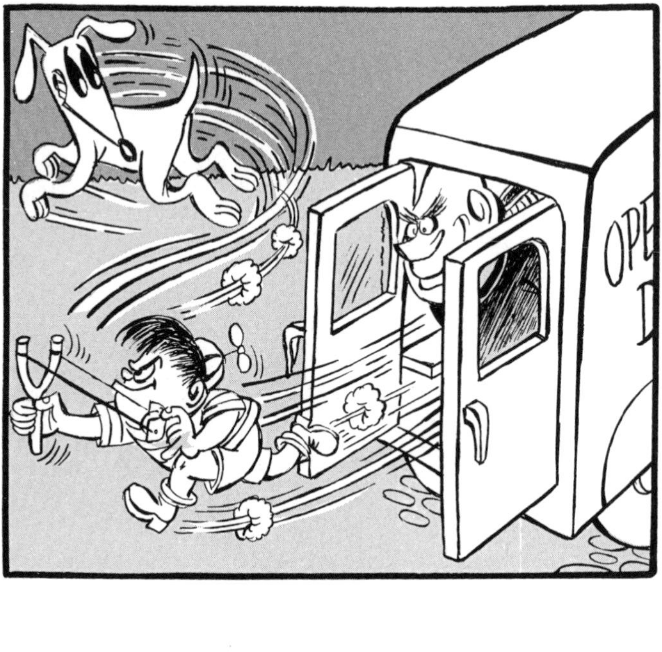

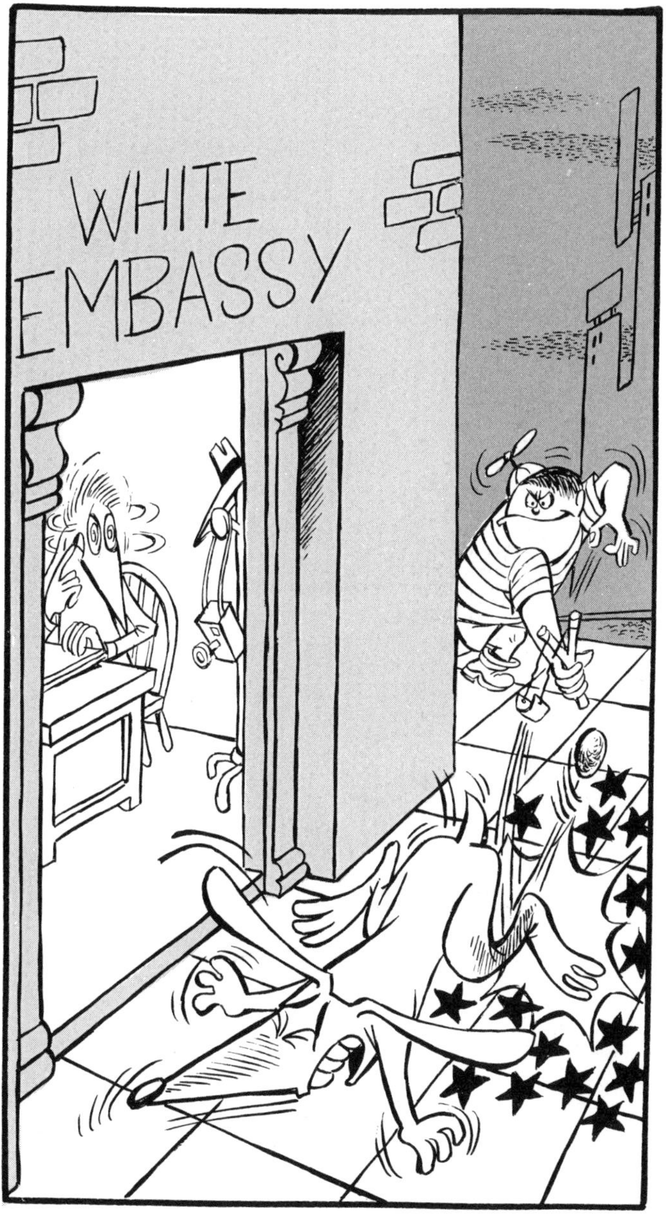
WHITE
EMBASSY

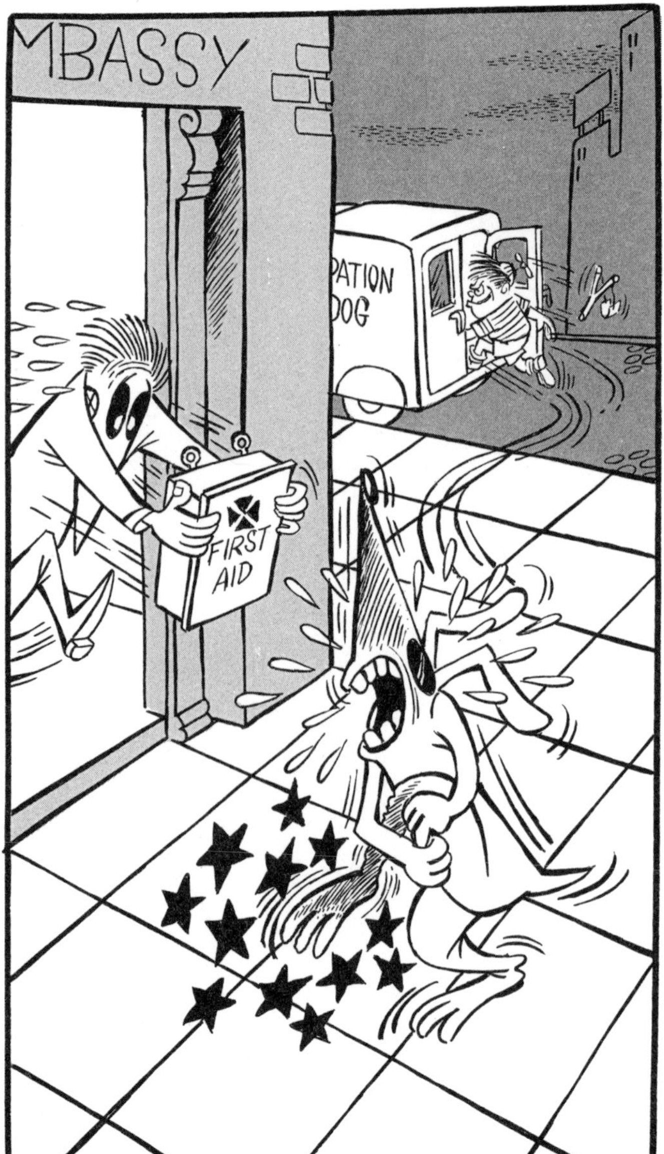
MBASSY
PATION
DOG
FIRST AID

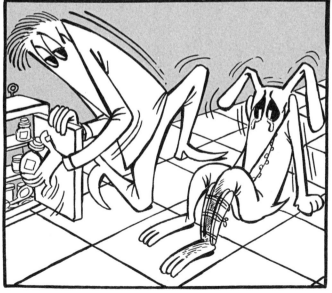

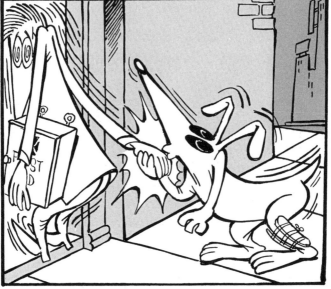

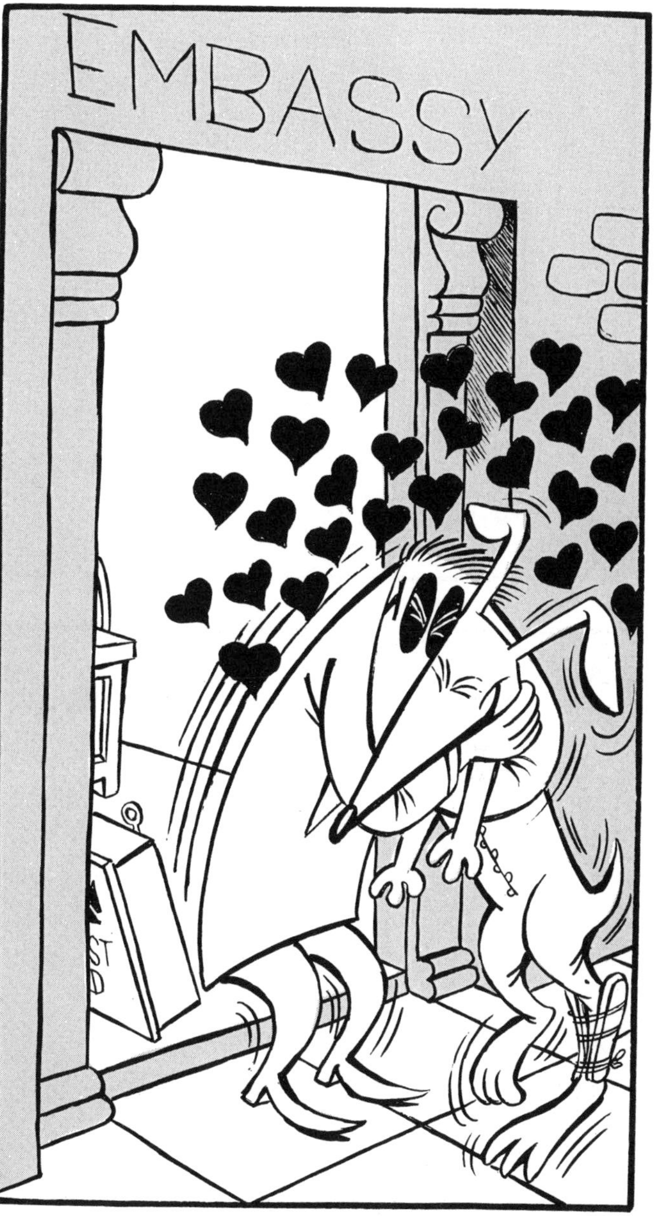
EMBASSy

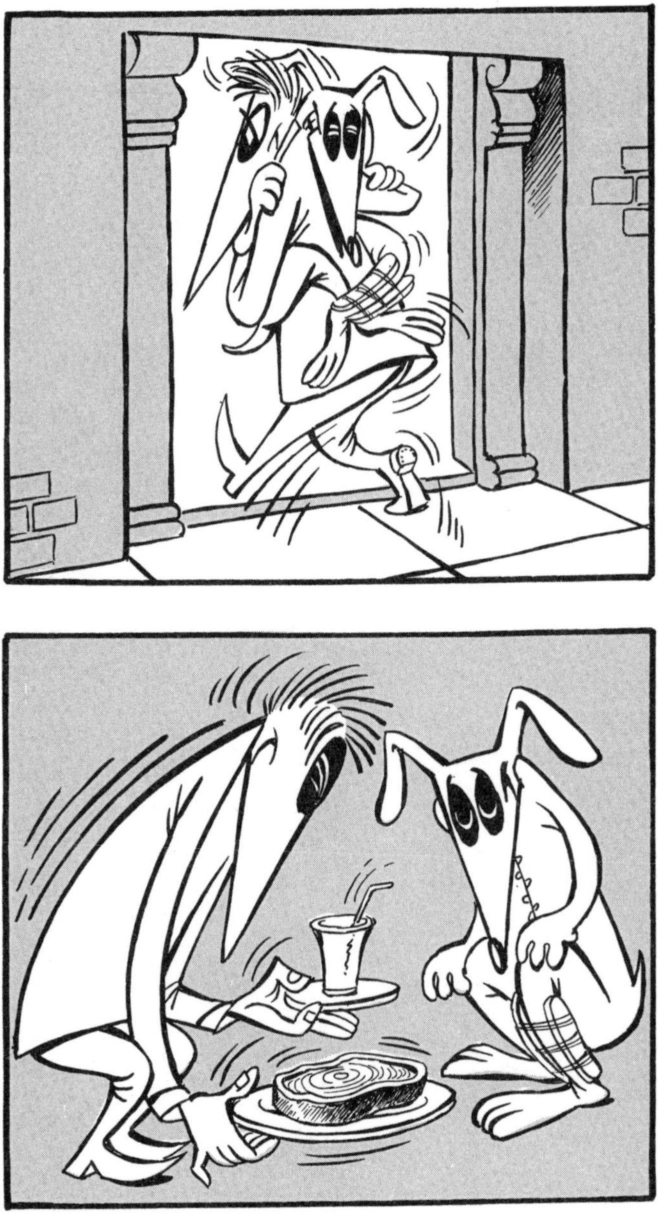

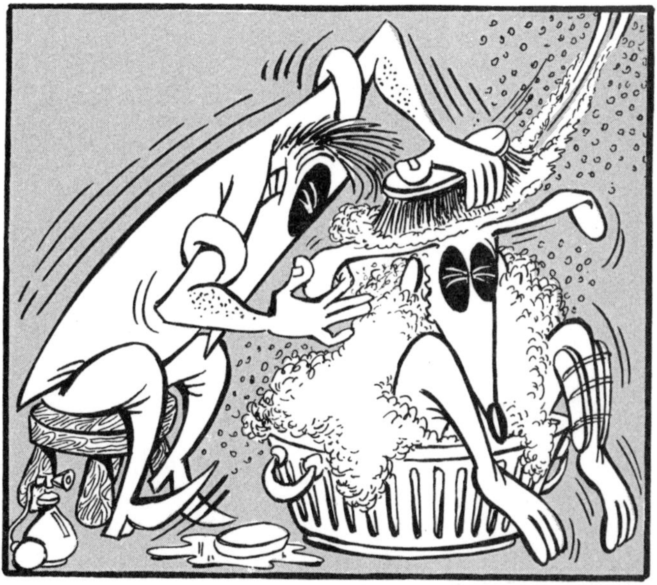

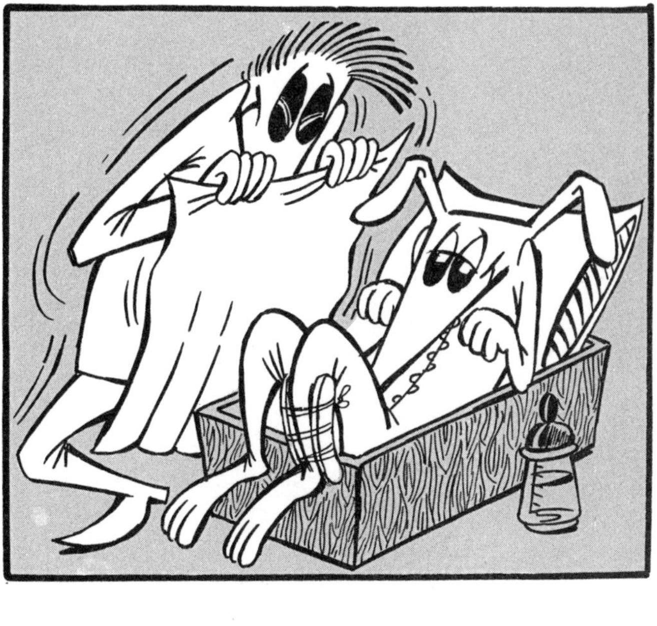

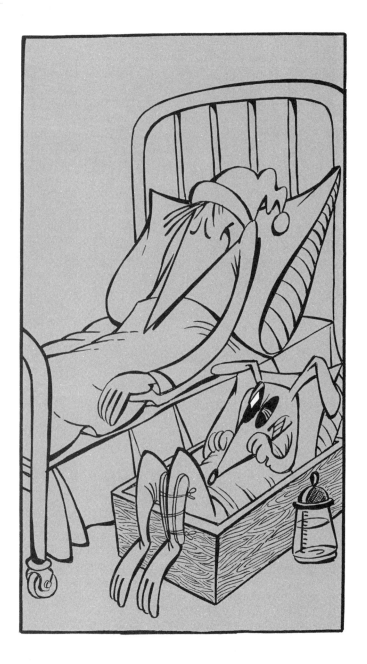

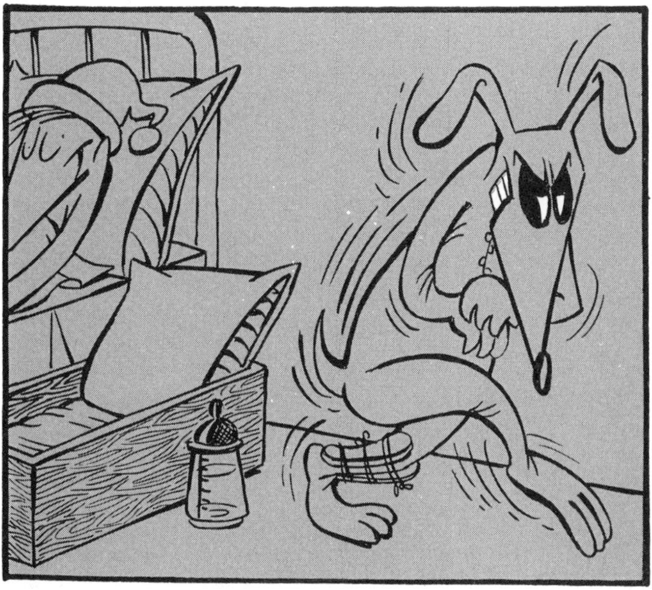

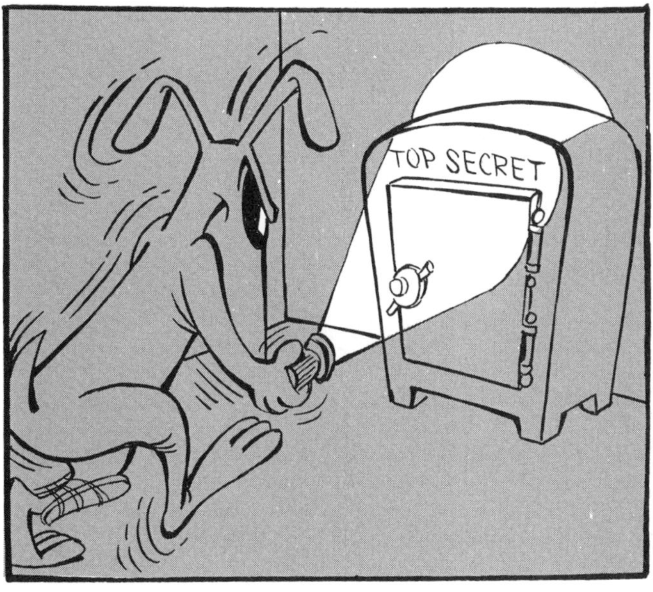
TOP SECRET

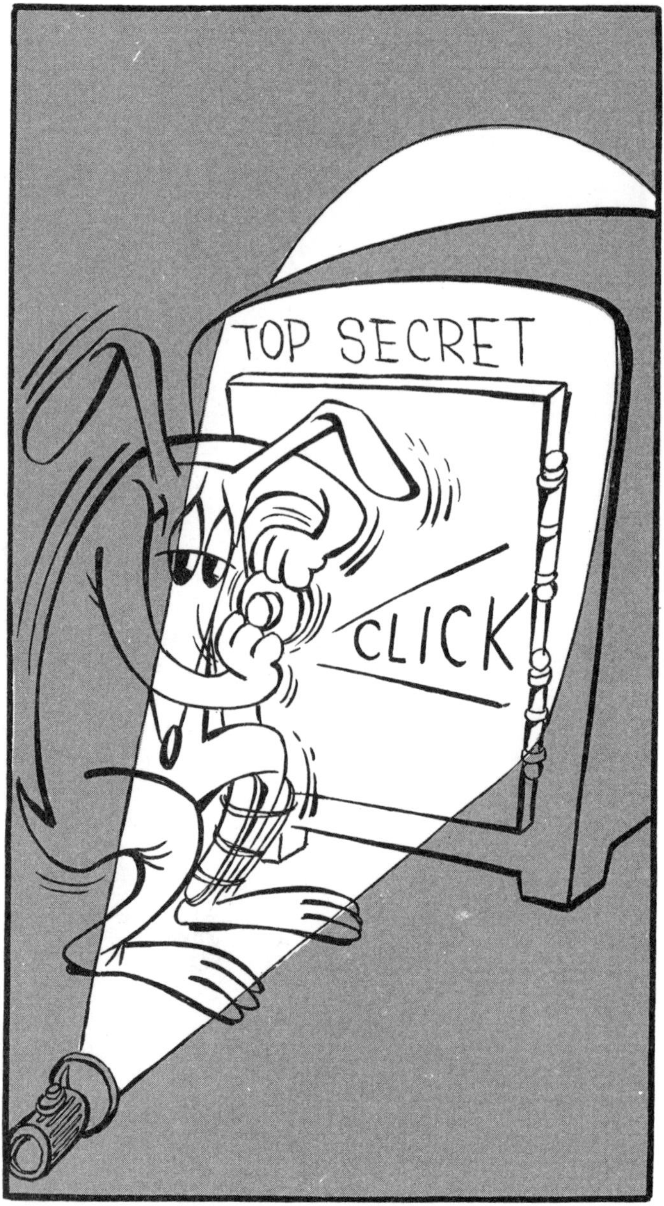
TOP SECRET
CLICK

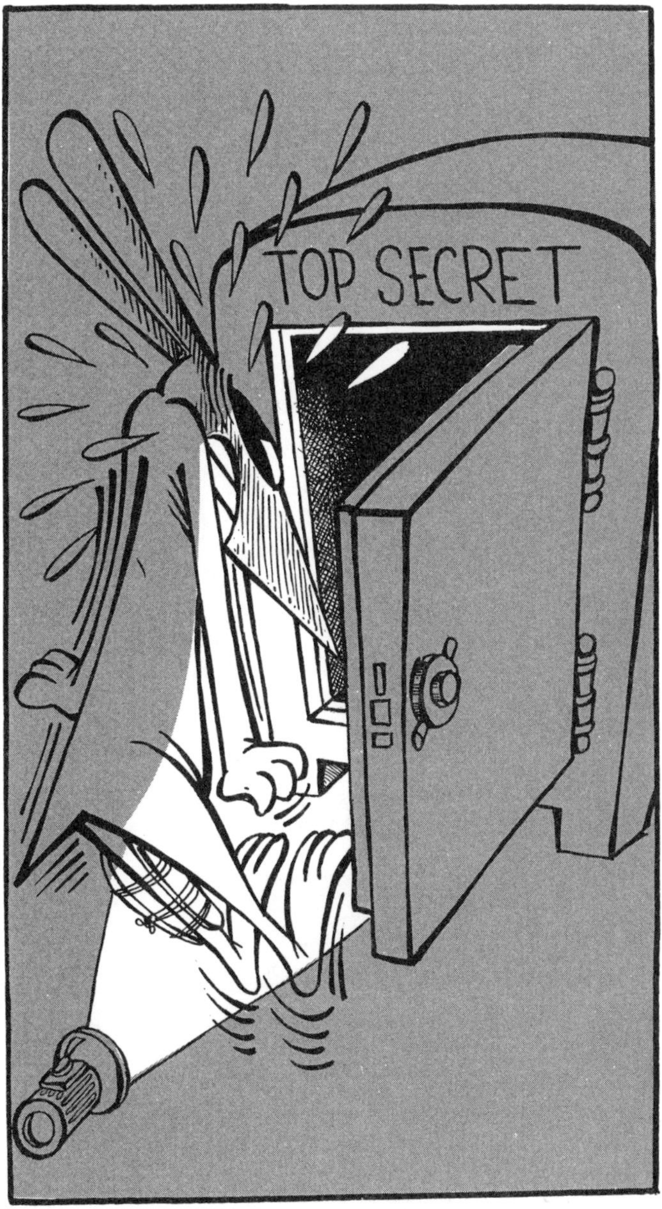
TOP SECRET

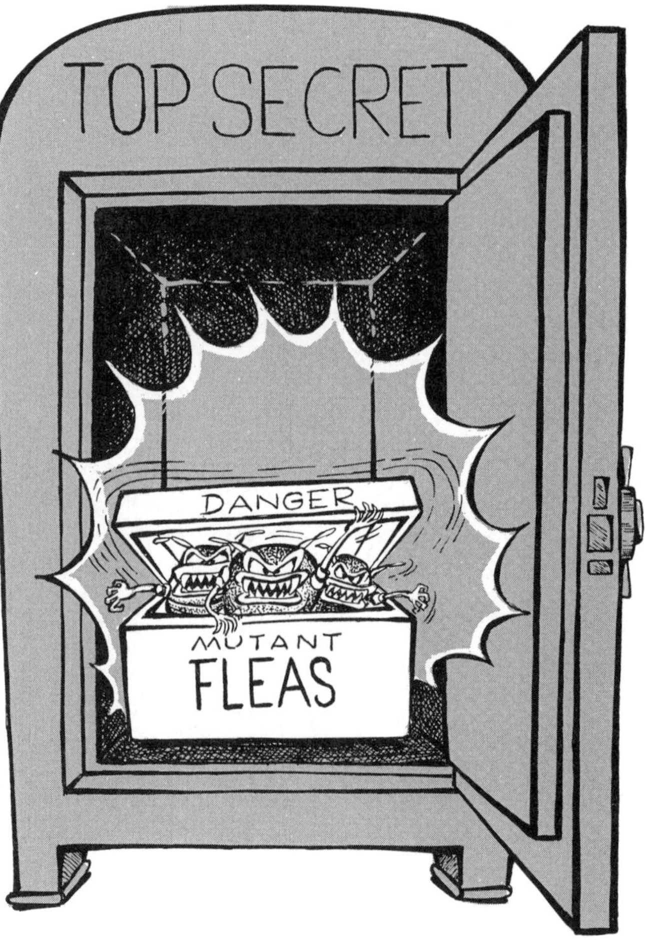
TOP SECRET
DANGER
MUTANT
FLEAS

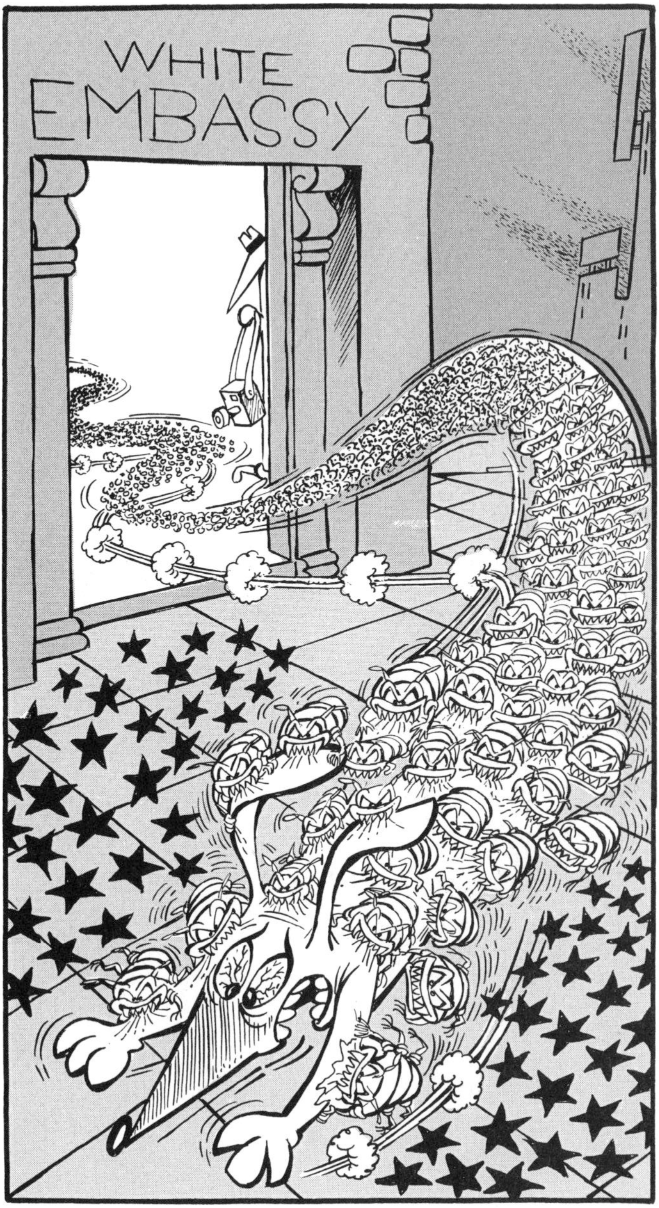
WHITE EMBASSY

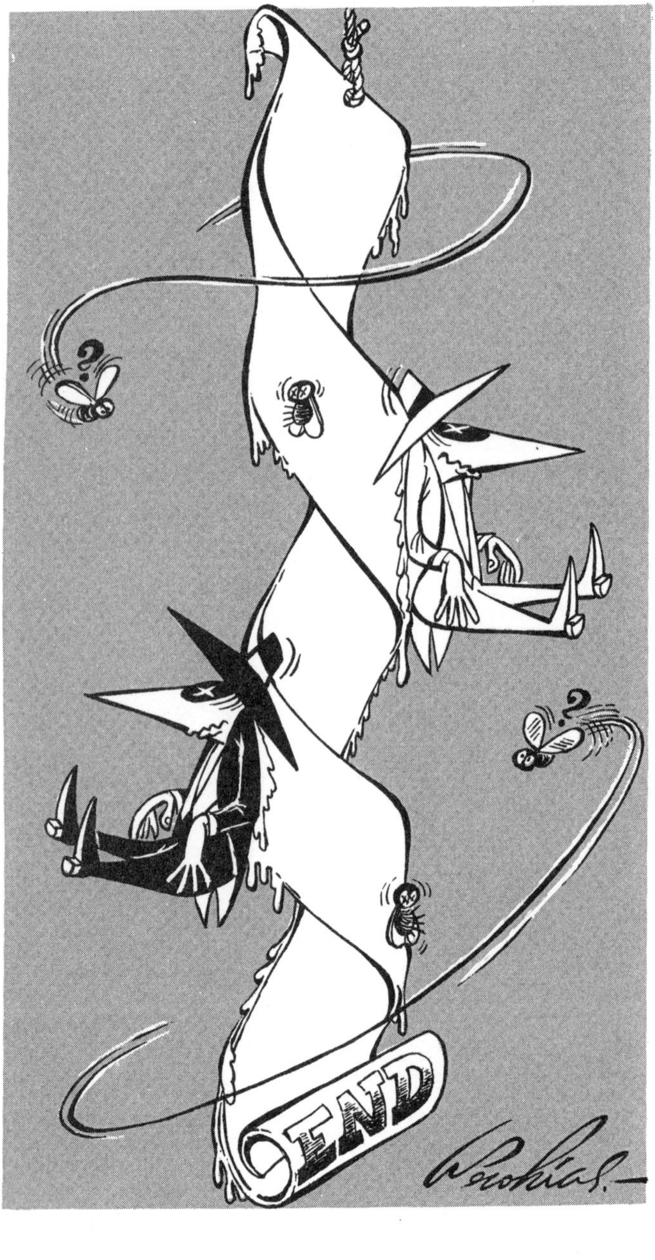
END
Prohias.